Queering Faith in Fantasy Literature

Perspectives on Fantasy

Series Editors

Brian Attebery (Idaho State University, USA)
Dimitra Fimi (University of Glasgow, UK)
Matthew Sangster (University of Glasgow, UK)

The first academic series with an exclusive critical focus on Fantasy, *Perspectives on Fantasy* publishes cutting-edge research on literature and culture that brings sophisticated discussion to a broad community of debate, including scholars, students and non-specialists.

Inspired by Fantasy's deep cultural roots, powerful aesthetic potential and reach across a broad range of media – from literature, film and television to art, animation and gaming – *Perspectives on Fantasy* provides a forum for theorizing and historicizing Fantasy via rigorous and original critical and theoretical approaches. Works in the series will cover major creators, significant works, key modes and forms, histories and traditions, the genre's particular affordances, and the ways in which Fantasy's resources have been drawn on, expanded and reconfigured by authors, readers, viewers, directors, designers, players and artists. With a deliberately broad scope, the series aims to publish dynamic studies that embrace Fantasy as a global, diverse and inclusive phenomenon while also addressing oversights and exclusions. Along with canonical Anglophone authors and texts, the series will provide a space to address Fantasy creators and works rooted in African, Asian, South American, Middle Eastern and indigenous cultures, as well as translations and transnational mediations.

The series will be alive to Fantasy's flourishing fan cultures, studying how audiences engage critically and affectively and considering the ease with which participants in Fantasy communities move from being readers and watchers to players, writers and artists.

Editorial board members
Catherine Butler (Cardiff University, UK)
Pawel Frelik (University of Warsaw, Poland)
Rachel Haywood Ferreira (Iowa State University, USA)
Robert Maslen (University of Glasgow, UK)
Ebony Elizabeth Thomas (University of Pennsylvania, USA)
Anna Vaninskaya (University of Edinburgh, UK)
Rhys Williams (University of Glasgow, UK)
Helen Young (Deakin University, Australia)

Queering Faith in Fantasy Literature

Fantastic Incarnations and the Deconstruction of Theology

Taylor Driggers

BLOOMSBURY ACADEMIC
LONDON • NEW YORK • OXFORD • NEW DELHI • SYDNEY

BLOOMSBURY ACADEMIC
Bloomsbury Publishing Plc
50 Bedford Square, London, WC1B 3DP, UK
1385 Broadway, New York, NY 10018, USA
29 Earlsfort Terrace, Dublin 2, Ireland

BLOOMSBURY, BLOOMSBURY ACADEMIC and the Diana logo are trademarks of
Bloomsbury Publishing Plc

First published in Great Britain 2022
Paperback edition published 2023

Copyright © Taylor Driggers, 2022

Taylor Driggers has asserted his right under the Copyright, Designs and
Patents Act, 1988, to be identified as Author of this work.

For legal purposes the Acknowledgements on pp. xi–xii constitute an extension
of this copyright page.

Cover design and illustration: Rebecca Heselton

All rights reserved. No part of this publication may be reproduced or transmitted in
any form or by any means, electronic or mechanical, including photocopying, recording,
or any information storage or retrieval system, without prior permission in writing
from the publishers.

Bloomsbury Publishing Plc does not have any control over, or responsibility for, any
third-party websites referred to or in this book. All internet addresses given in this book
were correct at the time of going to press. The author and publisher regret any
inconvenience caused if addresses have changed or sites have ceased to exist, but can
accept no responsibility for any such changes.

A catalogue record for this book is available from the British Library.

Library of Congress Cataloging-in-Publication Data
Names: Driggers, Taylor, author.
Title: Queering faith in fantasy literature: fantastic incarnations and
the deconstruction of theology / Taylor Driggers.
Description: London; New York: Bloomsbury Academic, 2022. |
Series: Perspectives on fantasy | Includes bibliographical references and index.
Identifiers: LCCN 2021037287 (print) | LCCN 2021037288 (ebook) |
ISBN 9781350231733 (hardback) | ISBN 9781350231740 (ebook) |
ISBN 9781350231757 (epub)
Subjects: LCSH: Fantasy fiction–History and criticism. | Queer theory. |
Christianity in literature. | LCGFT: Literary criticism.
Classification: LCC PN3435 .D75 2022 (print) | LCC PN3435 (ebook) |
DDC 809.3/8766–dc23
LC record available at https://lccn.loc.gov/2021037287
LC ebook record available at https://lccn.loc.gov/2021037288

ISBN: HB: 978-1-3502-3173-3
PB: 978-1-3502-3177-1
ePDF: 978-1-3502-3174-0
eBook: 978-1-3502-3175-7

Series: Perspectives on Fantasy

Typeset by Deanta Global Publishing Services, Chennai, India

To find out more about our authors and books visit www.bloomsbury.com and
sign up for our newsletters.

*For John, who shares my love of all things fabulous and monstrous and has shown me love, grace and 'joy beyond the walls of the world';
and for the women, queers and trans people everywhere who dare to dream and make manifest the promise of other worlds and other ways of being. This book is possible because of all of you.*

Contents

Series Editors' Preface	ix
Acknowledgements	xi
Introduction: Worlds of difference	1
Structure and methodology	5
Against apologetics	9
Deconstruction, theology and feminism	12
Fantasy: Definitions, critical approaches and figurations	17

1   Saving face?: Fantasy, ethical alterity and deconstruction   23
    Defining deconstruction, deconstructing definitions   25
    Vive la différance   28
    Theological deconstruction   30
    Deconstructive theology   32
    The call to advent-ure; or, Derrida among the dragons   34
    Deconstructing Christianity in *The Passion of New Eve*   40
    'Holy places are dark places': Facing the other in *Till We Have Faces*   44
    Breaking the circle: Religion without religion in *The Left Hand of
        Darkness*   55
    Conclusions   65

2   Dragons in the neighbourhood: The fantastic discourse of femininity   69
    'A world all her own': Hélène Cixous and *écriture feminine*   70
    Is fantasy feminine?   77
    The laugh of the dragon   80
    Mère Christianity: Women's language and holy wisdom in *Till We
        Have Faces*   84
    'The fecund darkness': 'Bisexual' religion and society in *The Left
        Hand of Darkness*   94
    Conclusions   101

3   Hetero-doxies: Fantasy and the problem of divine womanhood   103
    Riddles in the dark: Luce Irigaray's feminist mysticism   105
    Becoming Psyche: Identity and Eros in *Till We Have Faces*   113

	'Her own mythological artefact': *The Passion of New Eve* and the theatre of divine womanhood	126
	Conclusions	136
4	Drag(on) theology: The queer strangers of fantasy	137
	Queer(ing) definitions	139
	Queering theology	144
	Undressing orthodoxy: Althaus-Reid's Indecent Theology	145
	Theology of failure: Tonstad's queer messianism	153
	Drag(on) theology: Queer incarnations and fantastic embodiment	158
	Double drag: Sacred parody in *The Passion of New Eve*	164
	Queer failure in/as worldbuilding: Mystical perversions in *The Left Hand of Darkness*	169
	Walking the Dragons' Way: Sacred multiplicity in *Earthsea*	176
	Conclusions	183
Monstrous messianisms: Conclusions		185
	Divine speech and matter: Ann Leckie's *The Raven Tower*	187
	Swimming against the tides: Neon Yang's *Tensorate* series	191
	Gods and seduction: N. K. Jemisin's *Inheritance* trilogy	195
	Awaiting eucatastrophe	200
Notes		203
Bibliography		213
Index		223

Perspectives on Fantasy
Series Editors' Preface

It has traditionally been difficult to reach a consensus definition of Fantasy. Critics generally agree that fantasies deal with the impossible, but beyond this, they have directed their attention variously to arcane subsets of literature or vast swathes of cultural production. That Fantasy powerfully evokes different meanings at different times for different people is one of its virtues as a vector for exploring culture. Depending on one's approach, Fantasy can be said to arise in our earliest myths and legends, to build on 'taproot' texts that abstract and crystalize human hopes and fears or to represent a relatively contemporary means of negotiating with pasts, presents and futures through retrenchment, reconfiguration or visionary reforging.

Fantasy's flexibility has brought it to particular prominence at the dawn of the third millennium. Successful film and TV series have adapted classic and modern works and created deep and dazzling new worlds on screen. Innovations in aesthetics, artifice, media, narrative, improvisation and play have re-energized Fantasy with modern modes, tropes and techniques, and the rise of the internet has allowed for unprecedented forms of community collaboration. These developments have created myriad new fantasies and amended, resynthesized and extended a powerful tradition in which the impossible is evoked to contrast with, probe the limits of and call into question our mundane realities.

However, despite this burgeoning richness, academia has been slow to develop a set of tools for addressing Fantasy as a major cultural form. Fantasy lags considerably behind science fiction, crime fiction and the Gothic in terms of critical attention. The *Perspectives on Fantasy* series addresses this lack by providing a space in which the best new scholarly and theoretical work can be drawn together to catalyse an increased understanding of a mode that is both artistically distinctive and deeply meaningful for a vast range of creators and audiences.

We chose the title *Perspectives* to reflect the fact that Fantasy is not a problem to which there is a single solution, but rather a range of territories that look different to different eyes, territories which we all explore better when we have a wide variety of lenses to look through. Our series is keen to extend the theorization of Fantasy, with a special focus on expanding and diversifying existing critical approaches. Important work has been done tracing the roots and emergence of modern genre Fantasy, but there is much more to be accomplished in this area and a pressing need for work that explores different cultures, politics, poetics, forms, tropes and methodologies. Though innovative monographs on major writers are very welcome, the series recognizes that Fantasy promiscuously crosses media. We therefore also encourage scholarship focusing on film, television, board games, role-playing games, video games, comics, art and animation. Within given groupings of fantastic works, we would like to see contributors examining themes and structural elements such as worldbuilding, the operations of magic systems, the construction of evil, the (re)negotiation of histories and creators' engagements with ethical, social, economic and ecological issues. We are eager for the series to be alive to Fantasy's flourishing fan cultures, exploring how audiences engage critically and affectively with fantastic creations and considering the ease with which participants in Fantasy communities move from being readers and watchers to players, writers and artists. Last, but not least, we are keen to provide a space for cogent critique. In considering how we imagine other worlds and peoples, the series will seek to be vigilant in exposing the limitations of fantasies, as well as the potencies of the equivalences they draw. Fantasy lets us rethink the world; in contemplating such rethinkings, we are keen to acknowledge oversights, exclusions and suppressions, as well as the flickering utopian potential of Fantasy's playful sidelong glances.

Brian Attebery, Dimitra Fimi and Matthew Sangster

Acknowledgements

A portion of this book's Chapter 1 was published in altered form as 'Archaeologies of the Future: Deconstruction, Fantasy, and the Fiction of Ursula K. Le Guin' in *The New Americanist* 1.3 (Autumn 2019), special issue 'Hobgoblins of Fantasy: American Fantasy Fiction in Theory', 103–26. I am grateful to *The New Americanist*'s editorial board and the American Studies Centre at the University of Warsaw for granting permission to reproduce part of my article here.

Excerpt(s) from *The Left Hand of Darkness: 50th Anniversary Edition* by Ursula K. Le Guin. Used by permission of Ace, an imprint of Penguin Publishing Group, a division of Penguin Random House LLC. All rights reserved.

Till We Have Faces by C. S. Lewis Pte. Ltd. 1956. Extracts reprinted by permission.

The Passion of New Eve by Angela Carter. Published by Virago, 1977. Reproduced by permission of the Estate of Angela Carter c/o Rogers, Coleridge & White Ltd., 20 Powis Mews, London W11 1JN.

This book began life as a PhD thesis at the University of Glasgow starting in 2015, and it has been the most profoundly life-altering project I have ever undertaken. I would first like to thank my family for their tireless support and encouragement, particularly my parents, Morris and Dawn Driggers, and my cousin McKenzie Bottoms, whose conversation was foundational to many of the ideas that sparked this research. I wish also to express my utmost gratitude to my former supervisors, Maria-Daniella Dick, Vassiliki Kolocotroni and Robert Maslen, for shepherding this project from its early stages, taking my joy and passion in this project on as their own and persistently reminding me to prioritize my well-being throughout my degree.

I am profoundly indebted to a number of colleagues and fellow scholars who read drafts and excerpts from this book at various points and offered judicious critiques and suggestions, including Brian Attebery, Vicky Gunn, Meg MacDonald, C. Palmer-Patel, Andrew Radford, Matthew Sangster, Alana M. Vincent, Sophie Vlacos and Heather Walton. Jonah Coman's friendship and seemingly boundless intellectual enthusiasm have buoyed me through the writing process and challenged me to be a better scholar; he has persistently reminded me that research can and should be a joyous pursuit. To everyone at the Centre for Fantasy and the Fantastic at the University of Glasgow I owe much thanks, especially Dimitra Fimi for her guidance and mentorship, and Marita Arvaniti and Mariana Rios Maldonado for their scholarly friendship and solidarity. This book is better because of all of these scholars' input and support; the errors are mine alone.

The writing of this book coincided with many changes and upheavals in my own personal life. I am eternally grateful to my 'found family' who have offered listening ears, affirmation and (where deserved) words of censure during this strange season, including Lazaro Mancilla, Lizy and Petri Simonen, Caitlin Wakefield, Naomi Berry, Colette O'Connor, Kristy Whaley, Jo Russell, the Rev Dr Ellen M. Barrett, OSB, Sr Alison Joy Whybrow, OSB, Soph Sexon, Joanna Helfer, and the late, great Debbie White.

Lastly, I would like to offer my endless thanks to my husband, John Driggers-McDowall. Your steadfast love, patience and support have been a life-giving source of joy for me as I have endeavoured to realize this project.

Introduction

Worlds of difference

Fantasy literature has long been celebrated within Christian communities for its ability to give narrative form to theology at a remove from the usual trappings of religion. Reflecting on his creation of a fantastical Gospel narrative in *The Chronicles of Narnia* (1950–6), C. S. Lewis comments that 'by casting all these things into an imaginary world, stripping them of their stained-glass and Sunday school associations, one could make them for the first time appear in their real potency' (Lewis [1956] 1982: 73). Kath Filmer has even gone so far as to say that 'fantasy *speaks* religion' (Filmer 1992: iii): that is, religion is not simply a part of fantasy's aesthetics, its narrative register or even its thematic content, but inextricably embedded within the form itself. Yet if fantasy's religious speech is often spoken in Christian registers, what remains to be examined is how it may do so for those of us who are marginalized by, or within, Christian traditions and institutions because of our genders, modes of presentation and sexual desires. How might the creation of fantastical alternate realities – or 'secondary worlds', as J. R. R. Tolkien terms them (Tolkien [1947] 2008: 52) – speak good news to those excluded and abused by the preachers of the Gospel in this world?[1] By 'stripping' theology of its institutional bearing points, can fantasy texts also 'undress', as the queer theologian Marcella Althaus-Reid has provocatively phrased it, the patriarchal, heterosexual and cisgender structures of doctrine (Althaus-Reid 2000: 18)? In the face of religious institutions that police and denigrate the desires and activities of our bodies, fantasy – in its fascination with fairies, dragons and other strange beasts – may provide a space in which bodies that appear monstrous, impure or 'other' are embraced as holy.

This book argues that fantasy literature carries a previously unexplored potential for articulating queer and feminist theologies and religious imaginaries. Taking up a deconstructive position within a Christian theological framework, it posits that fantasy texts can serve as fictional spaces in which theology can be re-imagined from queer and feminist standpoints. My argument considers fantasy as a genre with potential not only for communicating religious doctrines but also for interrogating them, holding them to account and transforming them. This deconstructive approach gives special attention to how the defamiliarizing strategies of fantasy can help us to re-figure God as the devalued and dehumanized 'other' against which dominant Western Christian subjectivity constructs and asserts itself. Using C. S. Lewis's *Till We Have Faces* (1956), Ursula K. Le Guin's *The Left Hand of Darkness* (1969), Angela Carter's *The Passion of New Eve* (1977) and, to a lesser extent, Le Guin's *Earthsea* novels (1968–2001) as case studies, I argue that fantasy can be understood as an act of theological re-visioning.

Re-visioning Christian theology from the margins of gender and sexuality is a task carrying urgency not only for women and LGBTQ+ people who profess Christian faith but for gender and sexually marginalized people living under Christian hegemony in general. Even during the writing of this book, numerous threats to the safety and well-being of women and LGBTQ+ people have arisen globally, and they have often been legitimized, as is so frequently the case, on theological grounds. From the election of the far-right Christo-fascist leader Jair Bolsonaro in Brazil,[2] to the stringent tightening of reproductive laws in several American states,[3] to the recent proliferation of 'LGBT-free zones' in Poland,[4] Christianity continues to be a shaping force in the lives of women and queer people internationally. As I argue, by imagining 'impossible' worlds different from our own, fantasy literature can subversively re-figure Christianity's conceptions of God, gender and sexuality, and demand that we more closely examine the story of a God who takes on a body and lives among the marginalized, whose ministry on earth takes place among poor sex workers and women cast aside by political and religious authorities. Furthermore, fantasy literature affords women and queer people a means to bypass both official doctrine and institutional barriers to religious participation, in order to reconfigure our understandings of Christianity and Christ per se.

With all of the former in mind, however, it should be stressed that this book is not about the inclusion of LGBTQ+ people (or lack thereof) in the church; it is also not only concerned with the surface-level representation of individual women or LGBTQ+ characters in fantastic texts. Linn Marie Tonstad has noted that the former debate 'extends rather than challenges normative distributions of power and recognition', manifesting as it does in the advocation of such reforms as 'sanctioning marriage and ordination for gays and lesbians', and as such it 'denies a real reconfiguration of structures of power and exclusion' (Tonstad 2016: 256). Campaigns for LGBTQ+ inclusion in the church tend to remain rooted in a theological triumphalism that privileges the sameness of self-identity. They often emphasize assimilation into existing and officially sanctioned forms of religious expression and social structuration, in which queer people 'turn out to be no different from anyone else' (Tonstad 2016: 256). This leaves intact the normative structures and fear of the 'other' that drive the exclusion of queer people in the first place. Meanwhile, the 2010s have given rise to an emerging sub-field of scholarship focusing on representations of marginalized identities and subjectivity in fantasy and other speculative genres, and non-normative gender and sexual identities have been no exception to this.[5] Without necessarily wishing to devalue this work and its importance, this book adopts an approach more focused on the systems of oppression and exclusion that structure self-identity in opposition to difference than on the validity of individual identity categories. In my examination of fantasy texts, it is not only characters that have the potential to be read as queer but often the secondary worlds themselves and the (im)possibilities that they present for embodiment, relationships and theology. Fantasy literature, in short, has the potential to bypass both existing religious institutions in our world and primary-world gendered and sexual identity categories – even 'queer' ones – in opening onto other ways of being and relating.

Throughout this book, the novels *Till We Have Faces* by C. S. Lewis, *The Left Hand of Darkness* by Ursula K. Le Guin and *The Passion of New Eve* by Angela Carter serve as close reading case studies, with discussion of other fantasy texts interspersed throughout. Most notably, a close reading of the final two novels in Le Guin's *Earthsea* sequence, *Tehanu* (1990) and *The Other Wind* (2001), comprises a sizable portion of Chapter 4, which focuses on fantasy and queer theology. With the exception of the latter novel, as well as Kai Cheng Thom's short story 'i shall remain' (2019), the majority of the texts discussed were published in the mid- to late twentieth century. This has been done partly in the interest of avoiding a presentist bias that is sometimes prevalent in discussions of gender and sexuality in fantasy fiction. Studies focused solely on representational optics can often give a false impression that, as Stephen Kenneally has claimed outright, '[t]he presence of LGBT [sic] characters in fantasy fiction, especially as main characters, is a relatively recent phenomenon' (Kenneally 2016: 8).[6] Such assumptions tend to ignore not only the fact that gendered and sexual identity signifiers, queer subjectivities and political categories are fluid and constantly shifting over time but also the conditions of censorship, discretion and closeted-ness under which queer writers, readers and critics of fiction often operate, either by necessity or by choice, for self-preservation.[7] This optics-based approach reproduces the assumptions and conditions of heteronormativity, under which all texts and characters are presumed heterosexual unless explicitly stated otherwise, and because of this it often participates in the very erasures it is intended to challenge. Contrary to this, my aim in revisiting earlier texts is to demonstrate that fantasy literature has, for much of its history, been deeply invested in gender, sexuality and religion, in ways that remain relevant to the social, political and theological landscape of the twenty-first century. Additionally, I hope to draw attention to the potential for subversive, against-the-grain readings of texts like *Till We Have Faces* that have been read conservatively up to this point. This strategy, I maintain, is in keeping with what Tolkien describes as fantasy's potential for 'applicability', in which interpretation 'resides in the freedom of the reader' (Tolkien [1954] 2011: xxii). *Till We Have Faces*, *The Left Hand of Darkness* and *The Passion of New Eve* were all chosen for this study because they represent widely different approaches to fantasy and a broad spectrum of possibility within the fantastic while also being driven, I argue, by similar theological impulses.

With the exception of C. S. Lewis, who is widely regarded as an author of Christian fantasy, as well as J. R. R. Tolkien, the majority of the authors under consideration in this study do not espouse Christian belief. Rather, their imaginary worlds pose serious challenges and carry potentially transformative implications for Christian theology as it currently exists. Even in the case of Lewis, *Till We Have Faces* is his least hospitable novel to straightforwardly Christian readings, and perhaps for this reason, it often receives little more than perfunctory attention in overviews of his work. Neither Le Guin nor Carter, meanwhile, would define their work as Christian, nor does this study make any attempt to do so. However, to the extent that Christian theology persists as a discourse that shapes Western cultures, *The Left Hand of Darkness* and especially *The Passion of New Eve* can at the very least both be understood as texts in conversation with Christianity and its inheritances. Even the title of the latter novel demonstrates that Carter takes Christian theology and iconography seriously as structuring myths in contemporary Western cultures and identity formation, although crucially it more often emerges in her fiction as a site of parody, deconstruction and fantastic re-invention than as earnest devotion. Le Guin's relationship to Christian theology is less immediately apparent, but both *The Left Hand of Darkness* and the *Earthsea* series engage in exploration and harsh critique of concepts familiar to Christianity: namely, prophecy, metaphysics and messianism in *The Left Hand of Darkness*, as well as divine sovereignty and the notion of an eternal afterlife in the *Earthsea* novels.

Implicit in this endeavour is an extension of poststructuralist theological reading practices such as those developed by Heather Walton, in which an account is given of discontinuities and contradictions between and within the literary imagination and theology, as well as the affinities between them. As Walton states, '[l]iterature resists being assimilated by theology [. . .] and is as likely to confound our understandings of faith as to confirm them' (Walton 2011a: 1). Although, historically, scholars of theology and fantasy literature have presumed this type of deconstructive positioning to be at odds with, or even threatening to, the aims of their studies, I posit that deconstructive readings align fantasy even more closely with Tolkien's theological longing 'to hold communion with other living things' (Tolkien [1947] 2008: 35) that are outside the realm of human understanding, including outside of theology per se. This book navigates uneasy alliances between literature and theology; between fiction and faith; between deconstruction and religious devotion; and between theology, feminism and queer politics, as it examines the myriad ways that fantasy can engage with queer and feminist religious imaginaries. These are elaborated over the course of four chapters, each of which focuses on a different facet of fantasy's relationship to queer and feminist theologies. Chapter 1 outlines a deconstructive approach to theology by way of fantasy writing; Chapter 2 examines the question of fantasy literature as the disruptive 'feminine' other to theology's 'masculine' logic; Chapter 3 engages critically with feminist incarnations of God in fantasy; and lastly, Chapter 4 considers fantasy from a queer perspective, as theology in drag. This structure should in no way be taken as a linear genealogy and certainly not as a forward-moving progression in which each succeeding theoretical framework supplants the previous ones. Rather, it acknowledges that the task of deconstructing God, sex and gender is always a multi-layered one.

Structure and methodology

Chapter 1 of this book, 'Saving face?: Fantasy, ethical alterity and deconstruction', elaborates a theory of fantasy as a deconstructive opening towards the other in theology by identifying deconstructive philosophy and fantasy writing as homologous structures. To do this, I discuss Derrida's writing with particular attention to its theological implications, referencing works like *The Gift of Death*, 'Faith and Knowledge' and *Rogues*, which explicitly engage with theological concepts, but also showing that theology was a key concern for Derrida as early as *Writing and Difference* and *Of Grammatology*. This point becomes even more clear when Derrida's work is considered as arising out of Emmanuel Levinas's ethics of alterity. This discussion of deconstructive philosophy is then brought alongside theories of fantasy articulated by J. R. R. Tolkien, Ursula K.

Le Guin and, most recently, Brian Attebery, in order to show both how fantasy texts deconstruct theology and how their own theological figurations can be read deconstructively. Tolkien and Le Guin are widely considered two of the most influential authors of fantasy, and they represent, respectively, explicitly religiously informed (Tolkien) and feminist and anti-capitalist (Le Guin) readings of fantasy that are nonetheless strikingly similar in their impulses. Attebery is included because, to date, he has most successfully navigated between fantasy's religious underpinnings and its potential for subversive theoretical and political projects, drawing on both Tolkien and Le Guin to do so. The chapter also demonstrates how a deconstructive relationship to theology is embodied within *Till We Have Faces*, *The Left Hand of Darkness* and *The Passion of New Eve*, and considers the implications of these readings for the fantasy genre more broadly.

Chapters 2 and 3 concern themselves with the theological facets of the deconstructive feminist projects of Hélène Cixous and Luce Irigaray and examines how they are embodied within fantasy literature. While Cixous's and Irigaray's projects have given way to more recent feminist theories, such as those espoused by Rosi Braidotti and Donna Haraway, that engage with the religious, my reasons for focusing on the former two in this book are twofold. First, there has been minimal engagement between this deconstructive branch of feminism and the study of fantasy literature, despite a shared vocabulary between them that I draw attention to throughout these two chapters. But second, the feminisms espoused by Cixous and Irigaray are among only a handful that offer ways of contending with existing patriarchal religious traditions without disavowing religion and theology altogether. Because Cixous and Irigaray approach the theological structures of Judaism and Christianity as sites not merely of critique and opposition but of deconstruction and potential transformation, and because they view this practice as fundamentally necessary for feminism, their work continues to be widely influential for feminist theologians and philosophers of religion today.[8] Nevertheless, claiming Cixous and Irigaray for feminist theology in the twenty-first century necessitates coming to terms with shortcomings and difficulties in their projects. As I demonstrate in these two chapters, fantasy texts can provide a means of realizing their potential, as well as navigating their openness to further deconstruction.

Taking Walton's discussion of literature as the feminized 'other' of theology as a starting point, Chapter 2, 'Dragons in the neighbourhood: The fantastic discourse of femininity', explores the relationship between fantasy and the concept of *écriture feminine* (feminine writing) developed by Hélène Cixous.

Its discussion of *Till We Have Faces* and *The Left Hand of Darkness* examines how the fantastic worldbuilding in these texts interrogates the possibility of a feminine theological subjectivity and disrupts the hierarchical, binary-gendered logic of patriarchy. Chapter 3, 'Hetero-doxies: Fantasy and the problem of divine womanhood', initiates a much more ambivalent engagement with Luce Irigaray's quest for a feminine incarnation of the divine. While Irigaray's project is indispensable for re-visioning the sexual and gendered nature of Christianity's theological imagination, it also shores up the difficulty of creating an alternative imaginary without re-inscribing patriarchal exclusions and hierarchies. In this chapter, an Irigarayan reading of *Till We Have Faces* demonstrates this difficulty while also showing how the novel's meta-fictional elements, which coincide with its fantastical impulses, can be seen to lend nuance to some of Irigaray's grander pronouncements. *The Passion of New Eve*, meanwhile, proves to be a much more thorough problematization of the viability of what Irigaray proposes for theology while still affirming the necessity of the gender-specific re-visioning she advocates.

These discussions open onto the further horizon of queer theology and fantasy. Chapter 4, 'Drag(on) theology: The queer strangers of fantasy', draws on the queer theologies of Marcella Althaus-Reid and Linn Marie Tonstad, as well as queer theories elaborated by Judith Butler and Jack Halberstam, to suggest that fantasy literature is theology dressed in drag. While debates on the blessing of same-sex unions and the inclusion of queer people in the church continue to rage, this chapter argues that fantasy literature provides a space removed from the immediacy of these discourses in which something more radical can emerge. Althaus-Reid's 'Indecent Theology' and Tonstad's queer messianism are presented as frameworks that facilitate a view of queer theological re-visioning as not merely a policy of inclusion but a provisional process of fantastic worldbuilding. This chapter clarifies its argument for fantasy as theology in drag by reading the curious embodiment of dragons in the later novels in the *Earthsea* sequence, *Tehanu* and *The Other Wind*, alongside Judith Butler's deconstruction of gender performativity. This emphasis on drag continues into a close analysis of language in *The Left Hand of Darkness*, highlighting how the novel embraces the failure of gendered vocabulary and the multiple meanings that proliferate from such failure, as part of its theology of alterity. Multiplicity and unsettledness are also on display in *The Passion of New Eve*, which contains the most literal instances of fantastic drag out of all these texts and finds openings towards transcendence, however fleeting, in its parodic play of symbols. My study concludes by identifying some of the implications of my arguments for the study of fantasy, theology and gender going forward, which will include highlighting more recent fantasy texts that can be understood in relation to the methodologies I develop in the rest of this book.

My use of Levinas, Derrida and Cixous – all philosophers writing from a distinctly Jewish position – as theoretical focal points in the first two chapters of a book primarily concerned with Christian theology raises the critical question of the role of religious alterity in this study. To be sure, it would be a mistake, as I elaborate further, to attempt to annex their respective projects into Christian theology or to simply graft their vocabularies onto Western Christian orthodoxy. To do so would mask the crucial fact that Levinas's, Derrida's and Cixous's respective interests in alterity, and in dismantling difference-suppressing symbolic and metaphysical orders, arise out of their own marginality in relation to a dominant culture that is at the very least implicitly Christian. In other words, the specificity of their Jewishness, bearing witness to long histories of violence and oppression at the hands of institutional Christianity, is integral to their philosophical and theological stances.

At the same time, dismantling the dominance of Christian doctrine necessarily involves rigorous engagements with, and habitation within, Christian discourses; as the first two chapters of this book will demonstrate, these are especially apparent in Derrida's and Cixous's writing. Moreover, attention to deconstruction's movements within structures, including religious and theological traditions, reveals that they are not one with themselves but rather heterogeneous. As Alana M. Vincent has noted, there is no such thing as a '"pure" Jewishness', or for that matter, a 'pure' Christianity, 'in isolation from and untainted by the influence of any other religious system' (Vincent 2012: 4).[9] This heterogeneity, revealed by careful attention to deconstruction, undermines institutional Christianity's claims of exclusive access to salvation which have manifested in much interreligious conflict and anti-Semitic violence. Furthermore, in revealing that the ostensibly unitary and fixed tenets of orthodoxy are in fact discontinuous and fragmentary, deconstruction unsettles appeals to divinely ordained law or tradition used to justify misogynistic, homophobic and transphobic theologies and practices. Thus, while religious alterity is not the primary focus of this study, it is understood to be implicitly linked to the practice of theological re-visioning from gendered and sexual axes of difference as well.

By this I do not intend to argue that deconstruction can or should save Christianity, especially its 'official' expressions, from itself. However, I still use the vocabulary of 'religion' and 'theology' throughout this book, and I do so primarily from the position of Christianity, with particular reference to the

Gospels and early church writings of the apostle Paul. I do this partly because it is the primary theological paradigm I inhabit, but also because of its continuing and far-reaching impact, as demonstrated in the examples given earlier, on the lives of those deemed 'other' in relation to its institutional manifestations. While in recent years there have been a number of studies giving attention to marginalized communities turning to fantasy texts to construct alternative theologies, spiritualities and religious practices, these have largely sidestepped the fact that those marginalized by Christianity cannot always, or even often, opt out of its material influence on their lives.[10] The transformation needed within both Christian theology and the theological study of fantasy literature, I argue, is not individual but systemic, although fantasy texts make critical interventions into these systems precisely because they bypass the official institutional channels. This is also why even the most idiosyncratic and heterodox concepts I examine are approached from the position of religion and theology as culturally shared discourses rather than the more nebulous and atomizing category of 'spirituality'. Nevertheless, this project is not undertaken with the intent of foreclosing other religious readings of fantasy or of any of the specific texts discussed. On the contrary, I believe that the deconstructive focus taken up here allows for not only a more rigorous but also a broader understanding of the theological workings of fantasy that is more open to ambivalence and multiplicity than has previously been the case. To the extent that this book does articulate a Christian theology, then, it is the theology of failure outlined by Tonstad which I discuss in Chapter 4: one that disrupts itself rather than promising its ultimate fulfilment or rehabilitation.

Against apologetics

At the time of writing, this is the first book-length study to examine fantasy's relationship to specifically queer and feminist theologies, although recent years have seen a number of journal articles, book chapters and blog posts that suggest a growing scholarly interest in their affinities.[11] Most theological research on fantasy has been concerned with positing fantasy almost as a form of religious apologetics, offering readings of fantasy as a literary form uniquely suited to the propagation of orthodox theological truth by a relatively narrow range of authors. (Among those whose works tend to be the most commonly discussed in this context are Lewis, Tolkien, Charles Williams, George MacDonald, G. K. Chesterton and Madeleine L'Engle.) Religiously oriented scholarship on fantasy to date has largely ignored, to its own detriment, the theological writing from gender and sexually marginalized standpoints that has proliferated from the second half of the twentieth century to today. The tone of theological fantasy criticism was set in the 1980s by Colin N. Manlove, who at that time argued that 'fantasy as it is generally known comprises a large group of directly or indirectly Christian works [. . .] many of which seek to produce in the reader a measure of belief in God' (Manlove 1982: 28).

In the early 1990s, Filmer similarly theorized fantasy as a refuge for the religious in 'a world in which scepticism and nihilism have more currency and are regarded as more valid than religious belief' (Filmer 1992: 2), even suggesting that fantasy texts and their authors serve a priestly function of spiritual renewal and moral instruction (Filmer 1992: 22). The assumption that fantasy shares a relationship with theology and religious belief that is superficially inventive but ultimately instructive, rehabilitative and dogmatically orthodox remains largely unchallenged in current criticism[12] (and, indeed, my own earlier scholarship itself has been content to rehearse this understanding).[13] A 2011 essay by Alison Milbank, for instance, turns to the usual suspects, Lewis and Tolkien, in claiming that '[w]e need estranging techniques [of fantasy] if we are to shock people into engagement with reality, so that they may appreciate the religious sense and we can begin to explain the Christian faith at all' (Milbank 2011: 38). Fantasy's purpose, according to this line of reasoning, is to reinvigorate the theological imagination as it currently exists and bring the unconverted to the light of divine truth, to which an orthodox understanding of the Christian tradition presumably offers privileged access.[14]

For many Christian readers, however, fantasy is not only a source of divine inspiration. Throughout the 1990s and 2000s, the same evangelical Christians who would happily read *The Chronicles of Narnia* or *The Hobbit* with their children also expressed consternation over the ostensibly corrupting, even demonic, influence of texts like the television series *Buffy the Vampire Slayer* (1996–2003),[15] J. K. Rowling's *Harry Potter* novels (1997–2007)[16] and the novels in Philip Pullman's *His Dark Materials* trilogy (1995–2000).[17] Fantasy's status as both divine and demonic, orthodox and heretical, profoundly religious and threateningly atheistic, makes it particularly a generative territory for subjects whose marginality in relation to dominant theological discourses demands a theology that navigates similar spaces between sacred and profane. The inventive possibilities offered by the secondary worlds of fantasy mean that the religious landscapes of fantasy texts also need not be beholden to the histories and heritages that mark them in the primary world, lending writers and readers the ability to speak new figurations of God and humanity, and new configurations of communion between them, into being.

A reading of fantasy as Christian apologetics first and foremost, then, is uninspired both as theology and as literary criticism. Because the focus of such studies has often been arguing for the validity of religious belief and Christian literary imagination per se, they have usually favoured a broad-strokes approach to Christian doctrine that tends to elide more specific points of theological inquiry and debate.[18] The result of this is that 'religious belief', 'Christian orthodoxy' and 'Christian literary imagination' are invoked as authoritative and unchanging unities, with the vagueness of their deployment paradoxically reinforcing specific prejudices and beliefs while conveniently avoiding their ethical and political implications. While the authors of some of these studies may express feminist values and be individually affirming of LGBTQ+ people, women and LGBTQ+ people cannot safely assume that any given theological project has our best interests at heart, for the reasons I have demonstrated earlier. On the contrary, upon closer inspection, these invocations of doctrine, orthodoxy and belief contain gaps and silences which betray a certain (patriarchal, cis- and hetero-sexist) understanding of gender and a set of moral and sexual values, which are either explicitly or implicitly taken at face value as divinely ordained. As I discuss further in Chapter 2, this especially rears its head in projects like Monika B. Hilder's, whose understanding of Christian theology relies heavily on a hierarchically gendered notion of divine sovereignty and therefore cannot fulfil its own stated feminist aims, salient though much of its textual analysis is.

These norms can also rear their heads in subtler ways, as in Milbank's reading of the final passages of *The Lord of the Rings*, in which Samwise Gamgee returns to his wife and children after bidding farewell to Frodo at the Grey Havens. In her estimation,

> [h]ere is reality as we know it: a fire in the hearth, supper, spouse, and a child on one's lap. And yet, long denied to Sam by his grim journey to Mordor with Frodo, these domestic details take on a new pellucid reality. Here is life as it should be lived, in relation to other humans but also with the inanimate world of chair and light. And even these simple elements of life lead us upward and further. If Frodo's ending gives us the opening to the transcendent, the blue flower of homesickness for heaven, Sam's opens us to the immanence of the real, and little Elanor is herself named for a flower in the magic forests of Lothlórien.
>
> (Milbank 2011: 42)

That Milbank chooses to highlight this domestic scene to demonstrate the imaginative potential for theology of a novel that features magic, wraiths, fell beasts, giant spiders, elves who commune with the natural world, and characters who struggle against their own capacity for evil, cannot help but feel, ironically, like a failure of imagination. At the very least, it is telling that for Milbank, 'the immanence of the real' is most keenly felt within the confines of monogamous, reproductive, heterosexual matrimony, which she goes on to gloss as 'life as it should be lived'. Such a reading forecloses the possibility that it may also be a matter of theological importance to dismantle sexuality, the gendered division of labour in the home and constructions of the family. In other words, the current approach to theology and fantasy does not consider how the fantastic imagination can remind theology of its calling to seek a life *other* than that prescribed within dominant understandings of reality, including constructions of reality in which Christian doctrine is itself complicit.[19] Those historically marginalized by the institutional church may also have radically different relationships to theological concepts such as the doctrine of incarnation, the notion of sacramentality and the redemption of creation than are usually available within the signifying structures of patriarchal, heterosexual Christianity. In this context, fantasy can become a mode of counter-storytelling to dominant theological systems. Understanding this is precisely the task taken up by this book, and it requires careful attention to deconstructive processes at work in theology, fantasy texts and understandings of the primary world itself.

Deconstruction, theology and feminism

Throughout this book, deconstruction as defined by Jacques Derrida will be crucial to understanding the subversive and transformative potential fantasy literature carries for theology. For many queer and feminist theologians, deconstruction has proved indispensable for dethroning oppressive and exclusionary readings of scripture and theology, demonstrating that such interpretations are not as authoritative as they may seem and pointing to sites where traditions may be open to subversion and rearticulation. As Althaus-Reid notes, '[w]e are used to a universal reading of the Scriptures [. . .] without suspecting that such an ample perspective excludes a lot of people from marginalized groups. The universal reading is really European, male and white' (Althaus-Reid 2004: 18). A deconstructive relationship to orthodoxy is thus necessary for many marginalized theologians, and this book draws on a corpus of existing writing that foregrounds this need.[20] Even so, deconstruction's implications for Christian theology have been a highly contentious subject from the moment theologians first became familiar with Derrida's work, and even now continue to spark debate, so much so that to offer an exhaustive account of discourse on Derrida and religion would be impossible. Nonetheless, the critical discussions undertaken in this study necessitate a brief historical overview of the various modes, and pitfalls, of engaging with deconstruction from the standpoint of Christian theology.

One of the most influential earlier theologians to write on Derrida was Thomas J. J. Altizer, who reads deconstruction 'as a contemporary expression of demythologizing' (Altizer 1982: 147) and 'a demolition of all the significations that have their source in the logos [. . . that] is only possible through the end of history or the death of God' (Altizer 1982: 156). Altizer's pronouncements are typical both of the 1982 collection in which they appear, *Deconstruction and Theology*, and of the 'death of God' theology in vogue throughout the 1980s, which posited that theology's only option in the face of growing secularization and cultural fragmentation was to embrace oblivion. They are also, as my discussion of deconstruction in Chapter 1 will make clear, based on an overdetermined misrepresentation of deconstructive philosophy as a primarily nihilistic pursuit.

While most writing on deconstruction and theology since the 1980s has not followed the line of interpretation taken up by Altizer and his cohort, his approach has been influential enough that most theological studies of Derrida must dedicate much space to dispelling the notion of deconstruction as inherently nihilistic. In actual fact, deconstructive philosophy is intimately concerned with religion and rarely ever in a straightforwardly antagonistic fashion. This is most clear in Derrida's later work; throughout the 1990s until his death in 2004, Derrida published many texts directly commenting on religious themes (such as death, the gift, sacrifice and hospitality) and their many intersections with philosophical history, ethics and global geopolitics.[21] This is to say nothing of the pieces of autobiographical writing by Derrida contending with his own ambivalent relationship to, and the liminality and undecidability inherent within, his religious identity as a Jewish man writing from the margins of a predominantly Christian society.[22] Yet even in Derrida's earliest writing on deconstruction in *Writing and Difference* and *Of Grammatology*, both published in 1967, theology and religion often come to the fore. Derrida's relationship to theology is complex. His insistence on the impossibility of universal and determined signification with its origins in the divine *logos*, his wariness of purity discourses and his tireless demonstration that traditions, cultures, nations and concepts are never fully one with themselves spell trouble for Christian theology as it has been historically conceived, and indeed for any religious tradition that claims privileged access to divinity through its signs and symbols. And yet, not only does Derrida refuse to do away with religion, he continually acknowledges a quasi-religious, messianic structure in his own concern for the radically other, which he holds to be the driving impulse of deconstruction.

This latter point has sometimes led to theological readings of Derrida that give the impression, explicitly or implicitly, that deconstruction is itself a theology or that deconstructive philosophy is inherently theistic. Hugh Rayment-Pickard, while taking care to acknowledge that 'Christianity does not share Derrida's anxiety about making positive theological statements' (Rayment-Pickard 2003: 150), nonetheless describes what Derrida calls *différance* as 'theology in a more pure, more total and irreducible form' (Rayment-Pickard 2003: 7) than metaphysical onto-theology. He goes further to argue that 'Derrida's deconstruction would be better thought of as a kind of *proof*, the demonstration of the *possibility* of God's impossibility' (Rayment-Pickard 2003: 144). Graham Ward, meanwhile, has gone even further than this, attempting to map Derrida's terms onto Karl Barth's *Church Dogmatics*, claiming that

> [i]t is the process of discourse, the logic of its referring and deferring in which the hermeneutical project is both disrupted and returned to, which is the focal interest of both Barth and Derrida. Discourse weaves a way of faith between the Spirit that questions, disrupts and promises and human attempts at representing this action. Discourse is the presentation of otherness *and* human representations of it; the Saying *and* the said, the Word *and* the words.
>
> (Ward 1995: 245)

Both Rayment-Pickard and Ward convincingly draw attention to the theological resonances in Derrida's writing on impossibility, messianicity, finitude and alterity. Yet while they are careful to acknowledge, at least nominally, deconstructive philosophy's distinctness from most Christian theology, they are just as apt to obscure this distinction by collapsing the vocabularies of deconstruction and Christian orthodoxy into one another, as if to suggest that Christianity was 'really' deconstructive, or deconstruction 'really' about Christ, all along. Such an approach domesticates the radicalism of Derrida's project and re-inscribes the same metaphysics of transcendence (for instance, in Ward's framing of an ultimate Word that not only transcends but is easily distinguishable from mere 'words') that deconstruction shows to be impossible.

Perhaps the most thorough and nuanced (and most widely influential) direct engagement with the religious implications of Derrida's work is John D. Caputo's *The Prayers and Tears of Jacques Derrida* (1997). Caputo's reading is much more successful than those offered by Rayment-Pickard and Ward, to the extent that it preserves much of Derrida's ambivalence towards any theological discourse, which is often lost or prematurely resolved in Christian readings. This is evident in his claim that '[d]ifférance does not settle the God question one way or the other; in fact, the point is to un-settle it, to make it more difficult, by showing that, even as we love the name of God, we must still ask what it is we love' (Caputo 1997: 13). These are the words of a scholar who has more fully taken on board the radical rethinking that deconstruction signals for theology, and indeed, Caputo's interpretation of Derrida has proven invaluable for my own arguments in the first chapter of this book. Yet in (rightly) pointing to the wide-ranging implications deconstruction carries for theology, Caputo, too, risks overstating his case. In his portrait of Derrida as a latter-day Augustine who 'rightly pass[es] for an atheist' even while 'praying and weeping over, waiting and longing for, calling upon and being called upon by something' (Caputo, *PT*, xviii), Caputo comes very close to reducing deconstruction to an ascetic spiritual practice.

Deconstruction is intricately bound up with theological concerns, and indeed its own underlying impulses are very close to the ones that underpin theology and religion. At the same time, it is irreducible simply to another theological discourse; rather, it is a movement already at work within theological structures, whether acknowledged or not. The challenge facing theological projects wishing to contend with deconstruction is resisting the temptation either to reduce deconstruction to a set of theological claims or to prescribe predetermined orthodox Christian doctrines as a corrective to Derrida.[23] This book adopts a deconstructive space within theology that takes cues from the influence of Jewish ethical philosopher Emmanuel Levinas on Derrida's work. Tracing Derrida's development of Levinas's writing on the other, it shows that Derrida's attention to the points at which structures, ideologies and discourses unravel arises out of primarily ethical and political concerns, and demonstrates how theology may be opened to disruption by the others it suppresses, excludes or hides away. The excellent essays found in Yvonne Sherwood and Kevin Hart's edited collection *Derrida and Religion: Other Testaments* (2005) remain among the best demonstrations of the radical possibilities that arise when theology is left utterly vulnerable to its others. Attending to the processes involved in the construction of theological concepts reveals that their claims to universality and access to the divine depend on the other that they must violently suppress in order to make such claims. Deconstruction shows that theological re-visioning is thus not merely a matter of making either theological discourse or religious communities more inclusive; the fundamental stories they tell about God, humanity, the church and the world must be reconfigured.

It is difficult to overstate the significance of Derrida's project for feminism and particularly the queer theories that have arisen out of feminist projects like Judith Butler's. Derrida himself directly commented often on feminist concerns with regularity,[24] and his consistent gendering of devalued alterity as 'woman' has proved alternately generative and contentious within feminist contexts. In the introduction to her 1997 edited collection *Feminist Interpretations of Jacques Derrida*, which gives a thorough overview of Anglo-American debates surrounding deconstruction and feminism, Nancy J. Holland summarizes the potential reasons for feminist trepidation regarding Derrida's work as follows:

> Although there is considerable debate among feminists about whether there is any 'essence' that defines women as such, it is also the case that much feminist thought continues to see itself as freeing women from the confines of patriarchal oppression so that we may realize our true inner natures. Given this perspective, to be told that both essence and truth must be 'deconstructed' seems to present a serious challenge to the feminist project.
>
> (Holland 1997: 7)

However, Derrida's point in designating as 'woman' precisely that which cannot be named, and which cannot claim a subjectivity for itself, is to show the extent to which the default subject in Western thought is male and how intimately the structures of Western language are tied to patriarchy. As he clarified in a seminar given at Brown University, later published as 'Women in the Beehive' (1984), 'when we say that the ego, the "I think", is neither man nor woman, we can in fact verify that it's already a man, and not a woman' (Derrida et al. [1984] 2005: 146). Consequently, '[i]n a given situation, which is ours, which is the European, phallogocentric structure, the side of the woman is the side from which you start to dismantle the structure' (Derrida et al. [1984] 2005: 146). For Derrida, 'woman' is not necessarily an eternal symbol of difference, but the position of 'woman' as she is constructed and subordinated within Western, patriarchal discourse can serve as a space from which to think deconstructively.

As Walton notes, many feminists have taken up the task Derrida implicitly lays out here in 'working to make manifest the relation between "woman" as a trope or rhetorical device and the creative struggles of women to refigure social and symbolic systems' (Walton 2007: 19). Chapters 2 and 3 draw respective attention to the ways in which Hélène Cixous and Luce Irigaray have found subversive potential for their own deconstructive projects in philosophical and theological invocations of 'woman' as a symbol, and relate these projects to fantasy texts' reconfigurations of gender in religious contexts. For women writing from the margins of feminism, deconstructive philosophy also creates opportunities for crucial interventions into feminist discourse. As these projects show, feminist desires to articulate a coherent feminist subject, whose needs and experiences form the basis for feminist action, shore up new and more complex erasures and sites of exclusion and oppression. Thus, deconstructive philosophy is invoked by Gayatri Chakravorty Spivak to show that 'women's subjectivity' is *white, Western* women's subjectivity[25] and by Judith Butler, who points out that the trope of 'woman' is almost exclusively *heterosexual, cisgender* and *feminine-presenting*.[26]

As generative as the position of 'woman' can be for inhabiting a deconstructive space within normative, patriarchal discourses, the category 'woman' is itself open to deconstruction. This study thus acknowledges that feminism's aims include the dismantling (and provisional reconfiguration) of the very identity designations, the very configurations of gender and sexuality, that render it both necessary and possible. Both by taking seriously the marginal position of woman-as-difference in dominant discourses and by demonstrating that the category of 'woman' conceals differences, contradictions and exclusions within itself, deconstructive feminism safeguards against re-inscribing patriarchal hierarchies and oppositions. Deconstruction, in Spivak's words, serves as a constant reminder that in speaking at all, even from the margins, 'we are involved in a structure that we must persistently critique' (Spivak 1989b: 213). While by no means reducible to either discipline, careful attention to deconstruction is therefore crucial for both theology and feminism, and especially in navigating between the two.

Fantasy: Definitions, critical approaches and figurations

Studies relating fantasy to deconstruction are scant, and the ones that do exist tend to subsume deconstruction within a broad characterization of 'postmodernism' (a term from which Derrida took pains to distance himself).[27] For this reason, a significant portion of Chapter 1 is devoted to a renewed and in-depth examination of the potential affinities between fantasy writing and deconstruction, particularly where theology is concerned. Before any further discussion of fantasy literature is possible, however, it is necessary to define the term 'fantasy' as it will be used throughout this book. The study of fantasy literature is still relatively new in the academy, having only been considered a viable subject of literary criticism in a substantial way since the late 1970s and only very recently has this work translated into any kind of institutional status.[28] In the field's early days, much ink was spilled in debates concerning how to define 'fantasy' and demarcate its borders, often employing increasingly idiosyncratic criteria for what does and does not qualify a text as fantasy. Kathryn Hume has noted that in any attempt to set rigid boundaries around fantasy, '[w]hat remains [. . .] is a small corpus of texts, all fairly uniform' that 'is duly declared to be "fantasy" – with little thought given to all the works that have departures from reality which somehow fail to fit the rules' (Hume 1984: 8).

Rather than endlessly rehearse these debates, then, this study follows Hume's precedent in seeking a definition of fantasy 'as inclusive and as flexible as possible' (Hume 1984: 20). Like Hume, this book understands fantasy in the broadest possible sense as '*any departure from consensus reality*' (Hume 1984: 21); moreover (and in a manner distinct from Hume's definition), fantasy texts are to be understood as texts for whom this departure is among their defining features. By 'consensus reality', Hume means a generally accepted, broadly normative understanding of reality that is nonetheless historically and culturally contingent, based on prevailing social norms. Fantasy, in other words, transgresses dominant prescriptions of reality and possibility, and it is this that I argue gives it deconstructive potential from positions of gendered and sexual marginality, as well as other axes of difference. Hume's desire for an expansive view of fantasy can also be observed in the work of many contemporary scholars and writers, such as in Hal Duncan's queering of distinctions between science fiction and fantasy in favour of his 'strange fictions' designation.[29] Along similar lines, Brian Attebery's definition of 'the fantastic' as 'creative and disruptive play with representations of the real world' (Attebery 2014: 32) invites a reading of fantasy as inherently deconstructive. Implicit in these wide-ranging and adaptable definitions of fantasy is the suggestion that its very contentiousness and undefinability is one of its defining features. As Lucie Armitt notes, fantasy is 'fluid, constantly overspilling the very forms it adopts, always looking, not so much for escapism but certainly to escape the constraints that critics [. . .] always and inevitably impose upon it' (Armitt 1996: 3).

Fantasy is a contention with *impossibility*; it confronts us with landscapes, creatures and events characterized by a heightened sense of the *other*; and it engages in fabulously disruptive play with cultural grand narratives both sacred and secular. Though the worlds represented within fantasy texts often appear to be self-contained and internally consistent at first glance, they frequently not only subvert the established norms of the primary world but also throw their own secondary-world representations into question. *Till We Have Faces*, *The Left Hand of Darkness* and the *Earthsea* sequence all contend with the impossibility of giving coherent accounts of the mysteries of their worlds, while in *The Passion of New Eve*, the line separating the world of fantasy from the world of 'reality' is fuzzy, permeable and ultimately revealed to be arbitrary.

This latter description could easily be applied to the borders of the fantasy genre itself, as my review of existing scholarship attests. In fact, all three case study novels I have chosen throw genre into question as well. While the majority of the scant scholarship that exists on the novel reads it as a fantasy, Doris T. Myers has argued that *Till We Have Faces* can and should be read according to 'the assumptions of all realistic fiction' (Myers 2004: 3), suggesting that '[t]he literary genre it most closely resembles is that of the historical novel' (Myers 2004: 5). Meanwhile, *The Passion of New Eve* is as likely to be variously described as magic realism, science fiction, erotic horror and postmodern literary fiction as it is to be aligned with fantasy and fairy tales.[30] Perhaps most problematically, *The Left Hand of Darkness* features interstellar travel, alien technology and interplanetary politics, all more traditionally viewed as hallmarks of the science fiction genre under which the novel is usually marketed. Yet it also contains unexplained mystical phenomena and continually disrupts its own narrative unity – and the reader's expectations of its world – with fragments of religious texts, mythic histories and folk tales, all of which are included in even the most conventional definitions of fantasy literature. As Attebery notes, fantasy's fluidity means that in any critical study, '[t]he interesting question about any given story is not whether or not it is fantasy or science fiction or realistic novel, but rather what happens when we read it as one of these things' (Attebery 2014: 38). Thus, while this study recognizes the scholarly utility of delineating, contextualizing and ideologically critiquing different subgenres of fantasy, as Farah Mendlesohn has most notably done in *Rhetorics of Fantasy* (2008),[31] it deliberately takes an open-ended approach that blurs these ultimately arbitrary, if discursively generative, distinctions.

What happens when we read a text like *The Left Hand of Darkness*, *Till We Have Faces* or *The Passion of New Eve* as fantasy, I argue, is that rethinking gender and sexuality becomes a matter not only of political but also of religious importance. That is, attention to gendered and sexual alterity is necessary for theology while also requiring a radical reconfiguration of theology, religious practice and community. Politically radical readings of fantasy are nothing new, be they psychoanalytic,[32] Marxist[33] or anarchist.[34] What sets the argument of this book apart from others is its specifically religious focus, which highlights fantasy's ability to subvert (and even to pervert) primary-world religious traditions, at the same time as it takes seriously religious quests for alterity. Moreover, it seeks to take the conversation on marginality in fantasy beyond the optics of representation and show that fantasy's construction of secondary worlds and creation of 'unreal' characters, creatures and events mean that in fantasy, theology and self-identity are already disrupted at the very moment of their articulation.

Whether this disruption is acknowledged by readers, or politically taken up in their interpretive strategies, is another matter. Fantasy always risks re-inscribing oppressive normativities and uncritically embracing exclusionary grand narratives. Many fantasy texts, whether intentionally or not, reinforce patriarchal ideals and hierarchical constructions of gender in the worlds they construct, and many fail to imagine secondary worlds sufficiently distinct from the conditions marginalized subjects experience as oppressive in the primary world. Recent controversies such as the right-wing, anti-diversity Sad Puppies campaign, which emerged with the express aim of swaying votes for the 2013 Hugo Awards and continuing through 2017,[35] have shown that fantasy's deconstructive potential does not necessarily translate to radical politics on the part of authors and readers. This is, however, the risk embodied by any deconstructive project, and it is furthermore a risk without which openness to the other would not be possible. Attebery has commented that even '[t]he mass-market paperback fantasy with a lurid cover is [. . .] outside the culturally defined norm' (Attebery 1992: ix), and a similar thing is true of the theological imaginaries articulated therein. While the radical potential embodied within fantasy is by no means inevitable, even the most conservative theologies reveal themselves to be open to subversive readings when placed in the context of a secondary world.

While the texts I discuss offer alternative theological orders, understandings of divine incarnation, configurations of gender and sexuality, and religious practices, none of these are to be taken as final, authoritative or prescriptive. As Brian Attebery has noted, a peculiar feature of fantasy is that

> [i]t denies its own validity; the one characteristic shared by all fantasy narratives is their nonfactuality. The fundamental premise of fantasy is that the things it tells not only did not happen but *could* not have happened. In that literal untruth is a freedom to tell many symbolic truths without forcing a choice among them.
>
> (Attebery 2014: 4)

By this, Attebery does not mean that fantasy participates in a blind relativism in which anything could be true; rather, fantasy's self-consciousness about its own unreality can act as a safeguard against theological claims to absolute authority. Although fantasy is characterized by its attention to alterity, it can do no more than gesture towards the other via reconfigurations of the familiar. For this reason, Rosi Braidotti's concept of *figurations* is immensely valuable for critical discussions of fantasy. According to Braidotti, '[a] figuration is a politically informed account of an alternative subjectivity' (Braidotti 1994: 1) that draws attention to its own status as 'a political fiction' (Braidotti 1994: 4). Figurations, in other words, are ways of giving speculative and provisional form to that which eludes representation within the set of available signs. Chapter 2 will discuss in more depth how fantasy participates in the construction of figurations when it comes to gendered and sexed theological subjectivity and embodiment.

A subset of figurations to which this book returns often is that of the monster. As Jack Halberstam notes, '[m]onsters are meaning machines. [. . .] [They] have to be everything the human is not and, in producing the negative of human, [. . .] make way for the invention of human as white, male, middle class, and heterosexual' (Halberstam 1995: 21–2). Monstrosity has been recognized by Halberstam, Braidotti and Jeffrey Jerome Cohen as a fantastic discourse of representation of the radically other, against which the Western human subject has been constructed. This has often included gendered and sexual difference but also intersects with other axes of difference such as race, class and disability. In a theological context, monstrosity can also stand in for the horror of the unknowable; at least part of the threat the monster poses stems from the way it breaks with traditional schemes of representation. This means that the monster is not simply reducible to a metaphor for difference but may also provide avenues into rethinking embodiment and subjectivity. As Halberstam puts it, '[t]he monster always represents the disruption of categories, the destruction of boundaries, and the presence of impurities and so we need monsters and we need to recognize and celebrate our own monstrosities' (Halberstam 1995: 27). This book elaborates how the religious imaginaries of fantasy texts make forays into the monstrous as part of their queer and feminist projects of re-visioning.

As I have already discussed, my use of the same three texts as my main case studies in each chapter attests that feminist practices of theological re-visioning are multi-layered; feminist and queer theologies arise out of common impulses and remain in constant conversation with one another. While discontinuities and incompatibilities will often become apparent, the self-consciously contingent and unsettled practices of queer and feminist theology mean that these impasses do not necessarily spell doom for the entire enterprise. As Althaus-Reid and Lisa Isherwood note, 'for [feminist theologians] the controversies are the life-blood, they signal that more unfolding is to be done' (Althaus-Reid and Isherwood 2007: 3). Nor is this project undertaken in an attempt to retroactively baptize any particular fantasy text or claim them definitively 'for' Christianity. What this book persistently affirms, however, is the need for theology take on board the challenges that issue from its margins, and to continually open the gendered and sexual realities it constructs, and the figurations of God and the body it offers, to disruption in the face of the other.

1

Saving face?

Fantasy, ethical alterity and deconstruction

Any attempt to articulate a theology from the position of gendered and sexual marginality must consist of more than simply saving face on behalf of religious orthodoxy. On the contrary, its entire relationship to orthodoxy must be fundamentally different to the established norm. A queer, feminist approach to theology specifically necessitates a resistance to the claims of absolute truth and exclusive access to the divine as *logos* that generally characterize patriarchal religious systems. It needs, in Marcella Althaus-Reid's words, 'to replace hegemonic divine concepts by deviant (unnatural) styles of thinking, helping people to develop their own identities outside the closure and boundaries of theo/social systems' (Althaus-Reid 2000: 175). Despite its common adoption as a tool for religious apologetics, which I outlined in the introduction, fantasy literature carries potential for disrupting representations of reality that religious orthodoxy both depends on and perpetuates with its claims to authority. The secondary worlds presented in fantasy texts can shake the foundations of the 'primary' world from which they necessarily draw influence – in other words, 'reality' as constructed within a fundamentally patriarchal, heterosexual and cisgender framework. This tendency, this chapter argues, is best understood in terms of the deconstructive philosophy put forth by Jacques Derrida. Likewise, many fantasy texts can be seen to dramatize deconstructive philosophy's attempts to describe a movement which it names 'deconstruction', one that consists, as Derrida puts it, in 'opening, uncloseting, destabilizing foreclusionary structures' (Derrida [1987] 1992: 341).

This chapter examines the ways in which fantasy literature can be read as deconstructive in relation to patriarchal religious structures. I will demonstrate that not only is deconstruction always already at work within fantasy texts and the religious structures they uphold, but also that some fantasy texts, such as those I am examining in this book, are also alert to their own deconstructive power, whether or not the texts themselves or their authors define this power according to such terms. The argument of this chapter is twofold. First, fantasy texts and deconstruction have homologous structures; both situate themselves in terms of impossibility and alterity, and therefore share a radical potential for the disruption not only of normative constructs but also of normativity per se. Second, both of them have relationships to religion specifically that equip them to inhabit a critical space within theology that affirms theology's language and concepts at the same time that it dismantles them. As discourses, fantasy and deconstructive philosophy are mutually illuminating; from one perspective, fantasy can give more concrete form to concepts and terms commonly associated with deconstruction, especially those related to religion, that may otherwise come across as esoteric. At the same time, reading fantasy's relationship to theology as a deconstructive one allows for a more nuanced understanding of the theological work that fantasy texts do and safeguards fantasy against the appeals to sovereign authority that exclude women and queer people from theology.

I will begin this chapter with a brief overview of deconstruction as theorized by Derrida. The theological implications of deconstruction will be crucial to this discussion and therefore particular attention will be given to how Derrida's discourse on theology relates to his interest in alterity. For this purpose, I trace a genealogy of influence between Emmanuel Levinas's ethics of the other and Derrida's work on deconstruction, particularly highlighting *Writing and Difference*, *Of Grammatology*, 'Psyche: Inventions of the Other', *The Gift of Death*, *Rogues* and 'Faith and Knowledge'. In these texts, Derrida foregrounds his project's nature as an advent of the other, and in doing so develops and extends Levinas's interest in the divine command towards ethical responsibility signified by the face of the other, who is utterly heterogeneous to the sovereign subject. While the definitions of 'alterity' and 'the other' will become complicated in later chapters of this book as queer and feminist theories and theologies draw from the language of psychoanalysis alongside deconstruction, for the purposes of this chapter these terms are to be understood in the theo/ethical sense that they are used by Levinas unless otherwise stated. In the second part of this chapter, I consider deconstruction alongside theories of fantasy elaborated by Tolkien, Le Guin and Attebery. I then turn to *Till We Have Faces*, *The Left Hand of Darkness* and *The Passion of New Eve* as case studies, conducting close readings that will demonstrate how each text not only uncovers sites of potential disruption by displacing theological structures into secondary worlds but also dramatizes the deconstructive power of fantastic storytelling in the process.

Defining deconstruction, deconstructing definitions

Derrida's fascination with God as a name for a disruptive ethical 'other' presents ample opportunity for troubling and transgressing normative religious doctrines and theological systems, particularly those situated within Western philosophical discourses, without disavowing theology altogether. Mentions of God pervade Derrida's philosophical writing, but these almost never occur in a clear-cut fashion, and they tend to be impossible to pin down to a particular faith commitment or even a rejection thereof. The closest Derrida comes to making an explicit statement about belief in God is in an interview with John D. Caputo, Kevin Hart and Yvonne Sherwood, in which he states that

> [i]f belief in God is not also a culture of atheism, if it does not go through a number of atheistic steps, one does not believe in God. There must be a critique of idolatry, of all sorts of images in prayer, especially prayer, there must be a critique of onto-theology – the reappropriation of God in metaphysics [. . .] In order to be authentic – this is a word I almost never use – the belief in God must be exposed to absolute doubt.
>
> (Derrida et al. 2005: 46)

The paradoxes and contradictions contained within this brief quotation, chief among them that between faith and atheism, and that of faith *as* atheism and vice versa, are a summation of the profound ambivalence with which Derrida approaches the question of God in his work. Throughout his writings Derrida is harshly critical of the God of classical theology figured as absolute presence, 'the absolute witness to the dialogue in which what one sets out to write has already been read, and what one sets out to say is already a response, the third party as the transparency of meaning[.] Simultaneously part of creation and the Father of Logos' (Derrida [1967] 1979: 11). As we shall see, such a God as is described here, who serves as source and determiner of all meaning, is to Derrida both impossible and an oppressive function of Western logic. And yet, for Derrida this is not the final word on the question of God; the question remains, and must remain, open for deconstruction to be possible. Elsewhere, in *The Gift of Death* (1992), Derrida also offers the name of God as 'the name of the absolute other as other and as unique' (Derrida [1992] 1995: 68). That is, God is utterly heterogeneous to what could be articulated as proper by any speaking subject.

Derrida's treatment of the name of God follows the premise that God is outside the realm of human understanding, a claim to which few theologians would object, but takes this in a far more radical direction than most theologians would. Derrida's invocation of the name of God as a name for the other serves at once to point to the absoluteness of the other's alterity and to unsettle the name of God. As Derrida elaborates in 'Epoché and Faith', 'God is not some thing or some being to which I could refer by using the word "God". The word "God" has an essential link to the possibility of being denied' (Derrida et al. 2005: 37). The very name 'God' points to the impossibility of what it names, since to invoke God is to invoke what would be alien to articulation within a language, a theology or a faith tradition. To believe in God, for Derrida, is to be an atheist because belief in God requires refusing the finality of any 'belief' in 'God' that could be stated. While acknowledging this is not the same as rejecting theology, it does demand that theology give up its dreams of absolute authority. To quote Althaus-Reid, 'theology has its own deconstructive forces, its own instabilities and imprecisions which always create tensions and open new ways of understanding' (Althaus-Reid 2000: 148), but these cannot be rearticulations of divine authority as it has been understood. It is for this reason that deconstruction also enables theologians marginalized by hetero-patriarchal and cis-sexist religious structures to radically challenge the underlying assumptions of orthodoxy on the grounds that hegemonic orthodoxy is not a unified whole, and already contains within itself the potential for rupture and transgression from a position of difference.

Althaus-Reid, Caputo, Walton and many others have extensively identified and made ample use of the opportunity for radical rethinking and re-visioning that deconstruction enables, even demands, for theology. Scholars of fantasy, however, have been more reluctant to take on Derrida's project. It has often been presumed that a deconstructive approach to fantasy would be inimical to theological or otherwise mystical readings of the genre. Insofar as common ground is identified, fantasy is positioned over and against Derrida's work to correct perceived flaws and shortcomings. Most famously, C. S. Lewis scholar Kath Filmer has dismissed deconstructive writing as a 'philosophical cloud-cuckoo-land' (Filmer 1989: 55) that consists of 'the disruption and denial of textual meaning' (Filmer 1989: 56). To Filmer, such a discipline 'depends on the absence of an objective reality; since there is nothing to be perceived, there can be no perception' (Filmer 1989: 57). As an alternative or antidote to such apparent nihilistic madness, Filmer presents mythopoetic fantasy as 'a kind of deconstructive activity which is every bit as radical as Derrida's, with the considerable advantage that the mythopoetic mode makes good sense' (Filmer 1989: 60). For her, the tangible forms of fantasy are far better equipped to challenge received notions of reality than the horrifying, alienating void that deconstruction apparently signifies.

Though not as strident in his position as Filmer, Marek Oziewicz has similarly grouped deconstruction together with a handful of potential approaches to fantasy he identifies as 'reductionist' (Oziewicz 2008: 4). Oziewicz categorizes 'reductionism' and 'holism' as two opposing approaches to fantasy, claiming that

> [w]hereas the former was interested in fantasy as a cultural practice which reveals political, historical, economic, gender and other entanglements that characterize human activities, the latter approached fantasy as a cultural practice whose meaning encompasses yet extends beyond those entanglements and aims to create a platform for imaginative representation of transcultural concepts and values. Whereas the former adopted as its allies relativism, biological determinism, naturalism, behaviourism, Freudianism and secularism and used them to examine fantasy, the latter aligned itself with the school of *sophia perennis*, antireductionism, essentialism, and Jungian, religious and spiritual perspectives.
> (Oziewicz 2008: 4–5)

Oziewicz's lists of values here are odd, given that they group together wildly divergent and often incompatible strands of thought on opposing poles of a culture war with little effort made to elaborate on them or to justify their alliances. The important point for Oziewicz's argument is, apparently, that approaches he deems 'reductionist' are inappropriate for fantasy in that

> [t]hey are anti-essentialist, relativistic, and politicized, besides asserting that reality is a linguistic construct, that all meanings are provisional, and that the concept of human nature, along with any talk about values or meanings in literature, must be distrusted as Euro- and andro-centric.
> (Oziewicz 2008: 29)

By contrast, 'holistic' approaches to fantasy, of which theological readings are one example,

> [see] fantasy literature – with its tendency for depicting unquestionably supernatural events and building stories on the protagonists' reactions to a reality suddenly flooded with the supernatural – as one of the ways modern humans express their yearning for mystery and continue to reflect on the meaning of life.
> (Oziewicz 2008: 5)

Even leaving aside the question of how allegedly 'reductionist' philosophies can be at once too relativistic and too staunchly political, Oziewicz's binary framing fails to consider how the supernaturally suffused realities presented in fantasy are blatant linguistic constructs; how 'the meaning of life' and any concept of divinity, transcendence and the human subject are always mediated through cultural, philosophical and linguistic presuppositions; and, most crucially, how the worlds presented in fantasy can unsettle such assumptions. In the following section, I map out some key points of Derrida's deconstruction in relation to questions of God and religion. This discussion will show that far from being reductionist, deconstruction opens onto a richer, more thorough engagement with religious themes, and with religious impulses in fantasy, than is possible within the narrow 'holism' that Filmer and Oziewicz advocate.

Vive la différance

Defining deconstruction is made difficult by the fact that 'deconstruction' refers both to a philosophical discourse and to what that discourse attempts to describe. This is partially because, especially in English, the word 'deconstruction' is easily misconstrued when used to describe the movement with which Derrida's writing concerns itself. As he states, '[the] word, at least on its own, has never appeared satisfactory to me (but what word is), and must always be girded by an entire discourse' (Derrida [1983] 1988: 3). Furthermore, Maria-Daniella Dick and Julian Wolfreys note that deconstruction's concern with disrupting and unravelling structures from within means that '[t]here can be no definition of deconstruction as a concept [. . .] to do so would be to traduce its movement, which would anyway already be at work within "itself"' (Dick and Wolfreys 2013: 55). In other words, any possible definition or even utterance of 'deconstruction' is open to the same disruptive movement which it describes. Deconstruction, as a movement within structures, does not supervene upon them from the outside; it is not a theory or a critical tool that can be applied because, according to Derrida, '[d]econstruction takes place, it is an event that does not await the deliberation, consciousness, or organization of a subject, or even of modernity' (Derrida [1983] 1988: 4).

One of the principal concerns of deconstruction as a philosophical discourse is the disruption of logocentrism, the metaphysical assumption that signifying structures have an essential origin in 'the logos or in the infinite understanding of God' (Derrida [1967] 1997: 11). Logocentrism and its derivative phonocentrism, or the belief in 'pure speech' (Derrida [1967] 1979: 9), hold that speech derives from a transcendental signified or original 'truth', inscribed as 'the logos of a creator God' (Derrida [1967] 1997: 14). For Derrida such a system cannot help but betray theological assumptions since conceptually '[t]he sign and [metaphysical] divinity have the same place and time of birth' (Derrida [1967] 1997: 14). Moreover, the authority that this divine truth denotes is unavoidably patriarchal. Derrida coins the term 'phallogocentrism' in order to establish a link between logocentrism and the phallic projection with which Freudian psychoanalysis characterizes the subject, with Spivak describing phallogocentrism as a metaphysics 'centred on the sovereignty of the engendering self and the determinacy of meaning' (Spivak 1992: 168). By contrast, Spivak summarizes deconstructive philosophy as the acknowledgement that

> in order to be able to speak, at the beginning of the discourse there was something like a two-step. The two-step was the necessity to say that a divided is whole. [. . .] This leaves something like a mark, a thumb print, a little design at the beginning which is covered over.
> (Spivak 1989b: 211)

This 'mark' of originary difference in the articulation of a whole is what Derrida identifies as the 'trace' (Derrida [1967] 1997: 46), which in his words 'retains the other as other in the same' (Derrida [1967] 1997: 62). By the 'same', Derrida means the apparently unified structure of sign-systems, as well as the apparent wholeness of the subject who signs; the 'same' in deconstruction refers to the apparent self-continuity within units. Where logocentrism takes this continuity as its predicate, deconstruction holds that meaning is made possible only through the simultaneous retention and obscuring of difference, and that 'without a trace [. . .] no difference would do its work and no meaning would appear' (Derrida [1967] 1997: 62).

It is understandable why, to the outside observer, such pronouncements seem to herald a nihilistic denial of meaning and death of God. Yet on the contrary, Derrida argues that his deconstructive project 'is not a question of "rejecting" these notions [of textual meaning]; they are necessary and, at least at present, nothing is conceivable without them' (Derrida [1967] 1997: 13). Derrida's claim is not that textual interpretation is impossible or to be discouraged, nor is it that reading is a free-for-all in which any interpretation is valid; rather, it is that textual meaning is not rooted in a monologic, unitary or closed signification. What makes meaning legible within signifying structures turns out, for Derrida, to be the very *'pure trace'* that renders their stability impossible and enables their deconstruction, and that Derrida terms '*différance*' (Derrida [1967] 1997: 62). Deriving from a verb that means both to '[suspend] the accomplishment or fulfilment of desire or "will"' and 'to be not identical, to be other' (Derrida [1972] 1982: 8), *différance* refers to 'the difference between two phonemes which alone permits them to be and operate as such' (Derrida [1972] 1982: 5). This, by extension, 'permits the articulation of signs among themselves within the same abstract order' (Derrida [1967] 1997: 63). In other words, '*différance* defers-differs*'* (Derrida [1967] 1997: 66), separating signs in time and space and allowing them to take on meaning in their differentiation from each other (thus enabling signification), while at the same time retaining the non-unity of signs within themselves (thus enabling deconstruction). Crucially, however, as the pure trace that precedes signification, *différance* is not itself part of the signifying structure, the letter *a* in its spelling (which distinguishes it from mere 'difference') dramatizing the heterogeneity it represents (Derrida [1972] 1982: 9).

Deconstruction, then, is not a destructive act wrought upon the text by an outside force, nor is it even a method of scholarly analysis; its destabilizing movements within texts, structures and speech acts do not preclude meaning but are instead inherently implicated in its production. Moreover, because deconstruction works within signifying structures, '[logocentric] concepts are indispensable for unsettling the heritage to which they belong' (Derrida [1967] 1997: 14). This is what Derrida means when, in *Of Grammatology* (1967), he famously proclaims that '[t]here is nothing outside of the text [there is no outside-text; *il n'y a pas de hors-texte*]' (Derrida [1967] 1997: 15). Deconstruction shows that any reading produced from a text is itself a text, reliant on *différance* in order to signify and thus necessarily incomplete, in that it cannot be closed off. It is concerned with the processes involved in producing knowledge and particularly the limitations and exclusions inherent in within these processes that are concealed by a logocentric understanding of meaning.

Theological deconstruction

As the latter point suggests, this is no mere abstract mind game or intellectual curiosity, and Derrida is no conjuror of cheap tricks. His deconstructive philosophy can be situated within wider efforts in Western philosophy, politics and culture to meaningfully contend with alterity and marginality (and crucially, alterity *as* marginality) following the devastation of the Holocaust and the Second World War, and the failure of Enlightenment liberal humanism that it demonstrated. Pertinent to any discussion of the implications of deconstruction for theology is Derrida's indebtedness to the work of Emmanuel Levinas, whose theological and ethical writing is emblematic of a post-Holocaust longing for 'the exaltation of a thought *other* than that of Aristotle, of a thought other than civilized' (Levinas 1999: 133). The primary theme of Levinas's philosophical project is the face of the other, a face 'from beyond the plastic forms that keep covering it up like a mask with their presence in perception' (Levinas 1999: 23), existing prior to and interrupting any mode of representation. This face, for Levinas, does not inhabit the mode of the visible and should not be confused with any system of features or characteristics that can be perceived. Instead, it is an ethical imperative towards an unlimited responsibility for the other. This responsibility destabilizes self-identity as defined by secular Western philosophy (Levinas 1999: 23) and opens towards a transcendent relation but one in which 'the difference between the I and the other remains' (Levinas 1999: 93). What then emerges, Levinas concludes, is a politics that envisions '[p]eace as relation with an alterity' (Levinas 1999: 137) rather than a sameness that erases and suppresses difference within the status quo. In religious terms, this is 'a new form of faith, a faith without triumph' (Levinas 1999: 109) always already obedient to the command and call of the other. After all, he postulates, '[s]hould we not call this demand or this interpellation or this summons to responsibility the word of God?' (Levinas 1999: 27). Levinas's 'faith without triumph' is therefore one in which God is not associated with the sovereign subject; rather, the word of God issues from beyond the subject and commands the subject to sacrifice its notions of sovereignty for the other.

For Levinas, the transcendent subject of Western philosophy failed to prevent the atrocities of the early to mid-twentieth century because its very articulation requires a violent disavowal of difference, so much so that difference per se eludes assimilation into systems and categories devised by Western thought even as it is inscribed along specific religious, cultural, racial, gendered and sexual lines. What leads Derrida to 'dream of [the] inconceivable process of dismantling and dispossession' (Derrida [1967] 1979: 82) that is deconstruction is the realization that this violence towards and erasure of the other is inherent within Western signifying structures and the logocentric assumptions underpinning them. This is apparent in the title of the chapter of *Writing and Difference*, 'Violence and Metaphysics', that marks Derrida's first in-depth engagement with Levinas. In Derrida's words, 'the system of war, [is] the only system whose basis permits us to speak, the only system whose language may ever be spoken' (Derrida [1967] 1979: 107). Of chief concern to both Levinas and Derrida is the critique of a sovereign selfhood that seeks to dominate, assimilate, erase or eradicate the other. Derrida defines sovereignty as 'the concentration, into a single point of indivisible singularity (God, the monarch, the people, the state or the nation-state), of absolute force and the absolute exception' (Derrida [2002] 2005: 154) that would suppress difference and subjugate the other. Once again, the apparently unified subject, which posits itself over and against the other in a binary relationship, is linked to the theological exceptionalism associated with a sovereign divinity. For Levinas, to claim alignment with such sovereignty is an 'internment within self-consciousness' (Levinas 1999: 126) that is not only idolatrous but also necessarily violent, since it claims authority over, and even ownership of, an other whose difference nonetheless always exceeds the understanding of the subject.

Thus, while Levinas identifies the face of the other with the word of God, he characterizes this not as a sovereign order issued from on high, but as 'initially [. . .] the relationship one has with one who is weaker' (Levinas 1999: 101). Indeed, for him the face of the other 'is all weakness and all authority' (Levinas 1999: 105), its authority stemming from its very weakness. In his commentary on Levinas in *The Gift of Death* (1993), Derrida sums up Levinas's theological stance with the seemingly tautological phrase, 'every other (one) is every (bit) other. *Tout autre est tout autre*' (Derrida [1992] 1995: 78). By this Derrida means that every other that the subject encounters is as alien, as completely and utterly other, as God, and more than this, if the face of the other is the command of God, distinguishing between God and the other becomes impossible. As Derrida elaborates, '[i]f every human is wholly other, if everyone else, or every other one, is every bit other, then one can no longer distinguish between a claimed generality of ethics [. . .] and the faith that turns towards God alone' (Derrida [1992] 1995: 84). This blurring of the boundaries between God and neighbour, this characterization of ethics as always a matter of faith rather than a prescriptive system, is necessary for a deconstruction of the hierarchies of divine sovereignty that can be appropriated in order to establish and maintain hegemony. It suggests a faith that would no longer be the dogmatic exercise of authority or an appeal to an 'original' orthodoxy, since these both depend on the sovereignty of the same. Instead, it would be characterized by constant attentiveness to the other and to alterity or difference.

Deconstructive theology

Derrida's deconstructive project, then, stems from a concern for the other that both intersects with theology in positing the relation with the other as a matter of faith and carries radical implications for the re-visioning of theology in which God can be thought in terms other than a dominant presence. At the same time, as I discussed in this book's Introduction, attempts to engage both theologically with deconstruction and deconstructively with theology must be wary of conflating deconstruction with a theology itself. Derrida's own writing on *différance* anticipates and pre-empts such an error. Derrida notes that his language concerning *différance* 'will resemble [that] of negative theology, occasionally even to the point of being indistinguishable from negative theology' (Derrida [1972] 1982: 6). Because *différance* cannot be defined in terms of the proper, the discourse surrounding it is comparable to apophatic theological traditions that can only speak of God by specifying what God is not. At the same time, Derrida distinguishes *différance* from 'even [. . .] the most negative of negative theologies' (Derrida [1972] 1982: 6). While negative theology resists positive representation in order to point to God's absolute sovereignty as well as God's alterity, *différance* precedes and resists any such characterization, forming 'the very opening of the space in which ontotheology – philosophy – produces its system and history' (Derrida [1972] 1982: 6). In other words, the negative theology that writing on *différance* resembles is still a metaphysics, which *différance* both engenders and opens to deconstruction.

Nonetheless, deconstruction opens up a space in which to inhabit and affirm theological concepts in order to dismantle them. This would be a non-hierarchical relationship with the other, in which the word of God is located within every other person, and particularly those others whose social and political marginalization marks them as signs of alterity per se. Derrida describes this as 'a hypercritical faith, one without dogma and without religion, irreducible to any and all religious and implicitly theocratic institutions' (Derrida [2002] 2005: 153). If the relationship with alterity, read after the fact as theological, cannot be appropriated by any systematic programme, this includes any religious institution that would attempt to give shape to it. And yet, as Derrida notes, the disruptive encounter with the other 'can [. . .] also *render possible* precisely what it appears to threaten' (Derrida [1996] 2002: 55). As I have already shown, deconstruction uncovers the other within the same, and attention is thus drawn to its movements not by rejecting representation but by 'constantly risking falling back within what is being deconstructed' (Derrida [1967] 1997: 14).

For the purposes of this book, a deconstructive approach to theology is understood as a theology giving particular attention to the contingency of its concepts, iconography and symbols, the processes involved in their construction and their inextricability from a variety of historical, philosophical and ideological conditions. It is resistant to claims of sovereignty and exclusivity and attuned to how these have contributed to the oppressive inheritances of theological traditions. Although, as I outlined in the introduction, deconstruction is by no means a Christian practice, its dismantling of Christian theology nonetheless involves affirming its vocabulary and concepts and following them to the point at which they break down and transgress themselves. Within this book, for instance, deconstruction will invite points of connection between discourses on the incarnation of Christ, the dictum that every other (one) is every (bit) other and the word of God issuing from one who is weaker. As later chapters will demonstrate fully, deconstructive theologies uncover sites where Christ appears as the other rejected, written off, written over and oppressed by the structures of Christianity. Indeed, Derrida has suggested that Western Christianity has failed to be sufficiently attentive to the challenge its incarnational beliefs should pose to its own metaphysical outlook, and that in this way 'Christianity has not yet come to Christianity' (Derrida [1992] 1995: 28). Derrida dismantles transcendent sovereignty and unity (of the human subject, of God, of 'sensible reality') not out of a desire for demystification but out of a longing for 'a certain experience of the impossible: that is, of the other' (Derrida [1987] 1992: 328). The affinity that Derrida identifies between the other and impossibility according to a 'sensible reality' constructed on normative terms will be particularly pertinent to analysing the deconstructive potential of fantasy literature with regard to theology, as well as deconstruction's own potential as an interpretive framework for fantasy.

The call to advent-ure; or, Derrida among the dragons

Despite the antipathy to deconstruction voiced by many fantasists, several scholars of fantasy have alluded to a potential affinity between fantasy, even popular genre fantasy, and deconstructive theoretical projects. Attebery, for instance, notes that 'because a major result of many of these [deconstructive] theories has been an overturning of class- and gender-based canons, they promise to be tremendously liberating to the study of non-canonical fantasy texts' (Attebery 1992: xii). Mike Gray has come closest to this study's argument in claiming that '[f]antasy fiction may not present an intentionally self-deconstructive text, but it creates its world and selves in such a way that suggests the task is particularly close at hand' (Gray 2013: 94). Nonetheless, these claims have not been sufficiently elaborated upon by the authors themselves, nor have they been taken up by other scholars, and thus there remains a need for more detailed critical discussion of fantastic worldbuilding as an activity with deconstructive potential, particularly for theology. As I noted earlier in this chapter, Kath Filmer posits fantasy as 'a kind of deconstructive activity which is every bit as radical as Derrida's, with the considerable advantage that the mythopoetic mode makes good sense' (Filmer 1989: 60). A closer look at the fantastic theories and practices offered by J. R. R. Tolkien, C. S. Lewis and Ursula K. Le Guin, all writers to whom Filmer appeals in her argument, reveals a closer affinity between their work and Derrida's than Filmer acknowledges. J. R. R. Tolkien's essay 'On Fairy-Stories', which began as a lecture delivered in 1939 and continues to influence critical discourse on fantasy fiction, also dreams of impossible encounters with the other in its desire to re-envision ancient myths and folklore. Tolkien's longing 'to hold communion with other living things' (Tolkien [1947] 2008: 35) and 'open a door on Other Time' (Tolkien [1947] 2008: 48) through the creation of secondary worlds eventually led him to create his Middle-earth *Legendarium*, with texts such as *The Hobbit* and later *The Lord of the Rings* helping to form the basis for what would eventually become the contemporary fantasy genre. Like Levinas's ethical project, Tolkien's longing for encounters with textual others in the pages of fantasy stems from crises arising within twentieth-century Western modernity. Tom Shippey has even gone so far as to characterize Tolkien and his fellow fantasists T. H. White, C. S. Lewis and, to a lesser extent, Ursula K. Le Guin as 'traumatized authors' (Shippey 2000: xxx) who turned to fantasy as an attempt to contend with the otherwise unspeakable atrocities they witnessed, as well as bring to light knowledges, voices and experiences erased or destroyed in their wake.[1]

Although Tolkien extensively defends the desire for escape and consolation which fantasy both fulfils and awakens, he is also clear that fantasy is not to be understood as purely escapist. Equally crucial to him is 'recovery', which he defines as

> regaining of a clear view. [. . .] I might venture to say 'seeing things as we are (or were) meant to see them' – as things apart from ourselves. We need, in any case, to clean our windows; so that the things seen clearly may be freed from the drab blur of triteness or familiarity – from possessiveness.
>
> (Tolkien [1947] 2008: 67)

Readers could be forgiven for interpreting the above as a purely conservative or normative claim; at the very least, 'seeing things as we are meant to see them' is a much more deterministic statement than anything found in Derrida. Yet I contend that Tolkien's resistance to possessiveness here, and his implication that fantasy is not so much a restoration of an ideal status quo as it is a disruption of familiar habits and assumptions, suggests an affinity between his characterization of fantasy and Derridean deconstruction.

In fact, what is so bizarre about Filmer's oppositional framing of deconstruction and fantasy is its investment in the same vague notions of 'sensible reality' towards which fantasists are notoriously sceptical. Although I have demonstrated earlier that Derrida is far from rejecting sensible reality outright, neither does he simply take it at face value and nor, for that matter, do most fantasy texts. As Attebery notes, fantasy has always been characterized by 'creative and disruptive play with representations of the real world' (Attebery 2014: 32), and much of it is engaged with contesting the grounds on which these representations are constructed. Tolkien, for one, balks at the definition of 'real life' adhered to by fantasy's most ardent naysayers. He argues that '[t]he notion that motor-cars are more "alive" than, say, centaurs or dragons is curious; that they are more "real" than, say, horses is pathetically absurd' (Tolkien [1947] 2008: 71). Le Guin, taking cues from Tolkien's theory of fantasy, goes even further in offering fantasy as a remedy to a homogenized, neoliberal capitalist reality in which 'there is no other, there is no escape, because there is nowhere else' (Le Guin [2003] 2018: 319). In her view, 'seemingly by a denial or evasion of current reality, fantasists are perhaps trying to assert and explore a larger reality than we now allow ourselves' (Le Guin [2003] 2018: 319), one in which not only gods and magic but alternative ethical, social, political and religious orders become thinkable. If fantasists are invested in 'reality' at all, it is in the same sense that deconstructionists are: as a construction, premised on consensus and stability, that needs to be rethought and represented as open to disruption in the face of the other.

It would be naïve and overly deterministic, of course, to conflate centaurs and dragons with alterity per se; fantasy texts, for all their preoccupation with the strange and alien, are still texts and thus open to deconstruction. From a deconstructive standpoint, it is most useful to think of secondary worlds, and the characters and creatures that inhabit them, as contingent figurations that can unsettle the reader's preconceived notions and gesture towards an alterity that is still yet to come. While this book focuses on fantasy texts that deliberately invoke this potentiality and dramatize its effects, such gestures are inherent to the structure of fantasy even if they are unacknowledged or even openly disavowed by the individual text. In this regard, a deconstructive understanding of fantasy shares an affinity with Jeffrey Jerome Cohen's reading of monsters as 'difference made flesh', across which 'any kind of alterity can be inscribed' (Cohen 1996: 7). Like its close cousin the monstrous, the fantastic explicitly marks out spaces where alterity has been covered over in textual representations of the primary world and draws attention to the deferral performed by all texts.

As Tolkien acknowledges, '[f]antasy is made out of the Primary World' (Tolkien [1947] 2008: 68) and can no more promise direct and unfettered access to actual other worlds or to alterity per se than any other genre of text. Yet its power comes from its overt gestures towards an ineffable alterity that Tolkien terms 'Faërie', which may share a homologous structure with Derrida's (non-)characterization of the other in that it 'cannot be caught within a net of words' (Tolkien [1947] 2008: 32), always eluding the textual forms and names ascribed to it. Attebery elaborates that 'the fundamental premise of fantasy is that the things it tells not only did not happen but *could* not have happened', and through this conscious invocation of impossibility it 'denies [. . .] [the] validity' (Attebery 2014: 4), by which I take Attebery to mean the finality or ultimacy, of its representations of reality. By rearranging habitual representations of the primary world into impossible figurations, fantasy texts draw attention both to their own fictitious constructions and to their openness to future disruption in the face of the other.

Even the most ostensibly conservative impulse Tolkien identifies within fantasy – the consolation of the happy ending – can on closer inspection be understood in terms of a deconstructive openness towards the other. For Tolkien, whose interest in fantasy is closely intertwined with his Roman Catholic theology and religious practice, the happy ending of a fairy story carries distinctly messianic overtones, serving as 'a far-off gleam of *evangelium* in the real world' (Tolkien [1947] 2008: 77). This manifests as 'a fleeting glimpse of Joy, Joy beyond the walls of the world' (Tolkien [1947] 2008: 75). Yet even though he couches this in highly theologically orthodox terms, Tolkien once again characterizes the happy ending not as the restoration of an ideal status quo but as a rupture in the perceived order of the text. The consolation of fairy stories is not primarily therapeutic but transformative, even cataclysmic. It is to be found in an event that Tolkien terms '*eucatastrophe*' – a word Tolkien coins from Greek roots to indicate a 'sudden happy turn' (Tolkien et al. 1981: 100) – which consists of 'a sudden and miraculous grace: never to be counted on to recur' and never, for that matter, to be fully anticipated in advance (Tolkien [1947] 2008: 75).[2] The eucatastrophic turn can be every bit as disruptive to the structure of a secondary world as the construction of that world can be for representations of the primary world.

The eucatastrophic turn in fantasy is framed in homologous terms to Derrida's description of deconstruction's impulse towards the other as the advent of an unforeseeable justice, always located in an inaccessible future. Although Derrida resists aligning the approach of the other with a specific theological tradition to the same extent that Tolkien does with fantastic eucatastrophe, he nonetheless ascribes an almost identically messianic structure to the former. In this case, it is a 'messianicity without messianism [. . .] without horizon of expectation and without prophetic prefiguration' (Derrida [1996] 2002: 56), since any messianic approach that could be fully encapsulated within a theological or philosophical programme would be part of the structure of the same. The other's approach, for which deconstruction unravels the presumably closed structures of texts, is a shattering 'event' (Derrida [1987] 1992: 340) that announces the other's arrival as 'impossible' (Derrida [1987] 1992: 341). Elizabeth Anderson has even criticized Tolkien's particular use of fantastic eucatastrophe in his fiction from this deconstructive standpoint, arguing that his texts' 'endgame' is 'a colonizing logic of sameness that focuses on the defeat of an evil Other [sic]' (Anderson 2016: 244).[3]

It is crucial to remember, however, that dismantling of the same in anticipation of the other does not mean rejecting it; indeed, without it neither signification nor deconstruction can take place. Nor does Tolkien, for all that he aligns eucatastrophe with his own religious beliefs, perceive fantasy as a definitive reflection of a metaphysical reality or deny its potential complicity in oppressive causes. On the contrary, he acknowledges that '[f]antasy can, of course, be carried to excess. It can be put to evil uses. It may even delude the minds out of which it came' (Tolkien [1947] 2008: 65). Nonetheless, what must be emphasized about eucatastrophe in adopting a theory of fantasy that shares deconstruction's ethical and political concern for alterity is its unpredictability, as well as its ability as a self-consciously fictitious figuration to resist the foreclosure of its own representation. Attention to these elements of eucatastrophe allows for readings of secondary worlds as exceeding the limits of their own textual construction, as well as the philosophical and ideological assumptions they belie. Understanding the structure of fantastic eucatastrophe in deconstructive terms means reading it not as textual closure but as an open-ended gesture towards the approach of the other, which in the context of my discussion here means both God and marginalized subjects.

Tolkien's theory of fantasy highlights fantasy's ability to subvert received assumptions about the primary world. Its positioning of fantasy texts as spaces that simulate encounters with textual others, as well as figurations of a future, catastrophic arrival of messianic justice that defer ultimate closure, can be seen to mirror the movements that Derrida identifies. I am far from suggesting that deconstruction and Tolkien's or any formulation of fantasy are reducible to one another, and I certainly do not wish to argue, as Filmer does, that the latter is a substitute for the former, or vice versa. However, careful attention to the shared conceptual vocabulary of deconstruction and fantastic storytelling opens a critical space where it is possible to think of fantasy as a genre concerned with hegemonic structures and habits of representation, even and perhaps especially the hegemonies re-inscribed either intentionally or inadvertently by fantasy texts themselves. By rearranging elements of the primary world and rendering them as unfamiliar secondary worlds, fantasy can be seen to participate in the deconstructive activity of 'bending [the] rules [of signification] with respect for the rules themselves' (Derrida [1987] 1992: 340) in order to draw attention to the other while retaining a sense of the other's alterity. In fantasy, we may discover that marginality in literature is not a simple matter of optical 'representation'; its figurations of fairies, gods, monsters and dragons remind us that in any relation we are encountering someone who is every bit other.

Further to this, many fantasy texts deliberately invoke, and often dramatize, their ability to articulate a deconstructive engagement with theology. As Attebery notes, what is peculiar about fantasy is its ability to 'recontextualize myths', including religious imaginaries, 'placing them back into history and reminding us of their social and political power' (Attebery 2014: 4). The remainder of this chapter will demonstrate that *The Passion of New Eve*, *Till We Have Faces* and *The Left Hand of Darkness* all embody critical engagements with theology and religious traditions that gesture towards disruption in the face of alterity and can therefore be understood as deconstructive. Although at times their characterizations of theological alterity differ significantly from those articulated by Levinas and Derrida, all three novels lay bare the mythmaking processes involved in their own textual construction. I take my point of departure from Attebery's assertion that many fantasy texts are 'stories [told] about, around, and upon mythic stories' (Attebery 2014: 4), in which the process of constructing textual, and especially theological, meaning is revealed to be a contingent one. While *The Passion of New Eve* uses its fantastic imagination to take up a deconstructive space within a self-consciously Christian imaginary, *Till We Have Faces* re-visions the Greek myth of Eros and Psyche as a tale of impossible encounter with alterity (albeit alterity still understood, anachronistically, within an implicitly Christian framework). The fictional religion of the Handdara in *The Left Hand of Darkness*, meanwhile, can be seen to dramatize the Derridean notion that *tout autre est tout autre*, that every other (one) is every (bit) other, in its extension of an apophatic spiritual practice into ethical and political relations with fantastic figurations of alterity.

Deconstructing Christianity in *The Passion of New Eve*

The self-consciously deconstructive play with representations of (un)reality present in Angela Carter's *The Passion of New Eve* is highly instructive for reading a deconstructive relationship to theology in fantasy texts. The apocalyptic fever dream that is Carter's vision of an America on the brink of destruction is populated by gods, monsters and all manner of figures that embody and rehearse biblical, mythic and fairy-tale roles. Theology and fantasy are blatantly conflated with one another in this novel. Carter's strange creations literalize the complex interplay of cultural fictions in shaping consensus reality, making manifest the processes involved in their textual construction and uncovering the erasures and violent acts performed within these processes. In her hands, 'primary' and 'secondary' worlds bleed into each other as the distinctions between them are revealed to be ultimately arbitrary; all realities are textual constructions, and fantasy carries immeasurable cultural and epistemological power in shaping and being shaped by the so-called primary world. While Carter is not the least bit interested in putting an end to mythmaking, her particular fantastic imagination is just as, if not more, likely to be the site of dark parody and re-invention than reverent repetition. Her writing generally scoffs at the idea of fantasy as a repository of ultimate truth or a clear pathway to transcendence. While much of the novel's fantastic deconstruction of theology is intrinsically linked to gender and sexuality, and thus will be discussed in later chapters, some general points about the role of religion in the text bear mentioning here.

Much of *The Passion of New Eve* is concerned with the sway that religious and mythic narratives hold over the Western cultural imagination, even and especially when they are unacknowledged. This is reflected in the arc of the novel, which follows stuffy Englishman Evelyn as he moves to New York and stumbles into a horrifying and awe-inspiring fantastic society on the cusp of collapse. The novel becomes even more strange and fairy-tale-like as Evelyn journeys into the desert and is kidnapped by a many-breasted fertility goddess named Mother, who forcibly transforms him into a second Eve in the hopes of redeeming the world. A textual landscape that at the novel's outset appears to be an only slightly exaggerated representation of the primary world is gradually revealed to be one 'in which life parodied myth, or became it' (Carter [1977] 2012: 74), to the extent that by the end of the novel the very notion of a 'primary world' becomes unsettled. This is hinted early in the text when Evelyn first arrives in New York. Expecting 'a clean, hard, bright city where towers reared to the sky in a paradigm of technological aspiration', Evelyn is confronted instead with 'a lurid, Gothic darkness' (Carter [1977] 2012: 6). Evelyn journeys to America, a nation founded on the principles of Enlightenment reason, expecting clear principles and monuments to progress uncomplicated by Europe's premodern inheritances, but throughout the text, the violences and erasures concealed within its lofty ideals continue to rear their heads. Where he hoped to see a vision of utopia, Evelyn finds instead a city whose 'skies were of strange, bright, artificial colours' (Carter [1977] 2012: 8) from air pollution, whose streets are overrun with homicidal rats and whose society is riven by racial injustice and conflict.

The re-emergence of the repressed others of Enlightenment reason and the sovereign subject is explicitly linked to the persistence of the religious within American life. Spiritual panic pervades Carter's New York. Evelyn rents his apartment 'from a young man who then went off to India to save his soul [. . .] and advised [Evelyn] to concern [himself] with spiritual matters, since time was short' (Carter [1977] 2012: 8). Another man approaches Evelyn to tell him that 'he had observed luminous wheels in the sea, which proved that God had arrived on a celestial bicycle to proclaim the last Judgement was at hand' (Carter [1977] 2012: 8). Outside, the streets are littered with '[g]roups of proselytisers [. . .] chanting psalms and prayers, selling a thousand conflicting salvations' (Carter [1977] 2012: 8–9). Noting the tension between the city's clear-cut, gridlike structure and the frenzied religious fervour of its people, Evelyn reflects that 'this city, built to a specification that precluded the notion of the Old Adam, had hence become uniquely vulnerable to that which the streamlined spires conspired to ignore, for the darkness had lain, unacknowledged, within the builders' (Carter [1977] 2012: 12). In the desolate landscape wrought by secular modernity, the old gods have re-emerged with a vengeance, having been built into the very structures that outwardly disavow them. 'The age of reason is over' (Carter [1977] 2012: 9), declares Baroslav, the Czech alchemist who lives in Evelyn's building, and indeed the world Carter presents is an alchemical blend of mythologies, religious orders and folklore living among modernity's ruins.

There are, in the presentation of this fantastic tableau, echoes both of a common motif in religious fantasy literature and of Derrida's critique of the metaphysics of reason. The clearest point of comparison to other fantasy texts is C. S. Lewis's *That Hideous Strength* (1945), in which the ostensibly hyper-rationalist N.I.C.E. plots to resurrect the body of Merlin in order to usher in a technocratic age in which Earth is ruled by 'pure' reason. Though the designs of the N.I.C.E. are presented as more overtly nefarious in Lewis's earlier text than those of the architects who built New York in Carter's novel, the parallels are difficult to ignore. In each text, attempts to build a world according to the laws of reason, which both texts associate with discourses of purity and cleanliness, inevitably draw from the wells of fantasy and religion (which in both novels are conflated with one another) that they outwardly dismiss as irrational. Yet while in *That Hideous Strength*, the resurrected Merlin turns out to be a latent power of the earth whom the N.I.C.E. cannot manipulate to their own ends and who ultimately destroys them, Carter's presentation of the relationship between myth and reason is much more ambivalent. Evelyn's observation that New York is 'uniquely vulnerable to that which the streamlined spires conspired to ignore' (Carter [1977] 2012: 12) can be read in two ways with reference to deconstructive philosophy. On one hand, both the New York and the America presented in Carter's novel are especially vulnerable to disruption by fantastic figurations of its subjugated others. It is notable that many of the fantastic and religious figures present in the text are embodiments of femininity, Blackness and queerness, and I will return to the discussion of some of these figures in more detail in later chapters. On the other hand, New York's establishment of itself as a city built on reason is also vulnerable to substituting one form of sovereignty for another. From his earliest writing, Derrida has maintained that logocentric reason, including notions of 'scientific truth', cannot be invoked 'without also bringing with it all its metaphysico-theological roots' (Derrida [1967] 1997: 13). In the same way, Carter hints that the rationalistic discourse of Enlightenment modernity and the fantastic discourse of theology are intricately co-implicated.

Myth, fairy tale and theology can all be figured according to violently phallogocentric structures, and phallogocentric reason itself fundamentally derives its structure from theological metaphysics. If this appears as a destructive carelessness in the dystopian New York at the outset of *The Passion of New Eve*, it emerges in the evangelical Christian child soldiers who kidnap Eve later in the novel as an active and genocidal drive to eradicate difference. The militia is led by the son of a Florida soda magnate who believes he was divinely summoned to California to fight 'the Holy War against Blacks, Mexis, Reds, Militant Lesbians, Rampant Gays, etc etc etc' (Carter [1977] 2012: 157). The child Colonel's will to demolish this endless list of 'others' is matched by his self-identification with divine sovereignty; his call to war came to him in a divine vision of '[t]he Son of Man, who looked, to his surprise, very much like himself, dressed in the uniform of the Green Berets' (Carter [1977] 2012: 156). Sovereignty of God and sovereignty of nation are also implicitly conflated with one another in the inscriptions on the medallions that hang from each of the child soldiers' pierced nipples, as '[t]he medallion on the left nipple was inscribed with the word: GOD and that on the right nipple, with the word: AMERICA' (Carter [1977] 2012: 153). In the outlandish figuration of the child soldiers, Carter's text directly satirizes American civil religion as a phallogocentric mythology that professes absolute devotion to a logic of sameness.

Carter's depiction of New York and her portrayal of the child soldiers both show the sheer extent to which the so-called primary world is suffused with fantastic ways of thinking. Conversely, within the novel's implausible events and playful satire lies a very serious warning against too hastily or uncritically adopting the figurations that populate either fantasy or theology as absolute or eternal truths. The Christianity of the child soldiers, while intentionally extreme in its depiction, literalizes the violent erasure and subjugation of difference in which the logic of Western Christian theology has too often been complicit. By contrast, Carter juxtaposes religious narrative with the tropes and trappings of fantasy precisely to undermine any theological claims to ultimate or 'natural' reality; the world of *The Passion of New Eve* is one in which 'myth is a made thing, not a found thing' (Carter [1977] 2012: 53). As Elaine Jordan notes, this insistence on the provisionality and artificiality of all representation is exemplified in the novel's 'strong interest in the fantastic power of the silver screen', which 'allegorises the business of making up stories' (Jordan [1994] 2007: 215). In constantly narrativizing its own mythmaking processes and revealing the constructed nature of its characters and settings, *The Passion of New Eve* reveals that there is no primary world that is not always already mediated by fantastic processes of textual construction.

And yet, this is not cause either for despair or for abandoning religious mythmaking altogether. If every primary world or consensus reality is a hegemonic textual construction, then the telling of fairy stories and religious narratives carries boundless potential for deconstruction. As further chapters will discuss in more detail, numerous 'others' within the text, including Mother, Leilah/Lilith, Tristessa and even Eve herself, participate in the processes involved in their own mythologization in order to repeatedly reinvent themselves, with varying degrees of success. In exposing every act of representation as fantastic invention, Carter affirms, rather than rejects, the art of fantasy and, in Jordan's words, 'insist[s] that we must know that a space must be kept for uncertainty and recreation' (Jordan [1994] 2007: 226). *The Passion of New Eve* blatantly demonstrates the profound risks of fantasy writing in its potential to reaffirm normative theological orders, and also claims fantasy as a site for deconstructive play and theological re-invention, with bombast and camp abandon. This double-movement can also be seen at work, however, in the more subtle engagements with theology in *Till We Have Faces* and *The Left Hand of Darkness*.

'Holy places are dark places': Facing the other in *Till We Have Faces*

Till We Have Faces is, like *The Passion of New Eve*, a novel about mythmaking as an act carrying theological weight, and the deconstructive processes at work in fantasy writing and theology are fully displayed within its narrative. As its subtitle signals, it is 'A Myth Retold', a re-visioning of the classical myth of Eros and Psyche that subverts and complicates many of the narrative beats of its source text. Set in the fictitious kingdom of Glome, the novel is narrated by Orual, princess and later Queen of Glome and half-sister to the beautiful Psyche, and divided into two parts representing two separate texts she writes. In the first, Orual makes a written complaint recounting a multitude of grievances against the gods, on both Psyche's behalf and her own. In the second, she finds herself revising and annotating that first narrative following a series of mystical visions that emerge from the act of writing.

Mara E. Donaldson has remarked that 'Orual's rewriting of her book deconstructs her previous writing' (Donaldson 2007: 160). Donaldson seems here to be using the word 'deconstructs' to mean 'subverts' or 'challenges' rather than a specifically Derridean movement. Nonetheless, I will demonstrate that the novel can be read as a deconstructive engagement with theology, and moreover articulates how fantastic worldbuilding can draw attention to the deconstruction already at work within theology and religious practice. Orual's narration of her struggles with the gods, understood as simultaneously the creation of a myth and the articulation of a theology, opens on an encounter with an ethical alterity that simultaneously precedes and disrupts the presumed unity of her narrative. Accordingly, *Till We Have Faces* also exhibits both the severe limitations of language in the face of the divine other and the power of language in shaping religious experience. Where earlier texts by Lewis, particularly the Cosmic Trilogy and *The Chronicles of Narnia*, would revel in the transcendent marvellousness of the mythic as divine encounter, *Till We Have Faces* is more hesitant when it comes to representing the supernatural, all the more so due to Orual's portrayal as an unreliable narrator. Encounters with gods and other mythic creatures are as shrouded in darkness and mystery as the temple of the fertility goddess Ungit in the narrative, either related after the fact with inadequate or paradoxical language, or accompanied by a rupture in the novel's setting and temporality.

One of the most consistent themes throughout *Till We Have Faces*, introduced early on in the text, is the breakdown of religious language. Psyche's beauty and grace attract the jealousy of the fertility goddess Ungit, especially after Psyche's kindness to the people of Glome during a plague earn her the reverence of the common folk, and the High Priest orders that she be sacrificed to the god of the Mountain, Ungit's son. In a divine mystery, Psyche is either to be married to the god as his bride or devoured as his prey, or both, for '[s]ome say the loving and the devouring are all the same thing' (Lewis 1956: 49). This offends the rational sensibilities of the Fox, a Greek slave who tutors Orual, Redival and Psyche. The Fox is an adherent of Stoicism, an ancient precursor to the modern 'sensualist empiricism or psychological atomism' that Levinas resists, calling it 'a psyche closed in on itself' (Levinas 1999: 125). In contrast to the devout superstition of Glome's Ungit-worship, he privileges dispassionate rationality, going so far as to be 'ashamed of loving poetry' (Lewis 1956: 8), as well as the divine sovereignty of the individual self, claiming that '[a]ll men are of divine blood, for there is the god in every man' (Lewis 1956: 149). Upon hearing the priest's words, he insists to the king that

> the Priest is talking nonsense [. . .] a moment ago the victim of this abominable sacrifice was to be the Accursed, the wickedest person in the whole land, offered as a punishment. And now it is to be the best person in the whole land – the perfect victim – married to the god as a reward. Ask him which it means. It can't be both.
>
> (Lewis 1956: 49–50)

The priest, however, ridicules the Fox's 'Greek wisdom' and his 'demand to see such things clearly, as if the gods were no more than letters written in a book' (Lewis 1956: 50). While the Fox demands a theology that can be clearly apprehended via textual modes of representation, the priest insists that 'nothing that is said clearly [about the gods] can be said truly' (Lewis 1956: 50). Gods have little time for the binary distinctions and clear-cut categories devised by reason; the incoherence of the priest's language may be nonsense to the Fox, but for the priest it opens a space in which to think radical otherness. As the priest reiterates, '[h]oly wisdom is not clear and thin like water, but thick and dark like blood' (Lewis 1956: 50). The strangeness of the gods cannot be so easily dismissed by the Fox's logic.

'Holy places are dark places' (Lewis 1956: 50), proclaims the High Priest. 'It is life and strength, not knowledge and words, that we get in them' (Lewis 1956: 50). The contradictory and paradoxical nature of the priest's language about the gods, and the reversals and ambivalences contained within it that frustrate classical reason, can provoke a reading of holy darkness in *Till We Have Faces* as a deconstructive discourse on alterity. It calls to mind Derrida's statement that the face-to-face encounter with alterity that Levinas describes 'cannot possibly be encompassed by philosophical speech without immediately revealing, by philosophy's own light, that philosophy's surface is severely cracked' (Derrida [1967] 1979: 90). Reason, most commonly figured as light within Western philosophical discourse, belongs to the same; in Derrida's words '[e]verything given to me within light appears as given to myself by myself' (Derrida [1967] 1979: 92). By contrast, the encounter with the other manifests in Levinas's work, and in Derrida's extension of Levinas, as an 'epiphany of a certain non-light' (Derrida [1967] 1979: 85). What this amounts to, in both Levinas and Derrida's work, is that the other cannot be directly translated into an order of signification or representation, without neutralizing the other's alterity and assimilating it into the same.

Ungit's temple is indeed very dark; Orual narrates that '[i]n the furthest recess of her house where she sits it is so dark that you cannot see her well' (Lewis 1956: 4). As for Ungit herself, '[s]he is a black stone without head or hands or face' (Lewis 1956: 4). And yet, for all that Ungit exceeds the limits of Greek philosophy, she still exists within a theological order in Glome. Moreover, Orual explicitly states at the outset of the novel that she must 'write in Greek' (Lewis 1956: 3) for a presumed Greek audience. From the very beginning, a dialectic emerges, nearly identical to the dialectic in deconstructive philosophy, between godhood as radical alterity and godhood inscribed as sovereignty within theology, cultural discourse and religious practices. Inscrutable and elusive though Ungit is, for instance, the religious practices dedicated to her worship also posit her as jealous and often demanding ritual sacrifice. This characterization is increasingly put into question as the novel goes on, however, as it slowly becomes apparent that the novel's narrative and worldbuilding are heavily mediated by the philosophical and theological frameworks in which Orual's narration is embedded. From an early age, Orual's Stoic education by the Fox is held in uneasy tension with the 'horror of holiness' (Lewis 1956: 54) that permeates both public and private life in Glome, exacerbated by the trials Orual endures following Psyche's sacrifice.

Things begin to change, however, when the old priest dies and the new priest, Arnom, begins 'learning from the Fox to talk like a philosopher about the gods' and 'proposes to set up an image of her – a woman-shaped image in the Greek fashion – in front of the old shapeless stone' (Lewis 1956: 234). Orual '[feels] that an image of this sort would be somehow a defeat for the old, hungry, faceless Ungit whose terror had been over [her] in childhood' (Lewis 1956: 234). Once Ungit becomes assimilated into a form of representation more pleasing to Greek reason and aesthetic sensibilities, the horror of her alterity is significantly diminished. By placing a statue of Aphrodite in front of the faceless Ungit and letting more light into the temple, Arnom makes the place more bearable for Orual but 'less holy' (Lewis 1956: 234); indeed to Orual it is more bearable precisely because of its masking of difference.

Horror, however, is not all there is to Ungit's holiness. Her presence, though troubling in its otherness, is a source of consolation for the faithful. From the time the image of Aphrodite is placed within the temple, Orual acknowledges that the stone still 'is, in a manner, Ungit herself' (Lewis 1956: 234) and irreplaceable by any image, however beautiful. However, the extent to which the common people of Glome hold this to be true does not become fully apparent until very late in the text. During the rite of the Year's birth, while Orual – now Queen of Glome – and Arnom keep their customary vigil in the temple, an old, poor woman comes to offer sacrifice to the goddess, praying and weeping. As she exits the temple, seemingly calmed, Orual questions the woman regarding her devotion:

> 'Do you always pray to *that* Ungit,' said I (nodding toward the shapeless stone), 'and not to *that*?' Here I nodded towards our new image, standing tall and straight in her robes and [...] the loveliest thing our land has ever seen.
> 'Oh, always this, Queen,' said she. 'That other, the Greek Ungit, she wouldn't understand my speech. She's only for nobles and learned men. There's no comfort in her.'
> (Lewis 1956: 272)

Greek wisdom, the old priest insists, 'brings no rain and grows no corn' (Lewis 1956: 50), and neither does it offer the provocation or consolation that can speak to the darkness of marginalized people's lived experiences. That the persistent religious practice of the marginalized – in this case, poor women – finds the greatest consolation the facelessness of Ungit, rather than the beautiful figures found in the reasoned discourse of learned men, places the text in the territory of a deconstructive faith. Where Orual sees in the stone Ungit an alterity that disturbs her construction of reality according to Stoic principles, the old woman finds a goddess in whom her vulnerability and marginality as one of society's 'others' is given voice.

The deconstructive movements at work within fantastic storytelling and theology are even further foregrounded in the events following Psyche's sacrifice to the god of the Mountain, which are in turns narrated by Psyche, Orual herself and a priest in the land of Essur. While the novel refuses to resolve or adjudicate between these various narratives, it gestures towards eucatastrophic openings in the stories, revealed in the very act of telling, in which they are deconstructed. Psyche's own acts of mythmaking are particularly fruitful when reading *Till We Have Faces* as an embodiment of deconstructive theological storytelling, especially considering Derrida's treatment of the figure of Psyche in relation to the advent of the other. From an early age, the Psyche of Lewis's text tells fairy tales about the Holy Mountain, declaring, 'When I'm big [. . .] I will be a great, great queen, married to the greatest king of all, and he will build me a castle of gold and amber up there on the very top' (Lewis 1956: 23). Later, on the night before the Offering, Psyche attempts to console a distraught Orual by repeating the story, convinced that the Offering will see it fulfilled:

> I am going, you see, to the Mountain. You remember how we used to look and long? And all the stories of my gold and amber house, up there against the sky, where we thought we should never really go? The greatest King of all was going to build it for me. If only you could believe it, Sister!
>
> (Lewis 1956: 75)

Once Psyche is bound to the Holy Tree on the mountaintop, however, the story turns out to be quite different. After their reunion in the valley of the gods, she relates back to Orual how the experience of being sacrificed strips her of all belief in her story. 'I couldn't believe in it at all', she recounts. 'I couldn't understand how I ever had. All that, all my old longings, were clean gone' (Lewis 1956: 109). What is left of Psyche's faith, she finds, is

> hardly a thought, and very hard to put into words. There was a lot of the Fox's philosophy in it – things he says about gods or 'the divine nature' – but mixed up with things the Priest said, too, about the blood and the earth and how sacrifice makes the crops grow. I'm not explaining it well [. . .] It was shapeless, but you could just hold onto it, or just let it hold onto you. Then the change came.
>
> (Lewis 1956: 109–10)

The 'change', as it turns out, is the god of the west-wind coming to carry Psyche away to the palace of the god of the Mountain, a palace that Psyche notes 'wasn't, you see, just the gold and amber house I used to imagine [. . .] [a]nd not quite like any house in this land' (Lewis 1956: 112–13). The eucatastrophic happy ending of Psyche's fairy tale, in which she is wedded to a king and in a palace fashioned after the whims of her own imagination, leads her willingly to the sacrificial act which breaks the narrative and with it her old faith in the gods. Rather than a fulfilment of her tale which would mean closure, Psyche's response to her story instead initiates a new faith, a new understanding of and relationship to the gods, one that exceeds any binary distinction between the 'faith' of her own people and the 'reason' of the Fox.

The manner in which Psyche's narrative of her gold and amber palace is interrupted by an other, who exceeds any pre-figuration of him either in Psyche's story or in the religious ritual she believes to be its fulfilment, remarkably anticipates Derrida's characterization of Psyche in his own work. In his essay 'Psyche: Invention of the Other', Derrida envisions language about the other as 'a large double mirror installed on a rotating stand' (or *psyche* in French) (Derrida [1987] 1992: 331), 'the rotating *speculum* that has come to relate the same to the other' (Derrida [1987] 1992: 333). (Readers familiar with the Christian theological tradition may also think here of St Paul's declaration that 'now we see in a mirror, dimly' [1 Cor. 13.12, NRSV].) The other's coming is, in this configuration, the spontaneous, impossible event that breaks that mirror (Derrida [1987] 1992: 340) and enables the ethical relationship.[4] Yet the *psyche* that is broken by the other's approach, Derrida tells us, is also 'necessary' (Derrida [1987] 1992: 342) for the deconstructive movements that allow the other to approach. For Derrida the *psyche*, that is, the mirror, becomes associated with the same Psyche of Greek mythology, of whom Lewis writes, 'the one who loses Eros, her betrothed husband, for having wished to see him in spite of prohibition' (Derrida [1987] 1992: 331). Derrida's ambivalent characterization of Psyche/*psyche* here tells us much about both the radical potential and the inherent risk in telling stories about the other. For both Derrida and Lewis, Psyche is invoked as an archetype of the human subject, and her stories, even the one she tells Orual after she is welcomed into the god's house, are necessarily mediated by the same. Psyche's stories open onto their own eventual dissolution, and yet, in Lewis's text as well as in Derrida's, Psyche's loss of Eros is also intrinsically linked to the theological stories that surround the god.

Although Orual is the primary narrator of *Till We Have Faces*, the text constantly draws attention to the mediated and contingent nature of her story in its clashes with the stories told by Psyche and the Essurian priest she encounters in a temple late in the novel. Orual's privileging of the light of reason over the darkness associated with the gods proves to have devastating consequences for Psyche. Following Psyche's sacrifice, Orual journeys to the Holy Mountain with the intent of retrieving whatever may remain of her. Instead of dead remains, however, Orual finds Psyche alive and well in the valley of the gods, claiming that the god of the Mountain is now her lover and that what Orual sees as wilderness is the god's house. Though Psyche has nightly sexual encounters with the god, she is 'forbidden to bring any light into his – our – chamber' (Lewis 1956: 123). Educated as she is in the Fox's Greek wisdom, Orual becomes obsessed with assimilating the gods' motives into a framework she can understand. Lamenting her separation from Psyche following Psyche's marriage to the god, she insists on finding answers and resolves to conclusively prove the truth or untruth of Psyche's tale. Again the light and 'visibility' of reason and the darkness of faith are contrasted, as Orual insists, 'If I'd had my eyes shut, I would have believed her palace was as real as this', to which the Fox replies, 'But, your eyes being open, you saw no such thing' (Lewis 1956: 141). Convinced that Psyche's lover is no god, but either some monstrous beast or a thief wishing to take advantage of Psyche, Orual journeys back to the Mountain and eventually convinces Psyche to enter the god's chamber bearing a lamp.

In this scene, the futility of appropriating the face of the other with the 'light' of understanding becomes literalized. As she watches from afar, Orual's sense of holy horror is quelled, as Psyche's lamp seems 'a homelike thing in that wild place' (Lewis 1956: 170). The sense of security does not last, as the god violently lays waste to the landscape in response to Psyche's transgression, and seconds later, Orual meets him face to face: 'Though this light stood motionless, my glimpse of the face was as swift as a true flash of lightning. I could not bear it for longer. Not my eyes only, but my heart and blood and brain were too weak for that' (Lewis 1956: 172–3). The god declares that 'Psyche goes out in exile' and 'must hunger and thirst and tread hard roads' (Lewis 1956: 173). At first glance, this seems to be a retributive punishment for wrongdoing and could be interpreted as a rearticulation of hierarchical sovereignty. Certainly, this is how Orual interprets the scene, claiming that '[h]e rejected, denied, answered, and (worst of all) he knew, all [she] had thought, done, or been' (Lewis 1956: 173). Yet as I have shown, this is a novel that foregrounds the inherent instability of any theological claim and moreover that is intimately concerned with the dialectic at play between God-as-other and divine sovereignty in theological discourse. As readers, we have ample reason, both from what has come before this scene and from events at the end of the novel, to take Orual's words with a grain of salt.

Significant for examining the god's outburst here is the fact that another name the people of Glome have for the god is one associated with monstrosity, the 'Shadowbrute' (Lewis 1956: 70). This opens a space for reading the god's violence not in terms of a sovereign authority but in terms of the deconstructive approach to monstrosity theorized by Cohen. Monsters for Cohen '[resist] any classification built on hierarchy or a merely binary opposition' (Cohen 1996: 7), emerging at sites of rupture within or exclusion from stable categories. Because of this, the power wielded by the monster is a deconstructive one:

> Like a letter on the page, the monster signifies something other than itself: it is always a displacement, always inhabits the gap between the time of upheaval that created it and the moment into which it is received, to be born again. These epistemological spaces between the monster's bones are Derrida's familiar chasm of *différance*[.]
>
> (Cohen 1996: 4)

Monsters are figurations of difference, but beyond this, in Cohen's estimation they also per se signify both the excess and absence that characterize *différance*, and alterity in a more general sense, for Derrida. This is theologically significant when reading Lewis, who not only adheres to the Christian belief in God incarnate through Christ but, more often than not, also portrays the divine as bestial and monstrous throughout his fiction. Most famously, his characterization of Aslan as 'wild, you know. Not like a *tame* lion' (Lewis [1950] 2001: 197) in *The Chronicles of Narnia* has also, as David C. Downing notes, largely been interpreted to 'refer both to his utter sovereignty and to his numinous qualities' (Downing 2005: 68). Although the portrayal of god of the Mountain lacks an explicit association with alterity as political marginality, the nature of the Shadowbrute aligns with Cohen's reading of monstrosity.

For Cohen, if radical alterity manifests as a body, it is one that 'always rises from the dissection table as its secrets are about to be revealed and vanishes into the night' (Cohen 1996: 4). In the same way, the god of the Mountain violently rises up just as Psyche is about to uncover the secret of his face – a secret which must not be appropriated by Psyche's gaze – then effectively vanishes from the text after Orual gets the briefest glimpse of him. It is with such 'obscured glimpses' – as well as 'footprints, bones, talismans, teeth, shadows' – that 'monstrous interpretation [. . .] must content itself', for these things 'stand in for the monstrous body itself' (Cohen 1996: 6). Unlike Aslan, the physicality and precise identity ascribed to the Shadowbrute are constantly shifting and far from cohesive; according to the priest, 'the Brute is, in a mystery, Ungit herself or Ungit's son, the god of the Mountain; or both' (Lewis 1956: 49), and '[m]any say it *is* a shadow' (Lewis 1956: 48). Interpreted through Cohen's theory, the Shadowbrute and the god of the Mountain expose the utter incoherence of rational categories, systematic theologies and even language itself in the face of the divine. In *Till We Have Faces*, human understanding of the gods can never be organized into a seamless whole but may be slippery, or pock-marked and fragmentary, or sharp and spiny like the skin of a monster.

This reading, which resists interpreting the god's violent outburst as the retributive justice of a jealous sovereign, is further supported by a mystical vision Orual experiences late in the novel. In the vision, she is standing on the banks of a river, with a herd of golden rams on the other side. Realizing that 'those [. . .] are the rams of the gods' and that 'if [she] can steal but one golden flock off their sides, [she] shall have beauty' (Lewis 1956: 283), she swims to the other side, only for the rams to charge at her and trample her, although Orual notes that '[t]hey were not doing it in anger. They rushed over [her] in their joy' (Lewis 1956: 284). While the comment about joy is unique to Lewis's text, Orual's realization that the rams' aggression stems from something *other* than anger answers and disrupts her understanding of the devastation wrought by the god of the Mountain earlier in the novel. In her words, '[w]e call it the wrath of the gods; as if the great cataract in Phars were angry with every fly it sweeps down in its green thunder' (Lewis 1956: 284). As the golden rams resist Orual's attempt to assimilate them and appropriate their attributes for herself, so also Psyche's lover resists her attempt to apprehend his alterity via the light of reason.

The latter portion of the novel also shows us discontinuities and incoherencies between Orual's version of events and the version told in an explicitly religious context. While journeying through the land of Essur, Orual comes upon a temple, which houses a statue of a young woman wearing a black veil. A priest tells Orual that the temple is to a 'very young goddess' (Lewis 1956: 241) named Istra – Psyche's name in the language of Glome – and begins to tell her the story of how she became a goddess. As his story goes on, Orual becomes enraged, as she recognizes her own story being told as if she could have seen the god's palace and as though she were merely jealous of the favour her sister had found with the god. To Orual, the outrage of the tale the gods seem to have handed to the priest is that 'if the true story had been like their story, no riddle would have been set me; there would have been no guessing and no guessing wrong' (Lewis 1956: 243). Aside from the blatant inconsistencies in the narrative details (for instance, the priest's tale depicts Orual's sister Redival journeying to the god's palace as well), Orual takes offence at the story because of the way it puts her on the spot and harshly challenges the responsibility of her actions, 'as if I had the very sight they had denied me' (Lewis 1956: 244).

It would be tempting to join Orual in reading the priest's tale as insipid and simplistic, and from a certain perspective this would be true. Having read the entire novel from Orual's point of view, we have seen that all the characters and situations are much more complex than the broad archetypes the priest sketches out in his narrative: the beautiful maiden, the amorous god, the 'wicked' (Lewis 1956: 244) and jealous sisters. I would suggest, however, that this story has the structure of a myth within a myth and demonstrates both the power and severe limitations of fantastical storytelling (and all narrative) in a religious context. Orual is more correct than she knows in claiming that 'it's a story belonging to a different world, a world in which the gods show themselves clearly and don't torment men with glimpses' (Lewis 1956: 243–4). Such a world calls to mind Narnia or, to a lesser extent, the Deep Heaven of Lewis's Cosmic Trilogy, where divine figures commune openly and visibly with mortals, unmediated by the inadequacies of religious ritual.

That the fantasy of such a world is here contextualized in a world where gods, by and large, do not inhabit the realms of the visible and comprehensible makes it instructive for how secondary (or in this case, tertiary) worlds may be interpreted through a deconstructive approach to religion. The priest's granting of visibility to holy things that Orual, in fact, could not see erases the gods' unknowability, as Orual is all too keenly aware upon hearing the tale, just as any representable fantastical other-world can only ever defer-differ to the unrepresentable alterity towards which it attempts to gesture. Yet the immediacy with which the gods in the priest's version of the story present themselves to Psyche, Orual and Redival is undercut by the fact that the tale is all part of the rituals that take place within the temple, rituals which are themselves a deferral of the end of the story which may be yet to come.

The priest's story continues beyond Psyche's exile, detailing that she

> falls under the power of Talapal [Ungit], who hates her. [...] So Talapal torments Istra and sets her to all manner of hard labours, things that seem impossible. But when Istra has dome them all, then at last Talapal releases her, and she is reunited to Ialim and becomes a goddess. Then we take off her black veil, and I change my black robe for a white one[.]
>
> (Lewis 1956: 246)

When Orual demands to know whether this redemption has happened yet or whether Psyche is still roaming in exile, the priest can only answer that

> the sacred story is about the sacred things – the things we do in the temple. In spring, and all summer, she is a goddess. Then when harvest comes we bring a

lamp into the temple at night and the god flies away. Then we veil her. And all winter she is wandering and suffering; weeping, always weeping[.]
(Lewis 1956: 246)

Orual realizes that '[t]he story and worship were all one in his mind', and while she takes this as a sign that the priest 'knew nothing' and 'could not understand what [she] was asking' (Lewis 1956: 246), astute readers may note that the priest shares Lewis's own conviction that mythic storytelling and religious practice come very near to the same thing. The seasonal rehearsals of Psyche's story through ritual, including the eucatastrophic turn of her eventual reunion with the god, is for the priest and the temple worshippers the language through which they articulate, however inadequately, their own relationship to alterity.

Moreover, hearing a version of her own life's story in which she is neither the victim nor the central figure in the narrative begins to disturb Orual's own understanding of her treatment by the gods, in the same way that fairy stories, for Tolkien, unsettle accustomed patterns of thinking through recovery. If Levinas must, in Derrida's reading of him, transgress the law against representation in order to draw attention to the other that breaks all representations, so, too, must the gods be spoken of in Lewis's world in order to continually disrupt characters' notions of them. Indeed, speaking of the gods seems unavoidable. Earlier in the novel, after Orual's first encounter with Psyche post-sacrifice, she asks her devout bodyguard Bardia what he makes of Psyche's story. Bardia responds that 'it's not [his] way to say more than [he] can help of gods and divine matters. [. . .] [T]he less Bardia meddles with the gods, the less they'll meddle with Bardia' (Lewis 1956: 135). Yet in his silence at Orual's persistent questions, Orual notes that '[h]e had a pebble between his thumb and forefinger and was drawing little scratches in the earth' (Lewis 1956: 136). Even in declaring that he must not speak of the gods, Bardia must inscribe something of his own theology, just as he leaves literal marks on the landscape around him.

In most of *Till We Have Faces* Lewis depicts the inevitable failure of language and religious doctrine in the face of profound alterity, but in the Essurian priest's story he suggests that even the most simplistic and reductive of myths can defer towards communion with the other. Viewed in this way, *Till We Have Faces* reads as a deconstructive affirmation of the provisional and contingent in theology, which heralds the reality-breaking event of the other's approach via its fantastic figurations and eucatastrophic structure. This is perhaps most clearly demonstrated late in the novel, when Orual emerges from the house of

Ungit after keeping her queenly vigil during an elaborate religious ritual. As she recounts,

> [i]t was the joy of the people that amazed me. There they stood where they had waited for hours, so pressed together they could hardly breathe, each doubtless with a dozen cares and sorrows upon him (who has not?), yet every man and woman and the very children looking as if all the world was well because a man dressed up as a bird had walked out of a door after striking a few blows with a wooden sword. [. . .] I saw two farmers whom I well knew for bitterest enemies [. . .] clap hands and cry, 'He's born!' brothers for the moment.
> (Lewis 1956: 273)

In this passage, Arnom's theatrical enactment of the birth of the new year, which is a self-conscious fiction retold as religious ritual,[5] manifests among the common people of Glome as a peace that breaks with everyday enmities and oppositions. As a text, *Till We Have Faces* is by no means naïve about religion's – or fantasy's – potential to do harm, to reassert violent notions of sovereignty and to tell simplistic stories that marginalize its subjects. As readers we are encouraged throughout the novel to take seriously Orual's deep uneasiness and horror at the institutions of human sacrifice and sexual subservience within Ungit's temple. Nonetheless, the deconstructive and transformative power of storytelling displayed within the novel shows that it is precisely in saying 'yes' to fantastic religious figurations of alterity that every other (one) is met as every (bit) other in loving and ethical relations.

Breaking the circle: Religion without religion in *The Left Hand of Darkness*

In *Till We Have Faces*, Orual and Psyche's contentions with the religious narratives that surround them, and the ways in which these are dismantled in their encounters with the gods, ultimately lead them towards a greater sensitivity to the radical alterity of others around them. In Lewis's novel this awareness manifests primarily in relations of interpersonal love (which later chapters in this book will examine in more detail). Ursula K. Le Guin's novel *The Left Hand of Darkness*, meanwhile, is comparable to *Till We Have Faces* in its use of fantasy to navigate relations with the other, but in Le Guin's text this relation takes on a more overtly political dimension. Much of the novel's story is told by Genly Ai, an envoy from the utopian Ekumen of Known Worlds, on a diplomatic mission to the wintry planet of Gethen in the hopes of making Gethen a part of the Ekumen's interplanetary alliance. While no gods rear their heads in the secondary world of Gethen, *The Left Hand of Darkness* can still be seen as a deconstructive exploration of love, ethics and politics as matters to be approached with radical faith and openness to the other. This will be made immediately apparent to theologically minded readers by virtue of the fact that 'Ekumen' is derived from the same Greek root (*oikoumenikós*) as 'ecumenical', a word often used, especially in Christian contexts, to describe fellowship across difference both within and among religious traditions. The gulf of difference that Genly must traverse is heightened by the Gethenians' alien physiology and lack of stable sexuality or gender identity, and the cultural norms that stem from these attributes. Moreover, the novel routinely disrupts Genly's narration with the voices of other characters, as well as excerpts from religious texts, folk tales and myths from Gethen that complicate, deepen and even jar with the reader's understanding of the novel's action. The novel's exploration of alterity in ethical and political terms is also intricately bound up with the two fictional religions presented in the text: the Handdara and the cult of Meshe (or Yomesh). While the faith of the Yomeshta is a religion based around the type of monolithic, all-knowing sovereignty that Derrida critiques, I argue that the Handdara can be read as a figuration of deconstructive religion without religion.

Before discussing *The Left Hand of Darkness* in depth, a brief note on the use of gendered pronouns in the novel, and how it will be approached in this book, is necessary. While the original text of Le Guin's novel mainly uses masculine-coded 'he/him/his' pronouns in reference to Gethenian characters, this book takes note of Le Guin's stated regret over this choice. (The precise reasons for this regret will be discussed in depth in Chapter 2.) As she comments in her 1987 annotations to her essay 'Is Gender Necessary?', the singular, gender-neutral 'they/them/their' pronoun 'should be restored to the written language, and let the pedants and pundits squeak and gibber in the streets' (Le Guin [1987] 1989: 15). While Chapters 2 and 4 examine the complex questions raised by the use of gendered pronouns as they appear in the text in more depth, the majority of this book uses singular 'they' pronouns to highlight the Gethenians' gendered and sexual 'otherness'. I have chosen to refer to the novel's characters in this way not in the interest of obscuring the text, but rather in order to further underscore its investment in alterity, particularly where gender is concerned.

From the outset of the text, political aims focused on alterity are described in religious terms. The Ekumen's politics, like Levinas's ethical project, represent 'an attempt to reunify the mystical with the political' (Le Guin [1969] 2010:

146), and Genly even makes the tongue-in-cheek suggestion that his mission on its behalf is for '[t]he enrichment of harmony and the greater glory of God' (Le Guin [1969] 2010: 35). In practice, however, Genly's attempt, on behalf of the Ekumen, to enter an ethical relationship with the Gethenian people proves difficult, as for much of the novel Gethenian cultures, political systems and social practices remain inscrutable to him. As a Terran (or 'Earthling'), Genly is the audience's surrogate in the novel, and the confusion and alienation he feels mirror our own as the secondary world of Gethen unmoors us from familiar bearing points. The text's approach to presenting its secondary world to the reader is confrontational, and the disruptive and jarring effect this creates serves to highlight the text's preoccupation with otherness.

As is likely discernible even from its title, the association of darkness with difference, and religious reverence towards it, permeates *The Left Hand of Darkness* in much the same way it does *Till We Have Faces*. In an early scene in which Genly meets with Estraven, the dim firelight of the room serves to underline Estraven's unknowability. Genly observes that Estraven '[leaves their] face in shadow' (Le Guin [1969] 2010: 16) and remarks that Estraven's political motives are the darkest of many 'dark, obstructive, enigmatic souls' in Karhide (Le Guin [1969] 2010: 20). The 'darkness' Genly identifies in Estraven, as with Ungit in *Till We Have Faces*, seems to evoke absolute otherness and illegibility, and thus opens a space in which to consider the text in terms of Derrida's and Levinas's approach to alterity, which similarly figures the other as eluding the 'light' of reason and the *logos*.

Genly's inability to navigate the sociopolitical order and cultural practices in the nation of Karhide in the earlier passages of the novel stems partly from the fact that Karhide, as if mirroring the shifting and unstable body morphologies of its inhabitants, lacks a coherent national identity per se. Genly observes that Gethenians in general, but Karhiders especially, seem to lack the ability to organize themselves around a unified collective identity and remarks that despite its nominal nationhood, Karhide remains a 'stew of uncoordinated principalities, towns, villages, "pseudo-feudal tribal economic units"' (Le Guin [1969] 2010: 106). While Karhide does play host to a slew of feuds and rivalries among its various clans and regions, war is unheard of on Gethen. As Estraven warns Genly, '*Karhide is not a nation but a family quarrel*' (Le Guin [1969] 2010: 6). Estraven themself repeatedly expresses antipathy towards national identity, describing patriotism as 'fear of the other' (Le Guin [1969] 2010: 20). Much later, they reiterate this point, asking, 'How does one hate a country, or love one? [. . .] [W]hat is the sense of giving a boundary to all that, of giving it a name and ceasing to love where the name ceases to apply?' (Le Guin [1969] 2010: 227–8). Where Karhide lacks national identity, it also displays an abundance of hospitality towards the other. Hospitality in Karhide is law, under which citizens are bound to provide food and lodging for up to three days for any passing traveller, and anyone passing through Karhidish domains is welcomed with open arms. Karhide's lack of a sense of national sovereignty and unified identity (at least in the first half of the novel), coupled with the value its culture places on hospitality, already invites some comparison to deconstructive critiques of sovereignty. The text's secondary world de-naturalizes, by positing self-consciously fictional alternatives, the same primary-world structures that Derrida must dismantle from within. The deconstructive nature of this facet of the novel's worldbuilding becomes even more pronounced when we consider its religious underpinnings.

Genly fairly accurately attributes the fragmentary but radically hospitable nature of Karhide's culture to the inimical climate on Gethen and the necessity of collective solidarity for survival in such a climate. However, it also becomes apparent through Estraven's narration and the excerpts from religious texts that these attributes are also woven through the theology and practices of Handdara. Genly describes the Handdara as a religion 'without institution, without priests, without hierarchy, without vows, without creed; I am still unable to say whether it has a God or not' (Le Guin [1969] 2010: 57). Its practitioners live in quasi-monastic settlements, or 'Fastnesses', where they devote themselves to a practice of unknowing and unlearning. Retreating to the Fastness of Otherhord after failing to secure the allegiance of Argaven, Genly believes that he is coming to understand Karhide better, noting that beneath the social and political surfaces of Karhide's culture 'runs an old darkness, passive, anarchic, silent, the fecund darkness of the Handdara' (Le Guin [1969] 2010: 63). While scholars have most often associated the Handdara with Le Guin's lifelong interest in Taoism,[6] it is also generative for imagining what form, in practice, a religion attuned to the deconstructive movements within theology might take. Several years before Derrida's philosophy would become mainstream in the Anglo-American academy, Le Guin's novel presents in the Handdara a religion dedicated to disrupting binary logics, showing that apparently unified significations are profoundly dependent upon their others or 'shadows' and acting according to the belief that every other (one) is every (bit) other. Like Ungit and the god of the Mountain in *Till We Have Faces*, Handdara 'is elusive. It is always somewhere else' (Le Guin [1969] 2010: 57), always retreating from the light of reason and understanding.

Handdara mysticism can be seen to embody what Derrida describes as 'faith without dogma which makes its way through the risks of absolute night' (Derrida [1996] 2002: 56), in which any belief must be predicated on a vulnerability to radical unbelief. As Faxe the Weaver explains to Genly at Otherhord, '[u]nproof is the ground of action. If it were proven that there is no God there would be no religion. [. . .] But also if it were proven that there is a God, there would be no religion' (Le Guin [1969] 2010: 75). Unproof and radical unknowing are the governing principles of Handdara; indeed, in Faxe's view the risk of unbelief is what makes belief possible in the first place. This is the same reversal performed within Derrida's own writings on religion, in which a culture of faith must be a culture of radical doubt if it is to avoid the violence associated with sovereignty and certainty. As in Derrida's writing, such faith in *The Left Hand of Darkness* is a hope, even hope against all hope, in the approach of a future justice and ethical relation with the other.

In their journal entries, Estraven, themself a practitioner of Handdara, explicitly links Genly's aim to bring Gethen into cooperation with the Ekumen to the Handdara embrace of unproof and transgression of binary oppositions. In the middle of a long stretch of exposition, detailing Genly's struggles to negotiate with the political leaders in the nation of Orgoreyn, Estraven's narration strays into a seemingly unrelated theological digression in which they state that

> [t]o be an atheist is to maintain God. His existence or his nonexistence, it amounts to much the same, on the plane of proof. Thus *proof* is a word not often used among the Handdarata, who have chosen not to treat God as a fact, subject either to proof or to belief: and they have broken the circle, and go free.
> (Le Guin [1969] 2010: 164)

This statement, which echoes and expands on Faxe's earlier words to Genly, also closely parallels Derrida's sustained discussion of God-as-other. Derrida writes in *The Gift of Death* that '[i]f the other were to share his reasons with us by explaining to us, if he were to speak to us all the time without any secrets, he wouldn't be the other, we would share a type of homogeneity' (Derrida [1992] 1995: 57). Similarly, a God who could be apprehended according to standards of fact or proof, which always fall back on the logic of sameness, would not be other and therefore not be God. That Estraven should invoke God in detailing Genly's mission signals that to the extent that the Handdara conceive of God at all, it is in recognition that *tout autre est tout autre*.

For the Gethenians, living on a planet without contact with or even awareness of the existence of other worlds for millennia, Genly's mission is one that must be met with the absolute risk of faith. He is as other and inscrutable to them as they are to him, and the future that his mission would bring about would profoundly disrupt Gethenian life as it is known. Estraven's support of his aims, and their willingness to say 'yes' to the uncertain and disruptive future of his arrival on Gethen heralds, seems to stem directly from their Handdara theology. Handdara is intimately concerned with the future. The most celebrated Handdara practice in Karhide is that of Foretelling, a ritual in which indwellers at a Fastness gather to answer a question posed to them. At first Genly approaches Foretelling with a degree of scepticism indicative of a scientific mindset oriented towards proof. As it happens, Foretelling is no mere fortune-telling scam or superstitious enterprise but a much chancier pursuit; the novel recounts multiple instances of Foretelling gone horribly wrong, and as the indweller Goss explains, not every question is guaranteed an answer.

While Genly's question regarding Gethen's eventual membership within the Ekumen is answered with a simple 'yes' (Le Guin [1969] 2010: 69), there is nothing in Faxe the Weaver's answer to tell Genly how this will come about and what the change will entail. For the Handdarata, Genly is the other whose approach, though it heralds the initiation of a new ethics and a new form of relation, requires the utmost risk in affirming. The way in which the Handdarata say 'yes' to the future Genly brings, without certainty or any guarantee of security, closely parallels how Derrida characterizes openness to the advent of the other as 'religious *faith* through a form of involvement with the other that is a venture into absolute risk, beyond knowledge and certainty' (Derrida [1992] 1995: 5–6). This is further accentuated by the name of the planet that founded the Ekumen, Hain-Davenant. James Bittner has speculated that '"Davenant" comes from the French *avenement* (coming, advent), or French *avenir* (future, future ages)' (Bittner 1984: 96), both of which are words Derrida also uses to signal the other's approach.[7]

The Handdarata's approach to the future is thus instructive of how, as readers, to approach the 'future' figured by Le Guin's secondary world: as a matter of risk in relation with the other. To take part in Foretelling is to '[go] together into the darkness' (Le Guin [1969] 2010: 45), to turn one's attention to what cannot be absolutely prefigured or guaranteed. As Faxe explains to Genly after the Foretelling, the Handdarata practice Foretelling '[t]o exhibit the perfect uselessness of knowing the answer to the wrong question' (Le Guin [1969] 2010: 74). In acknowledging unproof as the ground of all speech, all theology and all action, the Handdara is a religion that is attentive to deconstruction within its own communities and relations. Handdara understands the future, ethics and God not as fixed points of certainty easily spoken of but as 'dark' matters of a faith inseparable from radical doubt and utterly dependent, ultimately, on vulnerability and receptivity to the other.

Estraven is not the only one to couch Genly's presence on Gethen in theological terms, however. In Orgoreyn, devotees of the cult of Meshe seize upon the promises of his mission and attempt to manipulate them towards their own theological and political ends. Observing Genly's interactions with the Orgota politicians, Estraven comments that one politician 'interprets the coming of the Ekumen to Earth as the coming of the Reign of Meshe among [the people]', declaring that the people of Orgoreyn must purify themselves (Le Guin [1969] 2010: 163). Rather than the deconstructive eschatology embodied within Handdara theology and practices, Yomesh messianism (the name 'Meshe' even phonetically evokes 'Messiah') is of a kind much more familiar within the primary world, marked by sovereignty, purity discourses and triumphalism.

Goss explains to Genly that the Yomesh religion began as an offshoot from Handdara, when a Karhidish noble asked the Foretellers to tell them the meaning of life. Yomesh's figurehead, Meshe, was the Weaver in the ritual that followed. In Goss's recounting of the story, the ritual ended in disaster, with almost all of the Foretellers either dead or driven mad. The Yomeshta, however, believe that Meshe 'saw past and future clear, not for a moment, but all during [their] life' (Le Guin [1969] 2010: 71). An excerpt from the Sayings of Tuhulme, a Yomeshta holy text, elaborates on this point, proclaiming, 'In the Sight of Meshe there is no darkness' (Le Guin [1969] 2010: 176). Unlike the religion without religion of the Handdara, which emphasizes darkness, radical difference and unanswerable questions, the Yomeshta hold fast to the belief that '[n]othing is unseen' (Le Guin [1969] 2010: 174), and that in the eyes of their prophet Meshe is '[o]ne centre, one seeing, one law, one light' (Le Guin [1969] 2010: 176). The central pillar of Yomesh mysticism, therefore, is precisely the sovereign unity which Derridean deconstruction seeks to unravel and which practitioners of the Handdara resist.

This obsession with all-knowing, all-seeing sovereignty also translates into a stronger sense of national identity in Orgoreyn than in Karhide, as well as the presence of a heavily policed surveillance state. When Estraven finds themself suddenly banished from Karhide for assisting Genly in his mission and flees to Orgoreyn in exile, they remark that they 'must learn to live without shadows as they do in Orgoreyn' (Le Guin [1969] 2010: 84). Upon their arrival in the capital city of Mishnory, they note the state's intrusion into the day-to-day lives of the people. They recount that 'the Inspectors' cars were forever snooping and spotlighting those dark streets, taking from poor [people] their one privacy, the night' (Le Guin [1969] 2010: 86). Genly notes that the Orgota word that he must translate as 'commensal' or 'commensality' refers both to the nation's governing body and to its citizens, and that 'in the use of it for both the whole and the part, the state and the individual, in this imprecision is its precisest meaning' (Le Guin [1969] 2010: 116). Orgoreyn's sense of national identity and political unity is thus much stronger than that of Karhide; great emphasis is placed on the maintenance of borders and the documentation of citizens and residents. As Genly ruefully remarks, '[b]etter to be naked than to lack papers, in Orgoreyn' (Le Guin [1969] 2010: 119). It is not at all difficult to trace this political obsession with observation, documentation, order and unity back to the Yomeshta's reverence towards the all-seeing eyes of Meshe.

From the moment of Genly's arrival in Orgoreyn, Le Guin emphasizes the allure of a theology and political ideology that promises clarity and certainty. Strong parallels are drawn in the text between the familiarity with Orgota customs to Genly's Terran sensibilities and the physical comforts he experiences there. In Mishnory, Orgoreyn's capital city, Genly comments, 'everything was simple, grandly conceived, and orderly. I felt as if I had come out of a dark age' (Le Guin [1969] 2010: 123). The Yomesh emphasis on absolute knowing and perpetual light suffuses Orgoreyn's architecture, its politics and even its day-to-day luxuries, and from Genly's brief descriptions, it is easy to recognize Orgota culture as very close to rationalist, Enlightenment modernity in the primary world. Like Carter's depiction of New York in *The Passion of New Eve*, Le Guin's text makes manifest how theology and metaphysics are built even into political structures that, in the primary world, do not acknowledge the ways in which they are co-implicated. Orgoreyn is an example of what Derrida refers to as 'the nation-state figure of sovereignty' (Derrida [2002] 2005: 158), absolute divine authority translated into state power; and as Derrida also notes, '[t]he use of state power is *originally* excessive and abusive' (Derrida [2002] 2005: 156). While Genly hopes that Orgoreyn's existence as a more unified and orderly nation than Karhide will make them easier to negotiate with on behalf of the Ekumen, this turns out to be far from the case. The strength of Orgoreyn's self-identity and its easiness to mobilize also make its leaders paranoid at a time of brewing – and unprecedented for Gethen – international conflict, and they eventually arrest Genly and send him off to a labour camp at Pulefen Farm.

Richard D. Erlich has noted that the message sent by the novel here is clear: '[a]ccept the world view of the Yomesh [. . .] accept their ideas on time, darkness, and epistemology, and you are only a few hundred years away from a mobilizable, patriotic Orgota State [. . .] and prison farms' (Erlich 2010: 130).

For the Yomeshta, darkness and difference are problems to be expunged with the light of the *logos*. Le Guin's text symbolically demonstrates how untenable this notion is in a passage when Estraven and Genly, exiled and stateless, journey across the vast, empty expanse of the Gobrin Ice to contact an Ekumen ship. In one place, the white surface of the ice reflects the sunlight 'leaving the sky white, the air white, no visible sun, no shadow: and the snow itself, the Ice, disappeared from under our feet' (Le Guin [1969] 2010: 262). Genly recounts the horror of attempting to walk in such weather, which Estraven calls the 'Unshadow' (Le Guin [1969] 2010: 281) and in which variations in the terrain are rendered invisible. When we consider darkness and shadows in the novel as motifs symbolizing difference, the parallels with deconstructive philosophy become clear. For Derrida, signification is impossible without originary *différance*. Although Le Guin figures alterity in this instance in terms broader than the trace, the sentiment is nearly identical; in Estraven's words, '[i]t's queer that daylight's not enough. We need the shadows, in order to walk' (Le Guin [1969] 2010: 286). Here, Le Guin literalizes the Handdara belief that action is utterly dependent on darkness, on unknowing and on radical difference.

Ultimately, it is Estraven's Handdara theology, more than anything else on Gethen, that allows Genly to realize the full purpose and potential of his mission, which is a face-to-face encounter with the other that is nearly identical to the ethical and political project that Levinas describes. The necessity of a relationship in which the *I* is disrupted and its unity put into question by an infinite responsibility for an utterly alien *Thou* is communicated in the words of Tormer's Lay, a Handdara poem from which the novel takes its title: '*Light is the left hand of darkness / and darkness the right hand of light*' (Le Guin [1969] 2010: 252). In Handdara theology, light and darkness, self and other, are not figured as opposite poles of a binary, but as always intricately bound up with and dependent upon each other. Accordingly, the novel repeatedly emphasizes forms of community forged in darkness and profound awareness of the other's suffering, such as in the scene of the Foretelling and in a later passage where Genly is taken to the Orgota labour camp at Pulefen in a truck full of strangers. These instances culminate in the fully realized ethical relationship between Genly and Estraven, which serves both as a microcosm of the politics to which the Ekumen aspires and as a manifestation, in a fantastic context, of Levinas's ethics of alterity. Alone together on the ice, they enact the future they aim to bring about for Gethen.

As stated earlier, in the early passages of the novel much is made of the darkness and inscrutability of Estraven's face to Genly. The motif of the face resurfaces once Estraven rescues Genly from his imprisonment at Pulefen. As Genly watches Estraven sleep, '[t]he dark secret face was laid bare to the light, to [his] gaze' (Le Guin [1969] 2010: 215). Estraven's face confronts Genly in a way previously imperceptible to him; he reflects that he 'saw [them] now defenseless and half-naked in a colder light, and for the first time saw [them] as [they were]' (Le Guin [1969] 2010: 215–16). This passage repeats, almost verbatim, Levinas's characterization of the face of the other as 'mortality, mortality of the other beyond his appearing; nakedness more naked, so to speak, than that which the unveiling of truth expresses' (Levinas 1999: 127). In finally discerning and responding to the call towards responsibility issuing from Estraven's face in its utter vulnerability, Genly is also able to open himself towards the future justice he professes. Genly and Estraven's previously strained diplomatic relationship, marked by mistranslations, misunderstandings and seemingly impenetrable barriers of cultural and sexual difference, begins to give way to a deeper sense of community and intimacy born out of their mutual exile.

As Genly and Estraven begin to relate to one another more openly, Genly comes to understand, late in the novel, that this was the reason he was sent on his mission to Gethen alone. As he ruminates to Estraven, alone, he must be changed by Estraven's world instead of changing it; in this way, his mission 'is individual, it is personal, it is both more and less than political. Not We and They; not I and It; but I and Thou. Not political, not pragmatic, but mystical' (Le Guin [1969] 2010: 279).[8] Genly realizes, in the end, that the political project signified by the Ekumen cannot be a politics of generality and principle; it must pass through absolute night and unknowability in the face of the other, and his sense of self-identity will not emerge unscathed. The profoundly disruptive nature of Genly and Estraven's ethical relationship, upon which they both depend for their survival on the Ice, is signified by Genly's surname, Ai. In English, 'Ai' sounds like the letter 'I'; Genly is the *I* who is undone by the call issuing from the face of the other. To Estraven, however, 'his name is a cry of pain [. . .] from a human throat across the night' (Le Guin [1969] 2010: 247). Genly is also the other towards whom Estraven is infinitely responsible and to whose face they are readily attentive due to their long practice in the ways of the Handdara. In *The Left Hand of Darkness*, as in Derrida's and Levinas's philosophies, politics is a matter of faith, and relation requires opening oneself to 'darkness and Creation unfinished' (Le Guin [1969] 2010: 264).

This resistance to generalities safeguards *The Left Hand of Darkness'* secondary world against being merely a utopian or liberal fantasy of mutual cooperation. It is notable that Le Guin is not participating in a prescriptive politics; as in the

Handdara's Foretelling, the text concludes the moment the Ekumen arrives on Gethen. What follows from this eucatastrophic conclusion, which is mirrored earlier by the bond formed by Genly and Estraven, is left an open question. Nor does the text lapse into exceptionalism in depicting Karhide as a culture informed by Handdara principles. The novel is deeply ambivalent about the Karhidish monarchy throughout, and both Karhide and Orgoreyn are at fault in the international conflict that emerges in the text's second half. Nonetheless, in *The Left Hand of Darkness* we can discern the value of a deconstructive faith pursued with care and precision that turns away from sovereign commands issued from on high and towards the word of God in the face of the other.

Conclusions

In this chapter, I have argued that fantasy is a deconstructive form of literature in which theology can be both defamiliarized and confronted with figurations of its subjugated others. In doing so, I have re-evaluated the relationships between fantasy, theology and the deconstructive philosophies of Jacques Derrida. Deconstructive philosophy is not nihilism, it is not relativism and it is not obliteration. Especially when read in terms of its relationship to the ethical philosophy of Emmanuel Levinas, it is an attempt to contend with radical difference as a matter of faith in the impossible. Deconstructive theology does not spell an end of religion or death of God per se, but it does call for theology to acknowledge the inherent instability and contingency of its names, symbols and concepts, and most especially its concepts of divine sovereignty. In the face-to-face encounter with the other, 'the name of God would allow us to think something else, for example, a vulnerable nonsovereignty, one that suffers and is divisible, one that is mortal even, capable of contradicting itself or repenting' (Derrida [1992] 1995: 84). As Derrida notes, faith in such a God 'would be a completely different story, perhaps even the story of a god who deconstructs himself' (Derrida [2002] 2005: 157).

The deconstructive mythmaking of *The Passion of New Eve*, *Till We Have Faces* and *The Left Hand of Darkness* demonstrates the potential of fantasy for re-figuring theology in such terms. All three texts take full advantage of fantasy writing's self-reflexive awareness of its own textual constructions in order to dispel any notions of theological truth as absolute, universal and fixed. *The Passion of New Eve* and *The Left Hand of Darkness* both display the violence towards the other wrought by these notions and the ways in which they bolster hierarchical notions of divine sovereignty. At the same time, the three texts also employ fantasy in order to highlight (or perhaps more accurately, to add shades of darkness to) the absolute alterity encountered in the most quotidian of relations. The ambivalences and crises of representation that arise out of the impossibility of signifying the wholly other *as* wholly other, and the ease with which theological articulations fall back on concepts of sovereignty, are fully dramatized in *Till We Have Faces*. The dark holiness of Ungit and the incoherence of the god of the Mountain/Shadowbrute produce a monstrous theology in which love for the other also opens onto the horror of radical doubt. Yet the novel still affirms acts of mythmaking as opening onto the ethical encounter. In both *The Passion of New Eve* and *The Left Hand of Darkness*, theological storytelling and religious devotion are presented as virtually inescapable discourses that fundamentally shape all relations.

While fantasy can no more offer direct and unmediated access to God-as-other than any other literary genre, its playful rearrangement of elements of the 'primary' world points, I have argued, to the deconstructive movements within all acts of representation, both literary and theological. Careful and critical attention to deconstruction's ambivalent relationship to theology on one hand and the theological and ethical impulses that Tolkien, Le Guin and Attebery have identified in fantasy on the other reveals a common vocabulary and structure between these seemingly disparate discourses. Fantasy produces figurations of alterity that are self-consciously provisional but that nonetheless represent departures from consensus reality. As theorized by Tolkien, it also participates in the deferral of a disruptive messianic approach in the form of eucatastrophe, and parallels can be drawn between fantastic eucatastrophe and the way in which deconstruction opens structures towards the future advent of the other.

As *The Passion of New Eve* dramatizes in its meta-fictional portrayal of mythmaking, the deconstructive potential of fantasy does not guarantee that the theological stories told by fantasy texts will not re-inscribe oppressive norms and hierarchies. Yet the risk of falling back on logocentric, and phallogocentric, concepts is precisely what is necessary for deconstruction to take place. This risk can be identified in any fantastic act of theological (re)imagination and is summed up by a Handdara proverb that Goss quotes in *The Left Hand of Darkness*: 'Behold, we must sully the plain snow with footprints, in order to get anywhere' (Le Guin [1969] 2010: 60). Though Goss's choice of words presumes an *a priori*, pre-lapsarian state evacuated of discourse that Derrida would deem impossible, it still communicates a deconstructive acknowledgement that all writing is *over*writing, that to signify at all is at once to conceal the wholly other and to open oneself to deconstruction. In its disruption of consensus reality and its constant flaunting of its own artificiality, fantasy literature enables theological articulations that unsettle notions of God that are premised on the phallogocentric subject and its dreams of absolute sovereignty. In saying 'yes' to the messianic promise of eucatastrophe, fantasy's figurations open onto their own dissolution in ethical communion with the other.

2

Dragons in the neighbourhood
The fantastic discourse of femininity

Attending to fantasy literature's deconstructive potential reveals much about its ability to make theological gestures that unsettle received wisdom about God and uncover ruptures, discontinuities and silences within the presumed unity of Christian orthodoxy. In the previous chapter, I demonstrated some of the ways in which this movement allows fantasy texts to hold themselves accountable for the violence and exclusion implicit in their theological imaginations (along with their reliance on metaphysics, sovereignty and purity discourses) and, in some cases, to begin to imagine alternative forms that theology and religious practice may take.

Deconstruction's ability to critique the phallogocentrism of hegemonic discourses and the violence implicit in Western (male) subjectivity has led Spivak to characterize it as 'a "feminization" of the practice of philosophy' (Spivak 1992: 171) that carries widespread implications for the feminist critique of masculine authority. Yet, as Spivak also points out, a feminist theory, ethics and politics cannot end with Derrida's writing on deconstruction, not only because 'deconstruction cannot found a politics' (Spivak 1989a: 206) but also because '[Derrida's] point is that man can problematize but not fully disown his status as subject' (Spivak 1992: 171). If deconstruction calls the white, heterosexual, cisgender, male subject of Western discourse into question in the face of the (w)hol(l)y other, then the task of feminism is to call into question the designation of this other as other-than-male, to problematize her appropriation as a trope, archetype or metaphor and to ask how she may represent herself and become a speaking subject. Deconstruction may help us to understand how fantasy texts are able to break with hegemonic religious structures, but a feminist theological understanding of fantasy must look to fantasy's deconstructive as well as its imaginative power to envision ways in which women may claim new forms of subjectivity and engage with religion otherwise. This chapter argues for an affinity between fantasy literature and the discourse of *écriture féminine*, or feminine writing, theorized by Hélène Cixous. A resolutely feminist development of Derrida's critique of the phallogocentrism of Western theology and philosophy, Cixous's experimental philosophy is also driven by speculative impulses and a vocabulary that draws on the narrative tropes of fairy tales, both of which suggest an as-yet-unexplored potential for fantasy literature as a fabulously inventive counter-discourse to patriarchal theology. While Cixous's resistance to phallogocentric authority emerges as much from her religious marginality as it does her feminism, her destabilization of Christian metaphysics is critical for Christian theology to take on board. Indeed, Cixous's analysis of the binary relationships structuring Western discourse suggests that these tasks are inextricably linked and points to the possibility of dismantling the binary opposition between these different positions without erasing their specificity.

I will begin this chapter by detailing the fantastically disruptive intervention Cixous's philosophy makes into the question of woman as the 'other' of philosophical and theological discourse. Drawing, with some crucial caveats, on Heather Walton's and Brian Attebery's claims, following Cixous, that literature is theology and philosophy's subversive, feminized other, I will then consider fantasy literature's potential to offer figurations of a feminist theological subjectivity by way of *écriture féminine*. This will also involve forays into the territory of monstrosity as I consider the 'feminine' figurations that rear their heads in fantasy as, to mangle a phrase from Tolkien, 'dragons in the neighbourhood' of patriarchal consensus reality. I then offer close readings of *Till We Have Faces* and *The Left Hand of Darkness* with attention to the negotiations of femininity, writing and monstrosity involved in their articulations of 'feminine' theological subjects. As I demonstrate, Orual's relationship to Ungit in *Till We Have Faces* and Handdara theology in *The Left Hand of Darkness* both give narrative form to the peculiarly feminine experiences Cixous describes. Both of these texts thus demonstrate fantasy's potential for reclaiming figurations of feminized alterity for feminist theology.

'A world all her own': Hélène Cixous and *écriture féminine*

Derrida's critique of phallogocentric sovereignty and its relation to theology and metaphysics provokes an examination of not only how women are among those marginalized by Western discourses but also how women and femininity have long been appropriated as symbols of unholy and disorderly difference in general. This extends to the Western theological imagination as well; in popular Christian teaching, Eve shoulders the blame for the fall of man in the Garden of Eden, the hero Samson is emasculated and symbolically castrated by Delilah, and Lot's wife is harshly punished for looking back on the ruins of Sodom and Gomorrah by being transformed into a pillar of salt. Even Mary, the venerated mother of Jesus, is in Althaus-Reid's estimation 'an imitation of women which ever since has made difficult the existence of real women in Christianity' (Althaus-Reid 2000: 100), her humanity and sexuality erased to be replaced by the archetypal 'mother-virgin of divine sons': an 'impossible woman' (Althaus-Reid 2000: 101).

As I demonstrated in the previous chapter, fantasy is uniquely suited to a deconstructive mode of engaging with religion that locates God not at the centre of conventional Western theological and philosophical discourses but at their margins and sites of exclusion. Because of this, it is also equipped to be a vital resource for groups historically deemed 'other' by Western culture to imagine and articulate theologies that resist re-inscribing oppressive claims to absolute authority. Fantasy, which already offers fabulous re-visionings of what readers understand as 'real' while also drawing attention to its own impossibility, is particularly well suited for articulating feminist subjectivities while simultaneously contesting the grounds on which subjectivity and identity are constructed and represented. Because the sovereignty of the *logos* is constructed as inherently masculine, a feminism that does not challenge the logocentric order, that seeks merely to replace the male subject at the centre of metaphysics with a 'female' one, would cease to be a feminism at all.

Given all of this, to develop a feminist theological imagination at all is no small undertaking. It requires philosophical and literary discourses that take disruptive difference as their chief concern and dissolve the boundaries that partition off the sacred from the profane. As I noted in Chapter 1, this is not to conflate the radical alterity taken up by deconstructive philosophy with the non-mimetic modes of representation found within fantasy. Rather, it is to acknowledge that the way in which 'difference' is inscribed within the economy of the same is structurally analogous to the way in which fantasy encodes certain resistances to normative identities by drawing on elements from the primary world. Hélène Cixous notes that '[t]he paradox of otherness is that, of course, at no moment in History is it tolerated or possible as such' (Cixous [1975] 1986: 71), and thus within discourse 'what is called "other" is an alterity that does settle down […] in a hierarchically organized relationship in which the same is what rules, names, defines, and assigns "its" other' (Cixous [1975] 1986: 17). While Western discourses attempt to assimilate difference into the same through schemes of representation and categorization, deconstructive philosophy deliberately invokes the representational tropes and language in which 'difference' is inscribed so as to reveal their constructedness, instability and vulnerability to alterity. As I argued in the previous chapter, fantasy participates in a similar phenomenon by displacing these representations from their ordinary associations in the primary world and underscoring their strangeness.

Cixous's efforts to initiate a feminine form of writing are particularly generative when considering fantasy's potential for feminist theological re-visioning, since it takes the fantastic, mythopoetics and theology seriously as sites of discursive and political struggle for women's liberation. Her theory of *écriture féminine* – feminine writing – arises from her conviction that '[w]oman must write her self: must write about women and bring women to writing' (Cixous [1975] 1980: 245). Yet her deconstructive analysis of the extent to which women 'have been driven away [from writing] as violently as from their bodies' (Cixous [1975] 1980: 245) demonstrates what a difficult and precarious undertaking this was at the time of her own writing. Like Derrida, she argues that meaning in Western thought and language relies on binary oppositions that are structured according to metaphysical hierarchies. Her essay '*Sorties*' begins by identifying a list of key oppositions that govern signifying structures:

Activity/passivity
Sun/Moon
Culture/Nature
Day/Night
Father/Mother

Head/Heart
Intelligible/Palpable
Logos/Pathos.
Form, convex, step, advance, semen, progress.
Matter, concave, ground – where steps are taken, holding- and dumping-ground.
(Cixous [1975] 1986: 63)

For Cixous, these oppositions form a complex network of interconnecting axes of difference and subjugation, all organized according to the pervasive hierarchy of man over woman. For instance, 'masculine' culture is thought both to act upon 'feminine' nature – figured as a passive receptacle – and to transcend it in the hierarchy of mind over matter. In Cixous's words, '[p]hilosophy is constructed on the premise of woman's abasement. Subordination of the feminine to the masculine order gives the appearance of being the condition for the machine's functioning' (Cixous [1975] 1986: 65). Throughout her writing, Cixous thus reiterates and elaborates on Derrida's critique on phallogocentrism, often drawing on autobiographical experience to offer an explicit discussion of how women's subordination within (and indeed, erasure from) discourse manifests in their material oppression.

For Cixous, woman's marginality in discourse carries widespread implications for her ability to exist as an embodied subject; her discursive function as (man's) difference has also meant that '[s]he has not been able to live in her "own" house, her very body' (Cixous [1975] 1986: 68). At the time of her writing, Cixous felt that 'with a few rare exceptions, there [had] not been any writing that [inscribed] femininity' (Cixous [1975] 1980: 248), and that women thus had been denied a language for their bodily experience that was subordinated to the 'light' of masculine reason and the phallocentric gaze. Instead, they had been appropriated as symbols of difference within the patriarchal scheme. The denial of the female sex drive and the internalized misogyny of women under patriarchy, for example, both arise out of and serve to re-inscribe women's alienation from their own bodies and from discourse (and from the body as discourse). The result of this, Cixous argues, is that while there are many women who write, there have not historically been many women who write *from the position of* 'woman'. This sentiment is shared by Le Guin, who, reflecting on her early career, notes, 'I did not know how to write about women – very few of us did – because I thought that what men had written about women was the truth, was the true way to write about women. And I couldn't' (Le Guin [1988] 1989: 233–4). What is at stake in woman's relationship to writing is her relationship to her own body, her own femininity and to other women. Woman coming to writing *as* woman poses a fundamental challenge to patriarchal economies of representation.

Cixous frames woman's coming to writing in messianic (and therefore, for our purposes, eucatastrophic) terms, as a justice that cannot be caught within a theory or systematically prefigured. In coming to writing, woman-as-other inserts herself, discursively and bodily, into the domain that has historically belonged solely to the same and to the masculine. In Cixous's view, writing is inseparable from the body and thus she argues that

> [w]omen must write through their bodies, they must invent the impregnable language that will wreck partitions, classes, and rhetorics, regulations and codes, they must submerge, cut through, get beyond the ultimate reserve-discourse,

including [. . .] the one that, aiming for the impossible, stops short before the word 'impossible' and writes it as 'the end'.

(Cixous [1975] 1980: 256)

Women's writing is thus a 'return to the body' (Cixous [1975] 1980: 250), but by no means is this to be interpreted as a closure or restoration of a unified, prelapsarian state. Instead, it is 'the beginning of a new history, or rather a process of becoming' by which '[w]oman un-thinks the unifying, regulating history that homogenizes and channels forces' (Cixous [1975] 1980: 252). Woman's return to her body by writing (through) the body is a return for the first time, a 'shattering entry into history' (Cixous [1975] 1980: 250), from which she has been erased, that opens towards alternative articulations of (feminine) subjectivity. The 'recovery' of her embodiment also heralds an advent of the impossible that would 'threaten the stability of the masculine structure that passe[s] itself off as eternal-natural' (Cixous [1975] 1986: 65). In this regard, woman's coming to writing, like deconstructive messianism, is figured in terms that can be seen to parallel fantastic eucatastrophe; it is a making-right that is signalled not by the re-establishment of a pre-existing order, but rather by the interruption and breaking of it.

Crucially, Cixous takes care to acknowledge that 'difference is not distributed [. . .] on the basis of socially determined "sexes"' and that '[w]e have to be careful not to lapse smugly and blindly into an essentialist ideological interpretation' (Cixous [1975] 1986: 81). For her, feminine writing rests not on a binary division between man and woman, but rather a rehabilitation of qualities traditionally gendered as 'feminine' that resist assimilation by the patriarchal order that seeks to suppress and erase them. Although she frequently speaks generally of 'men' and 'women' or 'male' and 'female' throughout her work, these are to be taken not as essential demarcations of gender identity but rather as diagnoses of gender relations in the cultural context she inhabits. There are, after all, women writers 'whose workmanship is in no way different from male writing, and which either obscures women or reproduces the classic representations of women (as sensitive – intuitive – dreamy, etc.)' (Cixous [1975] 1980: 248). Likewise, 'there are some men who do not repress their femininity' (Cixous [1975] 1986: 81), and in fact Cixous cites both Jean Genet and James Joyce among the handful of writers who, in her view, practice feminine writing. Yet, unconcerned though she is with reducing her feminism to individual identity, Cixous still primarily views feminine writing as a project of women's liberation in particular, since it is primarily in women's oppression that this discourse manifests. For her, '[i]t is by writing, from and toward women [...] that women will confirm women in a place [...] other than silence' (Cixous [1975] 1980: 251).

Cixous makes the theological implications of her writing and its association with the fantastic explicit throughout her work. She compares women appropriated by the male subject to such fairy-tale characters as Snow White and Sleeping Beauty, '[sleeping] in their woods, waiting for princes to come and wake them up. In their beds, in their glass coffins, in their childhood forests like dead women' (Cixous [1975] 1986: 66). Elsewhere, she describes the simultaneous silencing and becoming-metaphor of woman as being 'riveted [...] between two horrifying myths: between the Medusa and the abyss' (Cixous [1975] 1980: 255), that is, between monstrosity and absence. The dense forests of Faërie represent for Cixous the dark realm of embodiment and desire that every woman is forbidden from exploring 'as soon as she begins to speak, at the same time as she is taught her name' (Cixous [1975] 1986: 68). Cixous is here suggesting that myths and fairy stories instil in women a fear of the woods and of the mysteries of their own desires that may threaten the masculine order and are thus heavily implicated in patriarchal systems; in her words '[m]yths end up having our hides' (Cixous [1986] 1991: 14–15).

And yet, it is precisely for this reason that the fantastic also holds such power for women writers. If the realm of Faërie consists of unholy monstrosities and representations of 'alterity' that transgress patriarchal constructions of reality, women coming to writing can find there a language for articulating their own subjectivity as other than masculine, particularly if, as Cixous argues, they are pre-emptively excluded from transcendence via a sovereign divinity. Cixous's personal essay 'Coming to Writing' chronicles her own sense of displacement as both a woman and a religious minority – a 'Jewoman' (Cixous [1986] 1991: 7), as she terms herself – in the French Algeria of her childhood. Strikingly, she narrates her exclusion from writing as synonymous with her exclusion from theological discourse and religious authority, specifically, reflecting that

> [w]riting is reserved for the chosen. It surely took place in a realm inaccessible to the small, to the humble, to women. In the intimacy of the sacred. Writing spoke to its prophets from a burning bush. But it must have been decided that bushes wouldn't dialogue with women.
> (Cixous [1986] 1991: 13–14)

Although Cixous uses vocabulary specific to Jewish religious authority here, it is not difficult to apply similar observations onto the Christian tradition as well, in which patriarchal sovereignty is upheld often even in instances where women are allowed positions of authority. Since they are barred from the authoritative *logos* of theology, Cixous suggests that women's writing resides instead in the fantastic and 'the straying into the forest' (Cixous [1986] 1991: 14–15). As complicit as myths and fairy stories often are in patriarchal prohibitions issued to women, Cixous also identifies in them Red Riding Hood's 'dangerous questioning addressed to the body of the Wolf: What is the body for?' (Cixous [1986] 1991: 14–15). For her, the fantastic is not merely an imaginative extension of theology and religious practice, but their subversive other, the neglected space for the exploration of the body that patriarchal theologies endeavour to escape and suppress. The dark and threatening spaces of Faërie offer a topography for women denied even the illusion of transcendence in the *logos* to be reunited with their bodies and examine the uncharted territories of desire they may find there. Le Guin, once again, notes fantasy fiction's potential for taking part in this radical project, arguing that '"[w]riting the body", as Woolf asked and Hélène Cixous asks, is only the beginning. We have to rewrite the world' (Le Guin [1988] 1989: 228).

Cixous's entire project, in fact, can be extended to include an exercise in speculative worldbuilding. It attempts to envision '[w]hat would happen to logocentrism, to the great philosophical systems, to the order of the world in general if the rock upon which they founded this church should crumble' (Cixous [1975] 1986: 65). Cixous even explicitly describes women's exploration of their sexualities as the imaginative exploration of another world, saying,

> I have been amazed more than once by a description a woman gave me of a world all her own which she had been secretly haunting since early childhood. A world of searching, the elaboration of a knowledge, on the basis of a systematic experimentation with the bodily functions, a passionate and precise interrogation of her erotogeneity.
>
> (Cixous [1975] 1980: 246)

Woman comes to writing not to usurp man's place at the centre of the phallogocentric order but to dismantle it and invent ways of relating to the body, to one's own desires and pleasure, and to others that are radically different from what came before. While she makes few definitive prescriptions, Cixous hints in 'The Laugh of the Medusa' that these may concretely manifest in a profound rethinking of the structure of human relationships. Women writing the body might allow them, for example, to 'get away from the [psychoanalytic] dialectic which has it that the only good father is a dead one, or that the child is the death of his parents' (Cixous [1975] 1980: 261). Familial and social relationships would be reconfigured such that there would have to be a recognition of each other, and this grateful acknowledgement would come about thanks to the *other*, of difference, without feeling threatened by the existence of an otherness, rather, delighting to increase the unknown that is there to discover, to respect, to favour, to cherish.

(Cixous [1975] 1986: 78)

Where patriarchal masculinity seeks to establish itself over the feminized other so as to assimilate or devour her, Cixous seeks to initiate an ethic of love in which alterity, and particularly sexual difference, is maintained as other.

Is fantasy feminine?

Despite the current dearth of scholarship on fantasy literature and feminist theology, both Brian Attebery and Heather Walton have laid crucial groundwork for an inquiry into fantasy's potential for developing a feminist theological imagination, taking partial cues from Cixous. Since both Attebery and Walton make arguments about gender that are heavily informed by poststructuralist feminism, they are important to consider as precursors to the argument I am making here concerning Cixous, theology and fantasy literature. Attebery identifies in fantasy's historical exclusion from the Western canon and its historical dismissal as 'unreasonable' a subversive potential, noting that this 'makes the fantastic resemble [. . .] women's writing' (Attebery 1992: ix) and even going so far as to claim that 'fantastic literature is a woman' (Attebery 1992: x). More recently, Walton has noted that 'in discussions of the relationship between literature and the "logocentric" discourses of theology and philosophy literature is constructed as female' (Walton 2007: 18) because of its perceived subversiveness.

According to Walton, the precise reasons for the gendering of literature as feminine in relation to theology are varied and can often be difficult to untangle, but one of the reasons she gives is that '[f]eminism is a peculiarly literary movement', and feminists have historically 'found in literature an accessible space in which it was possible to critique contemporary practice and engage in the imaginative construction of alternative worlds' (Walton 2007: 10). Walton is not exclusively referring here to speculative genres such as science fiction and fantasy, but it is not at all difficult to see how easily applicable her characterization of women's writing is to the construction of secondary worlds. Fantasy fiction's ability to serve as an imaginative dimension of philosophical and theological discourses, and its potential for envisioning alternative forms of religious community and practice – such as Le Guin's Handdara – are of a piece with the 'vivid and unorthodox namings of the divine' (Walton 2007: 11). Walton identifies within women's writing.

While Walton does not specifically engage with women writers' relationship to the genre of fantasy, she does note that '[t]he genres in which many women have chosen to write (e.g. gothic romance and detective fiction) have always been viewed as of lesser significance – hardly literature at all' (Walton 2007: 14). Given the troubled history of the depiction of women in popular fantasy literature, it would be difficult to argue that its exclusion from the canon is directly comparable to that of the genres Walton names. Even so, Attebery argues that fantasy 'has something special to offer to the woman writer, who is already defined by her culture as the irrational, the disruptive, the formless, the Other' (Attebery 1992: x). According to Attebery, women's writing and feminist reading strategies '[disrupt] some of the same hierarchies of value and conventions of form that the strategies of fantasy deconstruct' (Attebery 1992: ix) by defying mimesis, frustrating oppositions between the 'real' and 'unreal', and often (though certainly not always in fantasy's case) flouting the received wisdom of the primary culture.

Walton, too, observes that in most Western understandings of the two disciplines,

> [t]heology is placed on the side of spirit, reason, light, truth, order – the masculine virtues. Literature is associated with the body, desire, darkness, mystery – the feminine. Theology is the place where God and 'man' meet. Literature, like Lilith excluded from the garden, endlessly seduces and gives birth.
> (Walton 2007: 15)

The alterity and marginality revealed within both women's writing and fantasy texts – even, in the latter's case, when this is contrary to their authors' intentions – are intricately interwoven with these types of literature's embodiment of qualities traditionally devalued in intellectual discourses because of their perceived femininity, such as magical thinking and a suspicion of 'rational' categorization. Walton argues that 'theology seizes language to illuminate and instruct whereas literature leads us back towards the dark and damp, sacred places where words and forms disintegrate' (Walton 2007: 17). In this formulation, we may imagine literature as the dark and damp house of Ungit in *Till We Have Faces*, in which the 'Greek wisdom' espoused by the Fox and Orual loses coherence and meaning. Where much of Western theology seeks metaphysical transcendence through a sovereign divine power – think, for instance, of the apostle Paul's instruction to early Christians that they must 'put to death the deeds of the body' (Rom. 8.13, NRSV) – feminist writing directs readers' attention back to incarnation, even to a plurality of incarnations that would otherwise be unthinkable within the structures of patriarchal theology. The fantastic can underscore the alterity of these feminine incarnations, subjectivities and imaginings of God, and thus draw attention to their subversive power.

Even so, understanding fantasy literature as patriarchal theology's subversive, feminine other is not without its pitfalls. Attebery's declaration that fantasy literature 'is' 'a' woman in particular is too uncritical about the association it draws between women, unreason and unreality, and therefore risks merely re-inscribing patriarchal silencing tactics against women rather than subversively working through them. It also comes very close to implying that fantasy is inevitably aligned with *écriture féminine* when this is not necessarily the case, even for fantasy texts written by women and featuring principal women characters. For example, a text like Elizabeth Moon's *The Deed of Paksenarrion* (1988–9), though it chiefly concerns its woman protagonist's evolving understanding of her religious calling, does not re-figure its theology on feminine terms. Instead, it consistently figures Paksenarrion's enactment of her holy vocation as the violent military conquest of a demonic other, an impulse that Cixous associates with patriarchal masculinity. Walton is more cautious with her personification of literature, noting that deconstruction's continued association of femininity with alterity 'has been a controversial move in the eyes of many feminists who are suspicious of claims by male theorists to identify the "feminine" with that which is unrepresentable' (Walton 2007: 34). For many, this would seem to confine women to a space in which they are continually denied subjectivity. Additionally, the essentialism and heteronormativity implicit in Walton's gender-dimorphic configuration of literature and theology, which Walton herself briefly notes (Walton 2007: 19), is ultimately problematic for an account of feminist theology that seeks to dismantle these norms.

Claiming literature as a distinctly feminine site of re-invention does the important work of acknowledging the inherent masculinity of 'rational' discourses, the marginality and absence of women within them, and their devaluation and silencing of qualities traditionally gendered as feminine. As a space for feminist theology, literature can also give voice to religious experiences that both arise out of and exceed the limits and foreclosures of patriarchal religious structures, particularly as they pertain to desire and the body. To both these ends, the discursive and political power of the notion of woman as disruptive other cannot and should not be dismissed. What both deconstructive feminist writing and the fantastic allow for is the ability to invoke and work through the trope of woman-as-difference and the myriad ways it manifests in representation, while refusing to present these representations as essential or mimetic truth.

The laugh of the dragon

Cixous's contention with the fantastic figurations of 'woman' in the Western cultural imagination, particularly regarding the figure of the Medusa, signals that one of the chief ways in which fantasy can engage in feminist re-visionings of theology is through a rehabilitation of the monstrous. Though the Medusa, a monstrous woman with snakes for hair whose gaze turns men to stone, has historically articulated cultural anxieties about 'feminine' power, Cixous playfully insists that '[y]ou only have to look at the Medusa straight on to see her. And she's not deadly. She's beautiful and she's laughing' (Cixous [1975] 1980: 255). Rosi Braidotti further develops Cixous's engagement with feminine monstrosity. Like Cohen, Braidotti argues that the monstrous body lacks either a stable form or a presence within discourse, expanding on Cohen's identification of gender as a key site of monstrous difference by stating that '[t]he woman's body can change shape in pregnancy and childbearing' and therefore 'is troublesome in the eyes of the logocentric economy' (Braidotti 1994: 80) which seeks to fix objects within its gaze and assimilate them into the same.

Woman's resistance to the terms of the very discourse in which she is marginalized can in one sense be interpreted as a double bind, as Braidotti outlines:

> [w]oman/mother is monstrous by excess; she transcends established norms and transgresses boundaries. She is monstrous by lack: woman/mother does not possess the substantive unity of the masculine subject. Most important, through her identification with the feminine she is monstrous by displacement: as sign of the in between areas, of the indefinite, the ambiguous, the mixed, woman/mother is subjected to a constant process of metaphorization as 'other-than'.
> (Braidotti 1994: 83)

For Braidotti, the process by which 'woman' comes to represent difference is itself a fantastic one. Woman's simultaneous marginalization and transgressive potential in relation to logocentric discourse not only places her in a position analogous to that of fantasy literature in relation to the canon; she herself becomes a fantastic beast within the patriarchal economy. Of course, Braidotti's use of pregnancy and childbirth to illustrate this, while certainly encompassing many real women's experience, risks essentializing 'woman's' construction as a generalized term. Yet this, too, can be understood in terms of the double bind of monstrosity and alterity; the shapeshifting body of the pregnant woman threatens patriarchal unity even as women who are infertile, transgender or childless by choice are likewise characterized by patriarchy as aberrant creatures disturbing the social expectations of woman-as-childbearer. Woman – fantastic, monstrous figuration that she is – is forever disrupting the categories and attributes assigned to her and undermining any theory into which she may be caught.

Braidotti's analysis of woman-as-monster suggests that the fantastic is heavily implicated in violence against women, and indeed 'the whole fantastic discourse about the origins of monsters becomes considerably less amusing when we consider that women paid a heavy price for these wild notions' (Braidotti 1994: 85). Yet, difficult to untangle from its misogynistic appropriations though it may be, the monstrous also has the potential to be reclaimed as a site of subversion in terms of what Braidotti calls 'positive alterity' (Braidotti 1994: 46). Moreover, the feminist reclamation of monstrosity is just one example of how the fantastic can aid feminist theology, specifically, in negotiating between and dismantling the opposing poles of 'the sacred or the profane, of heaven or hell, of life or death' (Braidotti 1994: 83) into which women tend to be metaphorized in the Western theological imagination. As Cohen points out, monstrosity may well '[naturalize] the subjugation of one cultural body by another by writing the body excluded from personhood and agency as in every way different', but it also creates a plurality of representations through which 'difference, like a Hydra, sprouts two heads where one has been lopped away' and 'the possibilities of escape, resistance, disruption arise with more force' (Cohen 1996: 11).

Contemporary fantastic literature can contend with and reclaim a vast array of divine and demonic cultural representations of women in positive terms, harnessing the threat that they pose to patriarchal structures while calling into question their 'essential' truth. Responding to criticism that fantasy in the modern era is a superstitious denial of the 'real' world, Tolkien points out that reading fairy stories as a child, he 'desired dragons with a profound desire', but that he 'did not wish to have them in the neighbourhood, intruding into [his] relatively safe world' (Tolkien [1947] 2008: 55). While Tolkien alludes to dragons to caution against conflating the figurations presented within fantasy with an absolute reality, reading his comments in light of the association of monsters with feminine alterity may prompt us to question the desire to commune with dragons while remaining safely separated from their monstrosity in the 'primary' world. Indeed, the history of woman-as-monster suggests that a feminist approach to the fantastic allows us to see women coming to writing as dragons rearing their heads in the sleepy suburbs of a reality structured on patriarchal terms. Nonetheless, Cohen reminds us that the monster's subversive power lies in its ability to contest the grounds of its own monstrosity, to 'bear witness to the fact that it could have been constructed Otherwise' (Cohen 1996: 12). By extension, 'fantastic' women, monsters and mother-goddesses alike, are violently robbed of subjectivity insofar as their liminality is appropriated as symbolic, but this liminality is also precisely what enables women to destabilize the settled patriarchal discourses that do so and tell their story otherwise.

Not only does the monstrous stand in for sexual difference, as both Braidotti and Cohen suggest, but monstrous women pervade fantastic literature and media, and in some cases their monstrosity draws attention to stolen, lost or hybrid subjectivities. Ursula K. Le Guin's *Earthsea* series is one example of a sustained, multivalent engagement with monstrous femininity. In the series' second novel, *The Tombs of Atuan* (1974), the character of Tenar is stolen from her home at a young age to be made the high priestess of the theocratic Kargad Empire. Her title Arha means 'the Eaten One' (Le Guin 1993: 181) and refers to the belief that her soul is devoured by the monstrous, nameless gods she serves the moment she becomes their priestess, completely given over to their power. Over the course of the novel, the pitch-dark, labyrinthine tombs which the Nameless Ones inhabit also come to symbolize Arha's own consciousness as she struggles to regain her subjectivity with the help of Ged, a wizard she has imprisoned within the tombs. The function of monstrosity in *The Tombs of Atuan* is complex; it emerges in the context of a community of women, but they are all in thrall to the patriarchal, theocratic empire of the Kargad lands. Their complicity in the erasure and repression of Tenar's subjectivity calls to mind Cixous's analysis of how women are themselves taught to fear and annihilate their own femininity under patriarchy. Her regaining of herself, and her name, in the dark corridors of the tombs likewise parallels Cixous's linking of woman's self-articulation to sexuality. Amy M. Clarke notes the overtly sexual symbolism of the labyrinth, commenting that '[t]he book even ends in an orgasmic collapse of the tombs' (Clarke 2010: 146–7). Even so, the novel stops short of dismantling phallogocentrism to the extent that Cixous does. Tenar's awakening to herself still requires the intervention of Ged's decidedly phallic wizard's staff, which floods the dark underground space with the light of reason and truth, and monstrosity is not something to be reclaimed but overcome.

Le Guin revisits the trope of feminine monstrosity in the series' fourth volume, *Tehanu* (1990), demonstrating both greater ambivalence than *Tombs* regarding the possibility of overcoming monstrous designations, as well as greater awareness of the disruptive power of reclaiming monstrosity for feminism. In this later text, Tenar's struggle to survive in the patriarchal world of Earthsea, and her drive to protect her adopted daughter Tehanu from the men who raped and sexually trafficked her, is continually aligned with the power of dragons. Shaking with rage after Tehanu's former captors break into her house, Tenar attempts to lighten the mood by asking Tehanu, 'Am I red? [. . .] Like a dragon, am I red?', to which Tehanu replies, 'Yes. You are a red dragon' (Le Guin 1993: 582). Throughout the novel Tenar's anger, often stifled so as to protect herself from further harm, manifests in the affinity she feels with Kalessin, a dragon so ancient as to have no discernible gender. When Tenar first encounters Kalessin, she muses that '[s]he had been told that men must not look into a dragon's eyes, but that was nothing to her. It gazed straight at her from yellow eyes under armoured carapaces wide-set above the narrow nose and flaring, fuming nostrils' (Le Guin 1993: 516). Afterwards, Tenar repeatedly dreams of being a dragon in flight and whispers Kalessin's name to herself in moments of need.

Clarke has directly compared the dragon motif in *Tehanu* to Cixous's reimagination of the Medusa, arguing that Cixous's challenge to simply look at the Medusa 'accord[s] with Le Guin's description of Kalessin, on whom Tenar is not afraid to look' (Clarke 2010: 148). As with the Medusa of Greek myth, the men of Earthsea dare not look a dragon in the eyes lest they fall under an enchantment, and dragons rarely ever speak to them, yet both Tenar and Tehanu are able to look at dragons straight on and openly converse with them. Just as Tenar dreams nightly of dragon flight, Cixous claims flight as a metaphor for the disruptive power of *écriture féminine*. In her words, women writing *as* women 'fly the coop, take pleasure in jumbling the order of space, in disorienting it, in changing around the furniture, dislocating things and values, breaking them all up, emptying structures, and turning propriety upside down' (Cixous [1975] 1980: 258).

If woman is to be understood as the fantastic dragon in the neighbourhood, and fantasy as 'woman', so as to foreground the alterity and disruptive potential of both, this personification extends to the notion that 'woman', like the fantastic, is persistently changing shape to push against, elude and deconstruct the stable categories that have been preordained for her. To say that fantasy literature is 'feminine' in relation to theology's masculine discourse on these terms is already to acknowledge the contingency of such a figuration. As writers, readers and interpreters of fantasy, the women whom theology attempts to fix with its gaze – either by idealizing them as mother-goddesses or by demonizing them as witches and monsters – can find a way to work through these representations, construct alternate modes of subjectivity from their component parts and imagine modes of engaging with religion and relating to God or gods that resist the patriarchal order.

As my brief discussion of feminine monstrosity in the *Earthsea* series demonstrated, modern fantasy fiction is able to participate in experiments with writing a non-phallogocentric feminine subjectivity similar to those undertaken by Cixous. Moreover, Tenar's reclamation of her subjectivity occurs in the explicit context of her embattled relationship to theology and religious community and practice. In the next two sections, I show how the fantastic narratives of *Till We Have Faces* and *The Left Hand of Darkness* respectively navigate the question of a 'feminine' theological subjectivity by placing them in conversation with Cixous's theory of *écriture féminine*. Viewed in this way, Orual's embattled relationship with the goddess Ungit in *Till We Have Faces* chronicles Orual's evolving relationship with her own femininity as well as other women and her struggles to articulate herself as a theological subject. Many aspects of Karhidish society and Handdara theology in *The Left Hand of Darkness*, meanwhile, prefigure the reconfiguration of social relations that Cixous advocates by attempting to envision, albeit imperfectly, a society without binary gender and the symbolic associations of values that accompany it. Both these texts demonstrate fantasy's singular potential for reclaiming, for feminist aims, discourses surrounding 'woman' within patriarchal theological traditions and transforming their meaning in disruptive ways.

Mère Christianity: Women's language and holy wisdom in *Till We Have Faces*

In Chapter 1, I argued that in C. S. Lewis's *Till We Have Faces*, Ungit's holy 'darkness' is indicative of alterity. For Orual, she specifically represents the 'dark continent' of femininity by which Orual is initially repulsed and to which she must eventually be reconciled. This section contends that Orual's initially antagonistic and increasingly complex relationship to Ungit represents a fear of her own femininity, and that her development as a theological subject parallels Hélène Cixous's characterization of the woman erased and devalued by phallogocentric patriarchal discourse coming to writing. As noted in the previous chapter, Orual's act of writing initiates a religious transformation, but this also coincides with a transformation in how Orual perceives and relates to other women and her own femininity. This is further complicated by the fantastic sense of mystery that accumulates around Orual herself after she becomes Queen of Glome and veils her face to the public. In this way, the fantasy of *Till We Have Faces* literalizes the difficulty of articulating theology from a position of femininity in a society in which 'feminine' bodies and subjectivities are figured as unrepresentable darkness and monstrosity, as well as the radical potential of reclaiming such figurations.

Brian Attebery's and Monika B. Hilder's recent studies of *Till We Have Faces* both lay crucial groundwork for placing the text in dialogue with Cixous's writing, with Attebery even directly invoking *écriture féminine* in his claim that the language of Ungit 'is women's language, her presence close and comforting, as well as smelly and stifling' (Attebery 2014: 93). This stands counter to much of the criticism of gender in both Lewis's oeuvre as a whole and *Till We Have Faces* in particular, most notably Filmer's argument that women in Lewis's fiction 'are either saints or sluts' (Filmer 1993: 88), and that *Till We Have Faces* 'is [. . .] entirely consistent with his belief that God is utterly Masculine, and that all else, in relation to God, is necessarily feminine' (Filmer 1993: 120). Hilder, meanwhile, has rightly identified a subversive potential in this metaphor, even going so far as to call Lewis's overall project one of 'theological feminism' (Hilder 2013: 20). However, her decision to continue to frame ethical asymmetry as a hierarchy, albeit a 'fluid, loving' one in which 'classical power relations are meaningless' and 'the paradoxes of harmony reign supreme' (Hilder 2013: 29), proves severely limiting not only for her reading of *Till We Have Faces* but also for her theological imagination more broadly. In this reading, God remains masculine and retains *his* position atop the logocentric structure; even if God were figured as feminine on Hilder's terms, her theological framework still maintains the structure of hierarchy. My reading of *Till We Have Faces* more radically perceives Ungit as a 'feminine' theological figuration who emerges in the text as a fundamental threat to all stable categories and hierarchies, although this potential is partially but never fully realized in the text itself.

Attebery's reading of Ungit is likely a reference to Cixous's characterization of the difference within women's subjectivity as 'more or less of the mother who makes everything all right, who nourishes, and who stands up against separation; a force that will not be cut off but will knock the wind out of the codes' (Cixous [1975] 1980: 252). For Cixous, 'mother' is one representation of what she hopes to reconcile with through feminine writing: 'body (body? bodies?), no more describable than god, the soul, or the Other; that part of you that leaves a space between yourself and urges you to inscribe in language your woman's style' (Cixous [1975] 1980: 252). While in Cixous this characterization of the (m)other who resides in the in-between spaces of subjectivity is a deliberate resistance to 'overbearing, clutchy' (Cixous [1975] 1980: 252) depictions, *Till We Have Faces*' use of narrative perspective means that Ungit becomes a site of contention between Orual's own femininity – her internal '(m)other' – and the misogynistic representations she has internalized from the patriarchal culture she inhabits.

Orual's relationship to her own femininity as she matures into adulthood is complicated by her lack of a mother and her purported ugliness, as well as the logocentric 'Greek wisdom' in which she is educated. The novel's narrative begins on the day of her mother's death when Orual is a young girl, and of her stepmother, Orual 'can say very little [. . .] for she did not live till the end of her first year in Glome' (Lewis 1956: 13). A profound absence of 'feminine' nurture or companionship thus pervades Orual's story. Denied any prospect of marriage on account of her supposed ugliness and continually abused by her father, the king, Orual takes solace only in the company of the Fox and Psyche, the latter being her only close bond with another woman. Following Psyche's banishment, Orual begins to live and present herself as an honorary man, stockpiling philosophical principles from the Fox, studying combat and the art of warfare with Bardia, assisting her father in the Pillar Room and eventually ruling over Glome as queen in the absence of a male heir. Orual's status in an almost exclusively male society is also accompanied by a distaste, jealousy and even hatred for other women, namely her nursemaid Batta, her sister Redival and Bardia's wife Ansit. While Filmer argues that the qualities these other women exhibit 'are consistent with those female characters and characteristics which Lewis denigrates' (Filmer 1993: 119), Orual's status as an unreliable narrator throws this reading into question, as the text invites readers to draw parallels between Orual's evolving relationships with other women, her supernatural relationship to the goddess Ungit and her struggle to articulate herself as a feminine theological subject.

While for most of the novel Ungit is characterized by faceless alterity, in the second part of the novel Orual clarifies,

I have said she had no face; but that meant that she had a thousand faces. For she was very uneven, lumpy and furrowed, so that, as when we gaze into a fire, you could always see some face or other.

(Lewis 1956: 270)

Ungit is thus not only a figuration of theological alterity, as discussed in the previous chapter; at this late stage in the novel, she herself is recontextualized as a repository for Orual's images of others and particularly other women. The face Orual perceives as she keeps vigil with Arnom in Ungit's house, for instance, is '[a] face such as you might see in a loaf, swollen, brooding, infinitely female. It was a little like Batta as I remembered her in certain of her moods' (Lewis 1956: 270). Batta, 'a big-boned, fair-haired, hard-handed woman' (Lewis 1956: 5), is the closest person Orual, Redival and Psyche have to a mother figure. Orual describes her as 'a busybody and tattler in grain' (Lewis 1956: 25), and even Batta's 'loving moods' are described in terms negatively associated with femininity, as Orual recounts '[having] run out into the garden to get free – and to get, as it were, freshened and cleansed – from her huge, hot, strong yet flabby-soft embraces, the smothering, engulfing tenacity of her' (Lewis 1956: 270).

This cloying and overbearing characterization of Batta's affection invites further comparison between (and interrogation of) Orual's perception of both. Even after Arnom becomes a priest and brings more light and order into it, the house of Ungit is 'an imprisoning, smothering sort of place' (Lewis 1956: 269) reeking of smells from ritual sacrifices: 'a temple-smell of blood [. . .] and burnt fat and singed hair and wine and stale incense' (Lewis 1956: 11). It is a warm, close, womb-like space damp with bodily fluids and thus evokes not only the similarly 'smothering' embraces of Batta (note that Orual uses this word to describe both) but also the 'darkness' which Cixous associates with female embodiment and through which Walton, in turn, claims that literature can find routes that logocentric theology forecloses. Indeed, Arnom, in his 'new way of talking about the gods which [he] and others had learned from the Fox' (Lewis 1956: 270–1), even conceives of Ungit's femininity in accordance with Cixous's analysis of patriarchal oppositions, claiming that 'she signifies the earth, which is the womb and mother of all living things' (Lewis 1956: 270). The personification of Ungit as mother and the association Orual draws between Ungit and her own mother figure suggest that the horror she feels within the house of Ungit is not simply the 'horror' of the numinous found in some of Lewis's other writings, such as *The Chronicles of Narnia*'s Aslan or the Cosmic Trilogy's Oyéresu, and certainly not indicative of a masculine divinity. Though irreducible to mere metaphor or allegory within the text, Orual's relationship to Ungit is a fantastical and theological extension of her alienation from femininity.

Arnom's explicit association of Ungit's femininity with the earth also calls us to re-examine Psyche's much earlier analogy in which religious belief is compared to the unacknowledged 'earth beneath' the 'city' (Lewis 1956: 70) of reason with which the Fox has educated them. Interpreted through Cixous, this not only positions Ungit and Ungit-worship as the 'feminine nature' to the Fox's 'masculine culture' (when both of these are understood as symbolic and arbitrary, rather than essential, designations) but also genders her tendency to transgress and frustrate systems of categorization, including the patriarchal authority that nominally governs religion in Glome. Thus, while religious practice is implicitly gendered as feminine within the novel, it is not necessary to interpret this in terms of submissiveness to a fundamentally masculine divinity; in fact, it is telling that although Orual's complaint is against the gods more generally and the god of the Mountain is gendered as male, it is the feminine Ungit who remains foremost in her theological imagination. Despite the novel's ancient setting, the gendering of religion in this way corresponds to Jantzen's argument that '[r]eligion can be seen as the repressed other of the secularist discourse of modernity' (Jantzen 1998: 10), with the Fox's Stoic philosophy standing in for the secularist discourses of Lewis's own era. Refusing containment within principles and structures, the 'holy wisdom' of Ungit permeates the text, causing the priest's language to double back on itself and transgressing the limits of Orual's understanding.

Orual's horror at 'holy wisdom' as defined by the priest can thus be read as a horror at the feminine, creating an implicit link between her hostility towards Ungit and her vilification of other women. In addition to Ungit, she is quick to blame both Batta and especially Redival for Psyche's sacrifice to the god of the Mountain, stating portentously that '[i]t was Redival who ended the good time' (Lewis 1956: 25) and later threatening Redival with torture when Redival turns to her for comfort after the priest's proclamation. Later, after being crowned queen, Orual has Batta hanged merely for being 'the pest of the whole palace' (Lewis 1956: 230). Orual's determination to shut out the holy horror of the gods with reason and discipline following Psyche's banishment is notably motivated by a desire 'to drive all the woman out of [her]' (Lewis 1956: 184). The devotion to upholding phallogocentric structures of rationality that Orual demonstrates coincides with suppressing her supposedly 'feminine' impulses, comparably to Cixous's hint that the social construction of manhood consists in alienating oneself from one's body and desires through appeals to abstract concepts. Even before Orual succeeds her father as ruler, she begins spending long hours attending to the business of the kingdom in the Pillar Room, which Hilder has pointed out is 'the seat of male authority' (Hilder 2013: 103). Aside from the obvious phallic imagery that comes to mind at the mention of pillars, the Pillar Room also invites associations with phallogocentrism due to the fact that it is the space in the palace reserved for writing. Like Le Guin's writing at the beginning of her career, the form Orual's writing takes is that of an honorary man; she writes in Greek according to the logocentric principles of Greek philosophy, and the implicit masculinity of this act is signified by the very space in which she works.

Additionally, Orual also resolves at this point to keep her face veiled at all times. Her stated reason for this is that '[i]t is a sort of treaty made with [her] ugliness' (Lewis 1956: 180–1), but it is possible to extrapolate from this statement that it is specifically a choice to hide away a femininity deemed unacceptable by the patriarchal world she inhabits. That it coincides with her attempts to become more masculine through reason, writing and combat invites comparison to Cixous's characterization of woman alienated from her femininity as a 'no-body that is dressed up, wrapped in veils, carefully kept distant' (Cixous [1975] 1986: 69). Indeed, the more Orual refuses to show her face, the more her identity as 'the Queen' asserts itself as 'Orual's' negation:

> I locked Orual up or laid her asleep as best I could somewhere deep down inside me; she lay curled there. It was like being with child, but reversed; the thing I carried in me grew slowly smaller and less alive.
>
> (Lewis 1956: 226)

The sense of suppressed femininity in particular – at least as defined by Orual's culture – is heightened in this passage by the reversal of the tropes associated with childbirth, nurture and motherhood. In the eyes of the Fox and Bardia, who serve as her chief advisors, Orual's ugliness means that 'they [do] not think of [her] as a woman', and she ruminates that '[i]f they had, it is impossible that we three, alone, by the hearth in the Pillar Room (as we were often) should have talked with such freedom' (Lewis 1956: 228). But to the general populace, the veiled queen becomes the subject of wild speculation, robbed of a subjectivity of her own and transmuted into all manner of fantastical and monstrous figurations:

> Some said (nearly all the young women said) that [my face] was frightful beyond endurance; a pig's, bear's, cat's, or elephant's face. The best story was that I had

no face at all; if you stripped off my veil you'd find emptiness. But another sort (there were more of the men among these) said that I wore a veil because I was of a beauty so dazzling that if I let it be seen all men in the world would run mad; or else that Ungit was jealous of my beauty and had promised to blast me if I went bareface.

(Lewis 1956: 228–9)

While her honorary maleness and her mythologization as 'the Queen' both grant Orual a measure of authority, as in her words '[t]he upshot of all this nonsense was that I became something very mysterious and awful' (Lewis 1956: 229), it comes at the expense of her own self-identification. Even the tales of her heroism 'have been mixed up with those of some great fighting queen who lived longer ago and (I think) further north, and a fine patchwork of wonders and impossibilities made out of both' (Lewis 1956: 226–7). Like Cixous's woman, Orual is ensnared by the same myths that grant her power over the men of her kingdom, caught between idealization, monstrosity and total erasure. In fashioning herself as by turns a 'masculine' hero and a veiled mystery, Orual, in Hilder's words, 'comes to fight her victimization with the very weapons which have wounded her' (Hilder 2013: 100).

Towards the end of the novel, however, Orual is forced to confront her own femininity and re-evaluate her perceptions both of Ungit and of other women. Her attempt to shut out 'feminine' impulses such as religiosity and vulnerability is one that inevitably fails, as she periodically succumbs to bouts of grief for Psyche, always accompanied by 'weeping and writhing and calling out upon the gods' (Lewis 1956: 184). Her religious faith, which coincides with her suppressed love for Psyche, continually overwhelms her reliance on patriarchal reason. Notably, the first of her visions that culminate in her religious transformation is charged with sexual imagery, and immediately follows the rite of the Year's birth in which she perceives Batta's face in Ungit and her conversation with the peasant woman worshipper. In the vision, Orual stands in the Pillar Room with her father, who instructs her to dig beneath the floor of the room and then commands, 'Throw yourself down' (Lewis 1956: 274). Orual and her father leap down into the chasm and land in 'another Pillar Room [. . .] except that it was smaller and all made (floor, walls, and pillars) of raw earth' (Lewis 1956: 274). Once again, Orual is commanded to dig and then throw herself down into the hole, and once again she finds herself 'in yet another Pillar Room; but this was of living rock, and water trickled down the walls of it' (Lewis 1956: 275). As the room begins to cave in on them, Orual's father leads her to a mirror and asks her, 'Who is Ungit?' to which Orual replies, 'I am Ungit' (Lewis 1956: 276).

The revelation that Orual 'is' Ungit is one of the most puzzling in the entire novel and, I would argue, one of the most widely misunderstood and oversimplified in scholarly readings of the text. Corbin Scott Carnell, for instance, has interpreted the novel conservatively, arguing that Ungit 'represents things-as-they-are, the world in travail for redemption' (Carnell 1974: 113) and that thus Orual's self-identification with the goddess signifies an awareness of her fallen state. Certainly, a cursory reading of the text would seem to bring forth ample evidence to support a reading of Ungit as representative of Orual's sinfulness or spiritual 'ugliness', which is reflected in Orual's own initial interpretation of the vision:

> Without question it was true. It was I who was Ungit. That ruinous face was mine. I was that Batta-thing, that all-devouring womblike, yet barren, thing. Glome was a web – I the swollen spider, squat at its centre, gorged with men's stolen lives.
>
> (Lewis 1956: 276)

For most of the novel, Orual perceives Ungit as a possessive and jealous goddess seeking to devour human lives, and so the revelation that she 'is' Ungit is, in part, a realization of her own possessive and jealous approach to love in her relationships with others. Throughout the narrative, Orual is shown to treat those close to her, particularly Psyche and Bardia, in ways that attempt to rob them of their will, keeping Bardia away from his wife Ansit for long hours in the Pillar Room and even going so far as to threaten suicide if Psyche does not sneak into the god of the Mountain's bedchamber with her lantern. The comparison of herself to a spider is even consistent with the motif Filmer identifies with evil women in both Tolkien's and Lewis's work. From these revelations Orual concludes that '[t]o say that I was Ungit meant that I was as ugly in soul as she' (Lewis 1956: 282) and endeavours to make her soul more beautiful so as to be pleasing to the gods.

A reading of Ungit that ends here, however, fails to take into consideration Orual's earlier encounter with the peasant woman and her own status as an unreliable narrator. At the initial moment of revelation, Orual identifies Ungit as 'womblike, yet barren', suggesting that Ungit is a perversion of motherly and nurturing qualities similar to the reverse-childbirth metaphor used to describe the queen, and yet the peasant woman's faith demonstrates that some in Glome do find nurture and comfort in Ungit where Orual finds none. This significant hint that all may not be as it seems with Ungit is given further weight by other revelations in the text which throw into question Orual's entire theological outlook and her perception of other women. A reading such as Filmer's rightly identifies that for much of the text, Ungit, Batta and Redival (and here we may add Ansit) are vilified and scorned, but Filmer ignores that many of these portrayals are openly challenged in the novel's second part.

Hilder's reading of *Till We Have Faces* identifies that the disapproving tone with which most women are described in the novel stems not from any inherent flaws that Lewis perceives in them but from the fact that the women of Glome inhabit a culture in which they 'learn to fear each other. Instead of cultivating empathetic companionship and sisterly resistance to sexism, these women more often than not perpetuate sexism' (Hilder 2013: 106). The enmity that exists between Orual and other women is defined by judgement according to patriarchal standards and stereotypes. As her beautiful younger sister Redival comes of age, Orual constantly shames her sexual promiscuity, commenting that '[s]he had always been featherheaded and now grew wanton' (Lewis 1956: 25), and dismisses Redival's guilt at having 'carried tattle about Psyche to the house of Ungit', saying that 'a new brooch, much more a new lover, would have had her drying her eyes and laughing in no time' (Lewis 1956: 63). The novel's second part begins, however, with Orual suddenly ruminating on the companionship she shared with Redival before Psyche's birth and lamenting 'how terribly she changed' (Lewis 1956: 254). Shortly after, she encounters Redival's former lover Tarin, who relates that Redival was 'very lonely' and 'used to say, "First of all Orual loved me much; then the Fox came and she loved me little; then the baby came and she loved me not at all"' (Lewis 1956: 255). While Orual remains 'sure still that Redival was false and a fool' after this encounter, she is nonetheless forced to admit that she has misjudged her sister's motives, having 'never thought at all how it might be with her when [Orual] turned first to the Fox and then to Psyche' (Lewis 1956: 256).

Likewise, Orual characterizes Bardia's wife Ansit as a bitter woman, jealous of the queen who participates in Bardia's masculine life, while Ansit is merely 'his toy, his recreation, his leisure, his solace' (Lewis 1956: 233). Ansit herself tells a different story, however, when the queen comes to visit her after Bardia's death: 'You left me my share. When you had used him, you would let him steal home to me; until you needed him again. [. . .] I'll not deny it; I had what you left of him' (Lewis 1956: 262). Ansit's bitterness stems not from some innate jealousy, as Orual had previously supposed, but because she bears witness to the toll that Orual's constant demands on Bardia, and her jealous drive to keep him at the palace instead of at home with his wife, take on him. Orual's first reaction to this revelation is to continue to appeal to the competitive animosity she feels towards Ansit and her own internalized feelings of inadequacy as a woman. Throwing off her veil, she cries out, 'Look, look, you fool! [. . .] Are you jealous of this?' (Lewis 1956: 262).

As Orual stands unveiled before Ansit, however, the first time in decades that she has bared her face to anyone, her grief and repressed desires are also laid bare, and both women's anger fades for a moment as Ansit realizes Orual's unrequited love for Bardia:

> She was weeping; and I. Next moment we were in each other's arms. [. . .] We spoke a language, so to call it, which no one else in the huge heedless world could understand. Yet it was a language only of sobs. We could not even begin to speak of him in words; that would have unsheathed both daggers at once.
> (Lewis 1956: 263)

As with her earlier revelation concerning Redival, the transformation in Orual's understanding is not yet total, and her companionship with Ansit in grief and love lasts only a moment, with Orual soon after resuming a formal demeanour and with it her veil. Nonetheless, it is a crucial precursor to her moment of self-identification with Ungit and inextricably linked to that event insofar as it awakens her and leaves her vulnerable to the love of the other woman. Orual's momentary intimacy with Ansit shatters every social convention – not just the hierarchy between the queen and the common woman but also the regulations which monogamous marital rites place on affection and desire – and takes both women to a realm for which they lack words. This encounter demonstrates that the jealous, devouring love that seeks to consume and assimilate the other, which Orual is accustomed to associating with Ungit and other women, and eventually comes to identify in herself, does not originate from femininity per se, but rather from the strain and strictures placed on it by a social order that isolates women from women and pits them against one another.

In fact, that the king still intrudes on Orual's spiritual awakening, even to the point of asserting his authority over it, is an especially significant parallel between the process of Orual's transformation and the emergence of Cixous's feminist project out of the poststructuralist and psychoanalytic traditions in which she is situated. Trom's dominance within Orual's vision signals the sway that patriarchal logic, and its fear of all that is 'dark' and feminine, still hold over Orual's perception of herself. Orual's theological ruminations on her vision thus reflect the sway that patriarchal law holds over her psyche. Elaborating on her assumption that Ungit's monstrosity reflects the inherent ugliness of her own soul, she posits that

> [n]o man will love you, though you gave your life for him, unless you have a pretty face. So (might it not be?), the gods will not love you (however you try to pleasure them, and whatever you suffer) unless you have that beauty of soul.
> (Lewis 1956: 282)

It is notable that Orual's identification of Ungit with wickedness shortly after her vision relies so heavily on the patriarchal standards of beauty against which she is judged, and that communion with the gods is figured in terms of heterosexual romance. Read against the transformation Orual undergoes in her relationships with other women in the text, it seems unlikely that we are meant to take these statements at face value (pun intended). Orual's temporary entrapment within patriarchal logics even as she begins to re-examine her relationship to femininity recalls Cixous's warning that 'the phallogocentric sublation is with us, and it's militant, regenerating the old patterns' (Cixous [1975] 1980: 255). The transformation in Orual's relation to femininity, to be a full transformation, would also require her to re-evaluate her perception of Ungit.

Unfortunately, this is a transformation that the text itself stops short of undergoing. Following the feminist reading of Ungit that I have undertaken to its conclusion would institute a shift in the gendered theological-symbolic order that in Lewis's fantastic imagination would be the site of great anxiety and may even be impossible. This is one potential explanation for the ambivalence of Ungit's portrayal within the text; in many ways, Orual's discomfort with Ungit may be Lewis's own, and thus it is still left somewhat unresolved by the end of the novel. As I elaborate further in Chapter 3, the novel's conclusion attempts to ameliorate the horror of Ungit's dark and fecund holiness, ironically in similar ways to the ones for which it challenges Orual and Arnom earlier in the text. Nonetheless, the more subversive reading remains possible due to the dissonances and paradoxes that surround Ungit's representation. Like Cixous's 'feminine', Ungit refuses to stay put; she is always eluding description and persistently evading, sometimes violently, any attempt to confine her within a stable category, and this extends even to the level of textual interpretation. Both sacred and profane, she represents both the anarchic and redemptive possibilities of articulating theology from the position of the feminine.

'The fecund darkness': 'Bisexual' religion and society in *The Left Hand of Darkness*

While *Till We Have Faces* concerns itself with women's language and with their relationships to their own femininity and to each other as feminine in a patriarchal religious context, *The Left Hand of Darkness* utilizes its fantastic worldbuilding to envision a world in which 'feminine' attributes are not repressed. Although, like *Till We Have Faces*, *The Left Hand of Darkness* was published before Cixous began her project of feminine writing, many of its speculative and fantastical elements can now be interpreted as literalizations of and even elaborations upon many of her ideas. The novel's central conceit of a society completely lacking in binary distinctions between masculinity and femininity engages many of the same questions Cixous grapples with regarding how religious, political and social life are structured around sexual difference, but as a piece of fantasy fiction it takes the opportunity to present a figuration of society without patriarchy that in hindsight gives detail and specificity to many of Cixous's speculations about sexual difference.[1] Of the various narrative voices the novel employs, only the Ekumenical ambassadors, Genly Ai and Ong Tot Oppong, are preoccupied with gender divisions, and both this fact and their observations serve to highlight the fundamental differences between the secondary world of Gethen and the primary-world culture in which Le Guin wrote. This use of narrative perspective to highlight gender differences in a context that otherwise lacks such a conceptual framework demonstrates one of the paradoxes inherent in Cixous's feminism: the rejection of binary hierarchies as a distinctly 'feminine' trait.

The most striking and explicit parallel to be drawn between *The Left Hand of Darkness*'s worldbuilding and Cixous's philosophy is found in Ong's field notes from her undercover investigation of Gethen. Her summary of the Gethenian social structure – or rather, what it lacks – reads as though it was lifted directly from Cixous:

> There is no division of humanity into strong and weak halves, protective/protected, dominant/submissive, owner/chattel, active/passive. In fact the whole tendency to dualism that pervades human thinking may be found to be lessened, or changed, on [Gethen].
>
> (Le Guin [1969] 2010: 100)

Like Cixous, Le Guin's text implicitly posits in this passage that gender is the axis of difference along which all other conceptual binaries and social hierarchies are structured, and thus the absence of a binary configuration of gender in her secondary world means that its social structure is organized in fundamentally different terms from the primary world. Importantly, however, the absence of a gender binary on Gethen is not the same as a total eradication of gender within the text, at least from the perspectives of Ong and Genly. As Ong notes, Gethenians 'are not neuters. They are potentials, or integrals' (Le Guin [1969] 2010: 101), susceptible to fluid sexualities and shifting body morphologies, especially during their monthly mating cycle, known as *kemmer*. This figuration of androgyny allows Le Guin to explore in concrete terms what Cixous describes as '[b]isexuality: that is, each one's location in self (*repérage en soi*) of the presence [. . .] of both sexes [*sic*], non-exclusion either of the difference or of one sex', not to be confused with 'the classical conception of bisexuality' (Cixous [1975] 1980: 254) which serves merely to re-inscribe phallogocentrism under the guise of neutrality. (It is worth clarifying here that Cixous is engaging with and re-visioning a particular understanding of androgyny or gender fluidity, rather than invoking bisexuality as a sexual orientation.) In a society in which the default subject is masculine, attempts to imagine a subject who is 'neutral' or genderless would always already be masculine as well. In practical terms, the organization of Gethenian society also enables the woman Ong to think otherwise about the gendering of labour (since the majority of the population 'is liable to be [. . .] "tied down to childbearing"'), psychoanalysis (there being 'no myth of Oedipus on Winter') and sexual violence (since 'coitus can be performed only by mutual invitation and consent; otherwise it is not possible') (Le Guin [1969] 2010: 100) as they relate to the world from which she hails.

For Ong and Genly, and for Le Guin as author in the primary world, the masculine and feminine thus continue to be significant to their and our understanding of life on Gethen even as they hold very little to no meaning to Gethenians. Le Guin describes her worldbuilding in the novel as arising from a desire 'to show a balance – and the delicacy of balance' (Le Guin [1981] 1989: 11) between values which our society would gender as masculine and feminine. As she elaborates,

> On Gethen, the two polarities we perceive through our cultural conditioning as male and female are neither, and are in balance: consensus with authority, decentralizing with centralizing, flexible with rigid, circular with linear, hierarchy with network.
>
> (Le Guin [1981] 1989: 11)

This sense of balance is immediately palpable in the nation of Karhide, where the novel begins. As I argued in the previous chapter, Karhide's position as a country without a unifying or totalizing identity, while certainly manifesting at times in infighting and contests of prestige, also coincides with the importance placed on hospitality and openness to the other in Karhidish culture. Moreover, the aphorism that Karhide is a family quarrel rather than a nation explicitly genders these qualities as feminine in Terran terms, embodying the anarchic principle that Le Guin notes 'has historically been identified as female', pointing out that '[t]he domain allotted to women – "the family", for example – is the area of order without coercion, rule by custom not by force' (Le Guin [1981] 1989: 12). Even housing within major urban centres like Ehrenrang is organized into '*karhosh*', an arrangement that mirrors the 'fundamental Karhidish institution of the Hearth' (Le Guin [1969] 2010: 10), a social order structured around genealogy and familial bonds. Karhide's existence as a gender non-binary society in which domestic and public life are virtually indistinguishable prefigures Cixous's re-visioning of 'bisexuality' as a social order in which either side of any binary construction is always inhabited by its other and that other is acknowledged as such.

Throughout the novel, Genly consistently associates these aspects of Gethenian tendencies in general and Karhidish culture in particular with femininity, often in ways which betray how deeply entwined the values and cultural assumptions of his native Terran society are with patriarchy. At dinner with Estraven, he justifies his suspicion of them by reflecting that 'Estraven's performance had been womanly, all charm and tact and lack of substance, specious and adroit' (Le Guin [1969] 2010: 12–13). Commenting on the absence of warfare on Gethen, and the proliferation of smaller, interpersonal squabbles and feuds in its stead, Genly comments that Gethenians 'behaved like animals in that respect; or like women' (Le Guin [1969] 2010: 51). Much later, when both are on the run across the Gobrin Ice, Estraven expresses their suspicion of patriotism to Genly, saying, 'What is love of one's country; is it hate of one's uncountry? Then it's not a good thing' (Le Guin [1969] 2010: 228). Even at this point, Genly notes in Estraven's attitude 'something feminine, a refusal of the abstract, the ideal, a submissiveness to the given, which rather displeased [him]' (Le Guin [1969] 2010: 228). Genly initially distrusts the order of Karhidish society because its nuances and particularities constantly elude his analytical anthropologist's gaze, and just as Orual does with Ungit, he projects stereotypes of femininity as defined by a phallogocentric culture onto the places where it retreats from Terran reason.

The 'feminine' anarchic principles embodied in the social structure of Karhide are also intricately interwoven with the theology and practices of the Handdarata. As with Ungit-worship in *Till We Have Faces*, Handdara mysticism in *The Left Hand of Darkness* is implicitly gendered as feminine within the text, although the latter consigns the existence or non-existence of a deity to undecidability. As in *Till We Have Faces*, the darkness that signals alterity in *The Left Hand of Darkness* is a distinctly feminine one. Genly describes the 'darkness' of the Handdara as 'passive, anarchic, silent, [and] fecund' (Le Guin [1969] 2010: 63), all traits that Cixous notes are associated with femininity in Western discourse. Even the Handdara's resistance to universal absolutes, its non-metaphysical theology and its lack of unified, hierarchical structure in its organization can be traced to the lack of gendered divisions in Gethenian society. As Erlich notes, 'Gethenians cannot give themselves totally to masculine transcendent projects because normal Gethenians go into kemmer every month (more or less), and all who are healthy have the privilege and risk of pregnancy, birthing and nursing' (Erlich 2010: 138). The leader of the Foretelling ceremony bears the title of 'Weaver', which immediately associates religious authority (though in accordance with Handdara practice it is non-hierarchical authority) with what has historically been designated as feminine labour in our world.

The Foretelling ceremony is also notable for the way it weaves the erotic excess which Cixous associates with women's language into the fabric of religious ritual. The Handdara Fastnesses at first glance appear analogous to monastic communities in the primary world (the Foretelling ritual even requires the presence of a celibate) but the atmosphere of the hall in which the ceremony is held quickly becomes suffused with frustrated sexual energy stemming in part from the celibate himself, who must be in full kemmer when the ritual is held.[2] Held within the web of silence that binds the Foretellers to one another, Genly finds himself transported into the private realm of sensuality. Being a man conditioned by the separations of a patriarchal culture, however, his reluctance to enter such an intimate relation with the other places him on the brink of hysterical horror at monstrous imaginings of the feminine.

As he struggles to maintain the coherence of his own mind amid the consciousnesses of the Foretellers, he is plagued by 'abrupt visions and sensations all sexually charged and grotesquely violent' of 'great gaping pits with ragged lips, vaginas, wounds, hellmouths' (Le Guin [1969] 2010: 69). The horror Genly feels in the hall of the Foretelling ritual is comparable to the holy horror Orual feels in the house of Ungit; both settings are suffused with an energy they perceive as 'feminine' and disruptive. For Genly, coming from a culture in which the feminine is still symbolically aligned with monstrosity and the abyss, the Gethenians' lack of fear of the feminine in their religious rituals is almost unbearable. The hallucination obliterates all sense of time and space, climaxing in a vision of Faxe the Weaver as a woman wielding a sword as they '[scream] aloud in terror and pain, "Yes, yes, yes"' (Le Guin [1969] 2010: 69).

This answer to Genly's question, which prophesies Gethen's future as part of the Ekumen of Known Worlds, can be seen to evoke not only the 'yes' with which deconstruction hails the other (and thus the impossible future) but also Molly Bloom's orgasmic repetition of ' . . . And yes [. . .] I said yes, I will Yes' (Joyce, quoted in Cixous [1975] 1980: 255), which Cixous claims '[carries

James Joyce's] *Ulysses* off beyond any book and toward the new writing' (Cixous [1975] 1980: 255). In this way, *The Left Hand of Darkness* acknowledges 'feminine' eroticism occupying the same space as the ethical, political and theological questions preoccupying the novel's narrative. At the same time, Le Guin is careful that the gendered associations in the text originate with Genly. This is crucial when, late in the novel, Genly draws a yin–yang symbol and shows it to Estraven, saying, '*Light is the left hand of darkness* . . . how did it go? Light, dark. Fear, courage. Cold, warmth. Female, male. It is yourself, Therem. Both and one. A shadow on snow' (Le Guin [1969] 2010: 287). This passage is another example of Le Guin incorporating Taoist elements into her texts, and most critics have taken it at face value. James Bittner, for instance, reads the yin–yang as symbolic of 'marriage' and gender 'complementarity' (Bittner 1984: xi), while Richard D. Erlich takes it as a symbol that we are to read Gethenian society, and Handdara values more generally, as 'a *closed* circle containing that most famous of binary (if dynamic) opposed pairs' (Erlich 2010: 143). Both of these readings ignore the emphasis the novel continually places, mainly through Estraven's narration, on the need to break circles rather than maintain them.

The yin–yang symbol may be a convenient figure for Genly in understanding life on Gethen, but it is one completely unfamiliar to Estraven or anyone else on Gethen. However much he tries, Genly cannot simply leap outside of the distinctions of gender familiar to him. Indeed, even after he comes to a better understanding of Gethenians and their culture, he still expresses that he feels a greater kinship with Estraven than with women, saying to them, 'With you I share one sex, anyhow' (Le Guin [1969] 2010: 253). Once again, this statement should be completely alien to Gethenian sensibilities. Le Guin's use of Genly's narration and dialogue as the main avenue through which the text addresses gender also draws attention to the limits of the fantastic imagination, shaped as it is by primary-world norms, in imagining a secondary world without binary gender and makes this struggle part of the narrative. Le Guin must fall back on the gendered language and representations that exist in our own even as she searches for a subversive space from which to dislocate them, and we as readers are made conscious of this through Genly's similar predicament. While Gethen lacks binary distinctions between the masculine and feminine, and any of the hierarchical relationships Cixous identifies with patriarchy, *The Left Hand of Darkness* was still written within a patriarchal culture and literary tradition and thus is available for critique from a Cixousian perspective even as it embodies many of her ideas.

While the novel engages thematically with ideas of feminine writing and relationality, its own writing marks the beginning of a transitional period between Le Guin's early, patriarchal writing and her gradual embrace of radical feminism. As she relates, this shift was brought about by what she describes as 'a certain unease, a need to step on a little farther' and a 'want to define and understand the meaning of sexuality and the meaning of gender' (Le Guin [1981] 1989: 8) just as second-wave feminism was gaining traction in the late 1960s. As a result, the terms on which it engages with gender and sexual difference have been the subject of widespread critique. Particularly problematic to some feminist critics at the time was Le Guin's use of 'he/him/his' pronouns to describe the Gethenians, causing them to read as men by default. (Indeed, this is one of the reasons why I have chosen to use 'they/them/their' pronouns in reference to these characters.) Summarizing her objections to the novel's worldbuilding, Joanna Russ wrote at the time,

> It is, I must admit, a deficiency in the English language that these people must be called 'he' throughout, but put that together with the native hero's personal encounters in the book, the absolute lack of interest in child-raising, the concentration on work, and what you have is a world of men.
>
> (Russ 1972: 90)

For Russ, the novel's use of pronouns is merely a symptom of a wider problem with Le Guin's worldbuilding, which nominally attempts to dismantle gendered associations but, in Russ's opinion, does not go far enough. The result, in her reading, is a novel full of characters who are *'masculine in gender, if not in sex'* (Russ 1972: 90).

Le Guin would later go on to acknowledge this criticism, conceding that her worldbuilding was 'messy' (Le Guin [1981] 1989: 10) in places and that particularly '[i]f [she] had realized how the pronouns [she] used shaped, directed, controlled [her] own thinking, [she] might have been "cleverer"' (Le Guin [1981] 1989: 15). Moreover, she critiques her own decision to confine the novel's action almost exclusively to traditionally masculine spheres of society:

> Unfortunately, the plot and structure that arose as I worked the book out cast the Gethenian protagonist, Estraven, almost exclusively in roles that we are culturally conditioned to perceive as 'male' – a prime minister (it takes more than even Golda Meir and Indira Gandhi to break a stereotype), a political schemer, a fugitive, a prison-breaker, a sledge-hauler.
>
> (Le Guin [1981] 1989: 15)

In her critiques of both her own use of pronouns and her structuring of the narrative, Le Guin comes very close to Cixous's analysis of the way in which Western culture and discourses are configured to uphold patriarchy by default. While Le Guin can write Estraven's feats of supposedly 'masculine' heroism and be 'privately delighted at watching, not a man, but a manwoman, do all these things, and do them with considerable skill and flair', she admits that 'for the reader, [she] left out too much' by never showing Estraven 'in any role we automatically perceive as "female"' (Le Guin [1981] 1989: 15).

Even acknowledging these shortcomings, however, *The Left Hand of Darkness* represents the potential of fantastic worldbuilding for provisionally figuring societies governed by a logic other than patriarchal phallogocentrism. While secondary worlds are by no means created ex nihilo and must inevitably rely on vocabularies and structures from the primary world, their play with representation locates sites in which the perceived naturalness or inevitability of gendered binary configurations can be disrupted. Le Guin's use of Genly as a narrator foregrounds this tendency within fantasy writing and saves the novel from lapsing into essentialism in its exploration of gendered attributes. As Erlich notes, 'Gethenian anatomy and physiology did not determine the philosophy of the Handdarata – but it made it easy to *think* that philosophy' (Erlich 2010: 138). Le Guin falls back on gendered vocabulary to demonstrate to her readers the extent to which binary gender organizes primary-world society and consequently how radical the transformation would be if society and theology were re-articulated from the position of the 'feminine'. This is very close to what Cixous argues in her own project of *écriture feminine*. At the same time, the use of gendered pronouns in the text, and the limitations that stem from it, demonstrates why insisting on the feminine, as a subversive space to inhabit within discourse, is crucial even as essentialism must be resisted. In both its worldbuilding and in the flaws and shortcomings inherent within it, *The Left Hand of Darkness* provokes reflection on the extent to which theology must be reconfigured from the position of femininity and the transformation that such an act could initiate in social and religious orders.

Conclusions

This chapter has considered the ways in which fantasy literature can function as a feminist counter-discourse in relation to phallogocentric theology. Drawing on Hélène Cixous's theory of *écriture feminine*, which itself arises out of deconstructive philosophy's critique of patriarchal discourse, it has mapped out some of the ways that fantastic writing crosses binary distinctions between the monster and goddess to produce figurations of a 'feminine' relation to theology. This movement in fantasy uncovers feminist theological subjectivities that realize the power of attributes traditionally gendered as 'feminine', and therefore devalued, to disrupt the patriarchal logic of theology and philosophy. As figured within fantasy, feminist theological subjects thus manifest as dragons in the neighbourhood of a reality fundamentally constituted by patriarchy. While there is always risk inherent in reclaiming woman's designation as monstrous other, Cixous is hopeful, saying that '[j]ust because there's a risk of identification doesn't mean that we'll succumb' (Cixous [1975] 1980: 257). Fantastic figurations of 'woman', such as woman-as-dragon or woman-as-monster, remind us that articulating a feminist theology must always be an unsettled pursuit so as to avoid re-inscribing the phallic sovereignty of the *logos*.

Both *Till We Have Faces* and *The Left Hand of Darkness* can be seen to point to the transformative power of inhabiting theology from a 'feminine' standpoint, as well as demonstrate fantasy's ability to come to terms with 'feminine' alterity. Read in conversation with Cixous, *Till We Have Faces* becomes the story of the theological formation of one woman, Orual, in which her relationship to the goddess Ungit parallels her relationship to femininity in a patriarchal society. Her journey from horror at Ungit to identification with her is thus accompanied by a long process of healing in her relations with other women. While Ungit's subversive potential never fully manifests in the text, her transgression of the binary distinctions between sacred and profane is generative when considering a feminine relationship to religion. *The Left Hand of Darkness*, meanwhile, envisions a society that can be seen to embody the rehabilitation of sexual difference that Cixous calls for. The nation of Karhide, as a society without binary gender, is structured fundamentally differently to societies in the primary world and thus demonstrates the extent to which gender structures all aspects of life, including religious life. While the limitations of the novel's worldbuilding are well documented, it nonetheless shows the potential of secondary worlds in articulating theologies structured according to a logic fundamentally different to patriarchy and phallogocentrism.

3

Hetero-doxies

Fantasy and the problem of divine womanhood

As a way of articulating a deconstructive philosophy that takes into account the particularity of women's experience without re-inscribing logocentrism, Cixous's theory of *écriture feminine* is particularly generative, especially when the full potential of its fantastical imagination is realized. Yet Christian theologians hoping to inhabit theology from a 'feminine' position are faced with another problem: that of incarnation. While the notion of a God who takes on a body, becomes mortal and enters into history carries endless potential for a deconstructive feminist practice of writing the body, the structure of Western Christology has historically severely limited whose bodies are associated with the body of Christ, to say nothing of how those bodies are discursively constructed. As Althaus-Reid and Isherwood argue, 'the figure of Christ has been so constructed by patriarchal thinking, as have women, that one gets left out of any reflection on the nature of the other' (Althaus-Reid and Isherwood 2007: 81). Feminist theology must therefore not only concern itself with the question of a feminine theological subject but also work to re-imagine the fleshly form taken by the God that Christianity proclaims. This has implications wider than communities of practicing believers; Althaus-Reid and Isherwood also note that 'it has to be acknowledged that this making of women has its roots in theology since the way in which men and women are meant to be supposedly reflects God's design for the universe' (Althaus-Reid and Isherwood 2007: 18).

Luce Irigaray is one feminist philosopher who confronts Christianity, and specifically the notion of incarnation, head-on, with results that continue to be formative within the field of feminist and queer theology. This chapter summarizes Irigaray's feminism as a project of cultivating a feminine relationship to divine incarnation that privileges women's erotic pleasure and non-hierarchical community. It argues that while Irigaray's writing is less self-consciously fantastic than Cixous's, her articulation of a female theological imaginary nonetheless makes her work an indispensable, if troubled, starting point for reading fantasy texts which share in her aims to imagine female incarnations of divinity. Morny Joy has described Irigaray's forays into religion as 'mythopoetic' (Joy 2006: 7), a term also frequently used to describe secondary-world fantasy, and Walton similarly notes that 'Irigaray has demonstrated that the "real world" is in fact the world of the male imaginary and that the female imaginary breaking into signification will sound strange, or even "unreal", in the beginning' (Walton 2007: 170). As I have argued up to this point, fantasy literature not only constructs realms which unsettle ingrained assumptions about the primary world and open onto 'unreal' figurations of devalued difference; it usually also draws on mythic and religious traditions that may be perceived as archaic in order to do so. In a similar way, Irigaray constructs a feminist religious imaginary which, while taking a re-visioning of Western Christianity as a starting point, seeks to initiate a mode of becoming divine previously unreal or unthinkable within patriarchal understandings of theology.

The creation of secondary worlds which still actively engage in dialogue with religious institutions and signifying structures in the primary world may on the one hand provide a textual space for feminists seeking to take up Irigaray's project and enter into theology on their own terms. On the other hand, both fantastic secondary worlds and the specific kind of feminist imaginary Irigaray proposes also have in common a risk of over-investing in archaic symbols and constructions of reality, and seeking eucatastrophic redemption through the recovery of a lost wholeness. Irigaray's writing on femininity and the divine often starts from a deconstructive position but eventually attempts to return to unified categories and essentialisms, in the process re-inscribing many of the exclusions and erasures perpetrated by phallogocentric, patriarchal theology. While Irigaray's idealization of a unified, divine 'woman' may give current feminist readers pause, close attention to fantasy texts whose theologies are analogous to her religious imaginary can offer a way of reading her work against the grain, taking her reliance on a certain prescriptive and universalist definition of 'woman' as instead provisional and culturally situated while retaining her crucial impulse to wed the sacred and the sensual and also to cultivate a divinity premised on values historically gendered as feminine.[1]

While there exist countless examples of fantasy texts from the latter half of the twentieth century that put forth representations of feminine deities, not all of these are fully compatible with Irigaray's theology of incarnation. Texts such as Marion Zimmer Bradley's *The Mists of Avalon* (1983) and Greer Gilman's *Moonwise* (1991) draw on various goddess myths and are concerned, to varying degrees, with values of nurture, community, feminine imagination and erotic pleasure, but they are more closely aligned with an Anglo-American feminist tradition that establishes itself in opposition to Christianity. By contrast, Irigaray, though certainly open to influence from other religious traditions, occupies a feminist space within Christianity, and there are many fantasy texts that take this as a point of concern as well. After summarizing key tenets of Irigaray's quest for a feminine divine and making note of the problems it raises for current feminist theologies, this chapter will detail how the analogous theologies presented in *Till We Have Faces* and *The Passion of New Eve* either implicitly or explicitly highlight and (in the latter's case) push against the limits and unified structure of Irigaray's definition of 'woman'.

Riddles in the dark: Luce Irigaray's feminist mysticism

Few feminist philosophers have been as influential, or as controversial, as Luce Irigaray. Her quest for a feminine religious imaginary and insistence on women's need to become divine on their own terms continue to define many of the ongoing debates in contemporary feminist theology.[2] Serene Jones notes that although Irigaray is not chiefly a theologian, '[a]mong feminist theorists, Irigaray holds particular promise for theologians because she explicitly takes up theological questions and calls women not to give up on God-talk, but to engage creatively in collective reimaginings' (Jones 2008: 397). Irigaray's critique of patriarchal constructions of reality, which extend to Western elaborations of Christian theology, leads her to counter-intuitively look for subversive opportunities within existing religious structures and discourses. Unlike her poststructuralist contemporaries, Irigaray remains invested in the sovereignty of the subject, in 'woman' as a unified category and in notions of femininity as *essentially* relational, communal and nurturing by nature of 'woman's' anatomical configuration. In her words, '[t]he feminine world is, by birth, more relational than the world of the boy, notably because of a privileged situation of the girl with respect to the mother, a same as the girl' (Irigaray 2009: 17) through, among other things, the shared experience of childbirth. This renders her work problematic for feminist theologians who are invested in the anti-essentialist politics that have been further elaborated by feminist, queer and trans theorists in the years since Irigaray began to put forth her project, although equally, her endeavour to figure a theology of incarnation that takes account of the sexual and gendered specificity of its subjects makes it indispensable to them.

Irigaray posits the need for a divine becoming of women as essential to their ability to exist as subjects. In her words, '[n]o human subjectivity, no human society has ever been established without the help of the divine. [. . .] If women have no God, they are unable either to communicate or commune with one another' (Irigaray [1987] 1993: 62). For this reason, she remains invested in divinity (and a particularly Christian divinity at that) for its significance in the formation of identity. Crucial to Irigaray's project are the deconstructive position she inhabits within her Roman Catholic faith and her adoption of the principle of irreducible sexual difference. In her view, '[t]he spirit of Roman Christianity can be summarized in two key principles: an incarnational relationship between the body and the word, [and] a philosophy and a morality of love' (Irigaray 2004b: 150). For Irigaray, both of these principles hold endless possibilities for women's liberation. However, she also argues that in practice the church has too often applied them unilaterally, assuming a masculine incarnation to be universal. She thus claims that

> as a feminine body subjected to a masculine Word going from the Father to the Son through Mary, I cannot truly love myself, nor the other, nor God. I become slave to a truth which is not mine, towards which I am an idolater, if it remains unique.
>
> (Irigaray 2004b: 150)

Women are partitioned off from the divine within a patriarchal religious order in Irigaray's view not only because the metaphysical order in which God is inscribed is inherently masculine but also, more simply, because a male incarnate God can form neither the basis for women's subjectivity nor the difference that engenders her relation with the other. This belief rests on Irigaray's insistence that men and women's subjectivities and ways of being in relation to the other are irreducibly different in their construction; in her words, '[t]hey cannot be substituted the one for the other, nor subjected to a hierarchical assessment' (Irigaray 2009: 14).

As her reclamation of divinity indicates, Irigaray departs from Derridean deconstruction in her approach to God not as 'an utterly faceless other' (Derrida [1996] 2002: 59) but as something to be cultivated in the subject, although as I point out subsequently it is a subjectivity always necessarily constituted in relation to the other. 'The other' for Irigaray refers both to irreducible sexual difference, as in the other gender, and to what has been repressed within the subject in psychoanalytic terms. Thus, rather than reclaim the positioning of woman-as-other, as Cixous does, Irigaray instead attempts to initiate the positive formation of a female divinity and subjectivity, arguing that '[w]hereas a woman too often abandons her own gender, man is too enclosed in his. The "sin" of each is not the same' (Irigaray 2004b: 155). In the context of Western Christianity in particular, she notes that '[h]oliness is often presented to women as being a relation to the other gender through self-abnegation' (Irigaray 2004b: 154). Irigaray thus frames women's quest for divinity as penance – though in a restorative rather than retributive sense – for failure or inability to love themselves.[3]

Of course, this basis for female subjectivity presumes the existence of an essential, *a priori* femininity which the patriarchal gaze forces women to abandon; for Irigaray, femininity is a lost wholeness to be recuperated. She insists that '[i]n order to become, it is essential to have a gender or an essence (consequently a sexuate essence) as *horizon*' (Irigaray [1987] 1993: 61). As I note further, this stance has been criticized by feminists who feel that it fails to solve the problem of women's idealization as stereotyped mother-goddesses within the Christian imaginary and attempts to place them atop the phallogocentric hierarchy without sufficiently challenging its structure. At the same time, the impulses particular to Irigaray's writing – namely, her endeavour to collapse the boundaries between the sacred and profane particularly as they pertain to sexual desire, as well as her attempt to think divine incarnation as it relates to femininity – are of such radical potential and significance to feminist theology that they cannot be dismissed out of hand. As my reading of *The Passion of New Eve* in particular will demonstrate, one of the things that fantasy texts which share these impulses can offer is the ability to inhabit a deconstructive position within Irigaray's project. Fantasy can draw attention to the conditions and processes involved in the construction of figurations of divine femininity, and their necessary inability to be universal, while affirming the necessity of imagining them.

One of the most significant tenets of Irigaray's writing for considerations of feminist theology and literature is her conviction that language – specifically its location within the body – is key to her quest for a feminine religious imaginary. This holds particular significance for Irigaray because of Christ's characterization as the word-made-flesh in Christian theology; as she comments, '[i]f the *word* is a vehicle of the divine, we have to take care that it will be deifying for us, that it incarnates us, as women, deifies us, as women' (Irigaray 2004b: 156). She thus claims that

> [p]utting myself in search of *my* word, my words, seems to be the first fidelity to a theology of incarnation. [. . .] Women have to discover their word(s), be

> faithful to it and, interweaving it with their bodies, make it a living and spiritual flesh.
>
> (Irigaray 2004b: 151)

For this reason, Irigaray turns to forms of speech historically employed by women existing within a patriarchal society, which rely heavily on 'riddles, allusions, hints, parables' (Irigaray [1974] 1985: 143) to transmit and preserve forms of knowledge that elude patriarchal discourse. By doing so, she argues, women can disrupt the habits of the patriarchal gaze that seeks to analyse and organize them into a theory, and thus create them in its own image. Irigaray identifies this elliptical way of speaking within 'what, within a still theological onto-logical perspective is called mystic language or discourse', noting that '[t]his is the only place in the history of the West in which woman speaks and acts so publicly' (Irigaray [1974] 1985: 191). Complicit though religious institutions and theological constructions may be in the erasure and subjugation of woman, to Irigaray they also provide consciousness with 'names to signify that other scene, offstage, that it still finds *cryptic*' (Irigaray [1974] 1985: 191): in other words, the historically female-gendered 'dark continent' of difference and desire. By invoking the intimate, sensual and paradoxical devotional language similar to that employed by medieval Christian mystics – many of whom are women – Irigaray similarly seeks to mark out a space within Christian spirituality not governed by a masculine logic. Irigaray terms this domain '*[l]a mystérique*' (Irigaray [1974] 1985: 191).

The radical potential of *la mystérique* lies in the sacredness with which it imbues repressed female desires and their ability to initiate a relationship other than understanding, ruled by a logic other than that prescribed by reason and consciousness. Like the mystics from whom she draws inspiration, Irigaray seeks a language that affirms and inhabits culturally ingrained notions of the divine to the point of transgressing and exceeding the limits of the institutional systems and structures which lay claim to them. This is not the same as claiming simply that mystical language allows women to articulate unholy sexual desires by displacing them into lofty expressions of longing for the divine. Rather, Irigaray's elaboration on *la mystérique* demonstrates that within an incarnational theology, the 'light' of divinity can be found and cultivated by journeying into the darkest recesses of the profane.

Irigaray locates divinity within a process of becoming in the midst of the ongoing fulfilment and re-awakening of desire that the other engenders in the material present. As she points out, her characterization of divine love embodied within the erotic and ethical encounter with the other means that the transcendental would not be immediately, but abstractly, deferred to the absolute 'you' of a God – who, in fact, then substitutes himself for the mother, the first other. The transcendental must unceasingly intervene between the other and myself – the 'you' and the 'I' – turning the sensible immediacy of relation into a cultivation of affect. [. . .] This will end in a transcendental feeling that remains, carnal, sensible, and which does not relate only to the mind.

(Irigaray 2009: 17–18)

This rethinking of divine transcendence as unfolding in relation to the other creates numerous challenges and possibilities for theological readings of fantasy literature. For one thing, it locates the religious desire for redemption that for Tolkien is articulated in fantastic eucatastrophe in (cisgender female) embodiment, lending it an erotic dimension that complements the way Cixous links female sexuality to writing and worldbuilding. For another, it challenges us to re-frame the messianic hope and longing for another world that fantasy both satisfies and re-awakens not as prefigurations of an ultimate redemption of the world outside of human agency but as opportunities for writers, readers and interpreters of fantasy to transform the primary world by allowing themselves to spiritually and sexually 'become'. Both of these become pertinent in this chapter's discussion of *Till We Have Faces* and *The Passion of New Eve*. Understood in terms of Irigaray's ethics of desire, eucatastrophe in fantasy becomes not a deferral towards a far-off messianic era, but an irruption of redemptive and transformative possibilities – for women especially – into the primary world. At the same time, fantastic eucatastrophe also challenges the assumptions of Irigaray's writing by framing redemption in terms other than a return to wholeness, and thus carries the potential to posit horizons of divine becoming which resist the strictures and closures to which she still confines femininity.

For Irigaray, this transcendental relationship with irreducible difference is most fully embodied by a heterosexual, cisgender couple. While this, once again, places limits and foreclosures on her philosophical project, neither is it to be understood as a rehearsal of heterosexuality as usual under patriarchy. Where within a patriarchal heterosexual order 'woman' is reduced to a commodity for man to possess, consume or even annihilate in service of his own passion, Irigaray's feminist re-invention of the erotic embrace as divine communion envisions 'a deeper unity' which touches

> [t]he bottom, the centre, the most hidden, inner place, the heart of the crypt to which 'God' alone descends when he has renounced modes and attributes. For this most secret virginity of the 'soul' surrenders only to one who also freely

offers the self in all its nakedness. This most private chamber opens only to one who is indebted to no possession for potency.

(Irigaray [1974] 1985: 196)

Divine love thus characterized by Irigaray is cultivated in the deepest, most hidden recesses of female subjectivity, paradoxically at the point where the boundaries of identity are most vulnerable to being set ablaze in a sustained burst of erotic passion. This space can only be touched by one of the other gender (man) who also renders himself violable to this intermingling of identity without assimilation. A feminine mode of becoming in relation to the other as defined by Irigaray envisions self and other in a different kind of duality, one that is subject to differences that are no less irreducible for their confluence and shifting borders. As I have already shown in my discussion of Cixous and Le Guin, this association of the feminine with non-hierarchical community and love of self and other was a common one in the 1960s and 1970s, and one which many feminists at the time felt important to reclaim.[4] For Irigaray they signify an ability to retain a sense of the sacred, the virginal and the divine while transgressing the strict boundaries placed around them by patriarchal theology and avoiding the purity discourses into which they are commonly inscribed.

Adopting a discourse that subversively inhabits women's fabled mysteriousness and the supposed 'dark continent' of their subjectivity is not the only way in which Irigaray seeks to invigorate the tropes and figurations of women that populate patriarchal Christianity with new and transformative life. The figure of Mary, mother of Jesus – specifically, her virginity and her silent acquiescence at the Annunciation – is also a focal point for the cultivation of divine love in the feminine subject. As discussed in the previous chapter, Mary has often been a troubling figure for Christian women, and Irigaray acknowledges that Mary as imagined within a patriarchal theological framework 'paralyzes the infinite of becoming a woman since she is fixed in the role of mother through whom the *son* of God is made flesh' (Irigaray [1987] 1993: 62). Nonetheless, Irigaray's re-visioning of the scene of the Annunciation positions Mary as a woman who cultivates divinity within herself as radical self-love that enables her love for the other. She attempts to read Mary's silence, which 'most women interpret only in a negative way', as 'a means of keeping self-affection as woman, and not losing herself in a discourse that is not fitting for her' (Irigaray 2009: 18). As with her subversive reinterpretation of the supposed mysteriousness of women's discourse, Irigaray's interest in Mary is an attempt to transform women's silence within patriarchal culture from a mark of their subjugation into a refusal to acquiesce to a discourse governed by patriarchal logic, and a choice to instead maintain unity with and affection for themselves in the face of a discursive order that seeks to alienate women from themselves and each other.

Irigaray argues that women's subjectivity and self-love is, by socialization and by nature, more driven towards communality and therefore exempt from the violence of phallogocentrism. This pronouncement not only denies women's capacity to be complicit in their own oppression but also relies on a biological essentialism that re-inscribes an archetype of 'woman' that derives from the *logos*. For Irigaray, the silence of Mary is represented by the meeting of her two lips, which refers not only to the lips of her mouth but also to the vaginal lips. Just as, in poststructuralist thought, the phallus is emblematic of Western patriarchy's tendency towards binary, exclusionary thinking, hierarchical domination and assimilation, Irigaray takes the two lips as a symbol of 'a privileged place of self-affection for a woman' (Irigaray 2009: 18), a way of relating not just to the other but to the parts of oneself that are repressed within a patriarchal logic. This exceptionalism regarding women's privileged relationship to the other is based on the idea that

> [t]he girl knows what it means to beget; it is a familiar experience for her, notably through intuition or feeling. Turning back to birth, or beyond, does not seem a dangerous abyss to cover, to veil, even with a God, as is the case for a masculine subject.
>
> (Irigaray 2009: 17)

In Mary's case, the two lips are the means by which she literally births a divine child. In Irigaray's redefinition of virginity as woman's ability to be in loving relationship with herself and the repressed difference within herself, Irigaray attempts to posit Mary as an archetype of the woman whose unique ability to bring forth divinity into the world is inscribed within her body, which is inseparable from the formation of her subjectivity.

Nevertheless, Irigaray's figuration of divine womanhood, as demonstrated by her characterization of Mary, is not sufficiently distinct from patriarchal theology's idealization of women as mother-goddesses for many feminists. Althaus-Reid, for instance, argues that '[t]he work of a liberative Mariological circle of interpretation is complex', involving not only a rehabilitation of traditionally 'feminine' values but also 'questioning our religious constructions of femininity' and 'unmasking God the white upper-class woman who has made of us passive supporters of a patriarchal system' (Althaus-Reid 2004: 43). Simply elevating women from scriptural traditions and turning God into a woman while taking their textual representation at face value is insufficient for a theology of women's liberation because feminist theology requires a further interrogation and problematizing of *which* women, fulfilling *what* definition of femininity, such an endeavour chooses to elevate. The anatomical features which Irigaray highlights as sites for woman's divine becoming, and the bodily processes in which they are involved, set up additional barriers of access to her notion of divine femininity. To the extent that Irigaray's writing emphasizes that theology is located in the body and is thus unavoidably gendered and sexual, however, it sets a crucial precedent for queer and feminist theologies whose figurations of divine becoming depart from or extend beyond those offered by Irigaray herself.

Indeed, Irigaray's tendency to rely on and attempt to rehabilitate already existing theological tropes has been widely commented upon and critiqued by most, if not all, current feminists even as they acknowledge her project's importance and legacy as well as the transformative potential it still suggests. Ellen T. Armour claims, for instance, that 'Irigaray's invocations of religious motifs constitute sites in her work where her attempts to think sexual difference seem to lose the radicality of that promise' (Armour 1997: 200). To Armour, '[s]uggesting that women project their own image onto the divine seems to run the risk of setting up an economy of sameness for women that would parallel the current phallocentric economy' (Armour 1997: 209). It is certainly a peculiar feature of Irigaray's writing that, while tireless in its hope for the divine redemption of the world through an ethics of love, the ways in which it imagines this redemption – and the representations of femininity and archetypes for love it involves – remain tethered to the very discourses and cultural imaginaries that Irigaray critiques and on whose themes she attempts to offer variations. From one perspective, Irigaray's development of a divine feminine in the hopes of liberating women from the specular gaze of the masculine often risks paralysing women within that same gaze in its own idealizations of femininity.

While the tendencies I have just outlined do necessitate an interrogation of and negotiation with Irigaray's limits and shortcomings for contemporary feminist theologies – which will be apparent in my following literary analysis – navigating such treacherous ground should not be unfamiliar to those practised in the deconstructive task of affirmation, which Spivak calls '[c]ollaboration with the enemy' (Spivak 1989b: 210). Nor will the structure of Irigaray's redemptive vision be alien to scholars of theology and fantasy used to negotiating between secondary worlds and the alterity they evoke, or between the eucatastrophic figurations of their redemption and the limitations of texts that can only rearrange elements of the primary world. In one sense, the questions that must be asked in any current adoption of Irigaray's incarnational theology are questions that must also be taken up in the study of fantasy texts that delve into mythic traditions and religious symbolism for inspiration. In this chapter, I will demonstrate that *Till We Have Faces* and *The Passion of New Eve* can be read in dialogue with Irigaray in ways that both reveal how each novel envisions divine incarnation for women and highlight or challenge the limited scope and essentialism of Irigaray's vision of divine womanhood. *Till We Have Faces* posits a female Christ figure in the form of Psyche, who, while ultimately deferring towards a 'higher' masculine divinity within Lewis's overarching theological scheme, nonetheless embodies Irigaray's vision of erotic religion in her relationship with the god of the Mountain and serves as a crucial intercessor for Orual's spiritual formation. Meanwhile, the complex web of Christian allusion and symbolism woven by *The Passion of New Eve* – especially the undecidability of its protagonist's status as a female messiah – casts Irigaray's theological imagination in a more ambivalent light that calls attention to its confinement within hetero- and cis-normative constructions of sexual difference and theological grand narratives.

Becoming Psyche: Identity and Eros in *Till We Have Faces*

As I demonstrated in the previous chapter, *Till We Have Faces*, like its narrator Orual, struggles to contend with the disruptive and decidedly feminine alterity ascribed to the goddess Ungit. While the text significantly challenges Orual's fear and distaste for femininity as it manifests in the other women in her life, often explicitly aligning this fear with the horror she experiences in the house of Ungit, it falls short of allowing Orual's understanding of Ungit herself to be radically transformed. Spiritual transformation in the novel comes not from Ungit but from Psyche, who Hilder argues 'is an emblem of the inferior "feminine" human soul [. . .] journeying toward fulfilment in relation to the superior and indeed perfect "masculine" God' (Hilder 2013: 125). Indeed, Psyche's beauty, nurturing spirit and vulnerability to others – particularly in her relationship to the masculine god of the Mountain – seem to suggest that she is an archetype of femininity less horrific, less threatening to patriarchal theology than Ungit is. However, interpreting Psyche's portrayal in the novel, particularly her relationship to Eros and her role as Orual's messianic redeemer, with attention to Irigaray's feminist attempt to reclaim these qualities creates an opportunity to read *Till We Have Faces* creatively. While Psyche, like Irigaray's attempt to prescribe a universal model of divine femininity, remains a problematic and limited figure from the standpoint of feminism in the twenty-first century, an Irigarayan reading of the text uncovers a subversive interpretation in which the novel attempts to challenge the phallogocentric theological hierarchies present in Lewis's earlier fantasy. Additionally, *Till We Have Faces* demonstrates how fantasy texts can use eucatastrophe and attention to the processes of mythmaking to emphasize the cultural contingency and openness to deconstruction of their own feminist theological imaginaries to an extent that Irigaray's does not allow.

My analysis will consider three aspects of Psyche's characterization in dialogue with Irigaray: her erotic encounters with the god of the Mountain, the blurring of boundaries between her identity and Orual's as they both make their journey towards reclaiming their divinity and, throughout both of these, the myths and archetypes of divinity which Psyche negotiates throughout the text. Psyche's sexual relationship with the god of the Mountain – none other than Eros himself – is already one of the most iconic archetypal depictions of the relationship between divine love and the human soul in the novel's mythic source material, but Lewis's depiction of their union invites comparison to Irigaray's particular characterization of *eros* in several significant ways. The parallels with Irigaray become even more apparent later in the novel as the boundaries between Orual's and Psyche's subjectivities begin to soften and, in the Fox's words, 'flow in and out and mingle' (Lewis 1956: 301) in a series of mystical encounters that disrupt the novel's sense of time and space and fulfil an earlier prophecy delivered to Orual by the god of the Mountain. In these encounters, Psyche, herself now a goddess in a perpetual process of becoming, plays the role of divine intercessor who is nurtured by Orual's labour to cultivate divinity in herself and ultimately enables Orual to love others. Crucially, however, the novel is also at least partially aware of the role of mythmaking and fantastic invention in the construction and interpretation of Psyche as a divine subject in the process of becoming, and it foregrounds Psyche's relationship to these social forces in ways that open the text to further interrogation and deconstruction.

As in the novel's mythic source material, Psyche's journey towards becoming a goddess begins with her literal erotic encounters with the god of the Mountain in darkness, but in Lewis's text her union with the god occurs via ritual sacrifice. The priest of Ungit designates Psyche as both the Accursed and '[t]he best in the land' (Lewis 1956: 49) and thus decrees that she must be sacrificed to the god of the Mountain. Psyche thus comes to encounter the god because, in the priest's view at least, she is sacred and pure to the point of profanity. Indeed, Psyche first begins attracting the attention of the house of Ungit when the people begin to worship her following a plague in which Psyche goes out among the crowd of the sick who have gathered outside the palace, in part to appease their folkloric belief that she possesses healing power because of her beauty:

> She touched and she touched. They fell at her feet and kissed her feet and the edge of her robe and her shadow and the ground where she had trodden. And still she touched and touched. There seemed to be no end of it; the crowd increased instead of diminishing. [. . .] I saw her growing paler and paler. Her walk had become a stagger.
>
> (Lewis 1956: 32)

Soon after, rumour spreads that Psyche is a goddess and even 'Ungit herself in mortal shape' (Lewis 1956: 32), and religious offerings begin appearing at the palace's doorstep: 'myrtle branches and garlands and soon honeycakes and then pigeons, which are specially sacred to Ungit' (Lewis 1956: 33).

As Doris T. Myers has noted, Psyche's healing of the sick establishes her as 'Christ-like' (Myers 2004: 24), evoking the numerous scenes from the Christian gospels in which Jesus heals the sick, but it notably does so in accordance with the 'feminine' virtues of care, community and vulnerability that Irigaray identifies as particularly conducive to divine love. Psyche is perceived as divine and pure because she does not partition herself off from (literal or figurative) contamination but instead places herself among the most vulnerable in her community. Likewise, Irigaray argues that '[t]he feminine divine never separates itself from nature', which here refers to the entire material world, including embodied human experience, 'but transforms it, transubstantiates it without ruining it' (Irigaray 2004: 167). While the question of Psyche's supposed power to heal is much more ambiguous in the novel than Christ's in the Gospel narratives that it calls to mind, it is clear that what is more important to Lewis is the non-hierarchical intimacy and sense of community her touch initiates between her and the common folk. Psyche's love is both sacred and scandalous because, in Myers's words, it 'includes [. . .] a compassion broad enough to encompass all the needy people of Glome' (Myers 2004: 25) and stands in stark contrast to the priests of Ungit who remain cloistered in their temple even as they nominally affirm Ungit's own connection to the matters of the material world. Like Irigaray's re-visioning of the mystics and other divine women from whom she draws influence, *Till We Have Faces* attempts to position Psyche within a space where divine incarnation overwhelms the authority of the theological structures and religious institutions that seek to regulate it.

Such is the excessive love that attracts the attention of the god, in whose house Psyche's cultivation of divinity within herself takes on an erotic dimension in the most literal sense. Although the god is personified as husband and Psyche as his wife in this figuration, the god in whose embrace she enters into her divine becoming is not understood in terms of the patriarchal God who, in Irigaray's words, 'would gaze upon his glorious unity, merging even the discrimination of his (self-same) attributes' (Irigaray [1974] 1985: 150), but Eros, bearing a name which refers not to a singular self but to a relationship cultivated between two. Thus, while Psyche is largely silent regarding the details of her nightly encounters with the god, Irigaray's depiction of *eros* makes it possible to read this silence creatively, of a piece with the darkness that hides their lovemaking from view. For Irigaray, silence can become for woman a source of strength; the woman who cultivates divinity in her sexual relationships is

> authorized to remain silent, hidden from prying eyes in the intimacy of this exchange where she *sees* (herself as) what she will be unable to express. [. . .] She is closed over this mystery where the love placed within her is hidden, revealing itself in this secret of desire.
>
> (Irigaray [1974] 1985: 200)

In this reading, the darkness within the god's chamber and the narrative elision of detail regarding Psyche's nightly sexual encounters with the god both retain the sacredness of the couple's caresses, not necessarily to keep Psyche ignorant of sacred things too 'high' for her comprehension but to keep both lovers away from a clinical or voyeuristic gaze that would stifle their divine becoming, and to preserve the possibility of more intimate ways of 'seeing' and 'knowing'. Understood in terms of *la mystérique* and Irigaray's archetype of the sacred couple, 'the holy darkness' (Lewis 1956: 123) of the god's chamber is a space in which both Eros and Psyche enter into a wholeness in which they overspill the boundaries of their identities and mingle without assimilation or incorporation.

Indeed, when Psyche does attempt to speak of her relationship to the god, her words disappointingly diminish the radical potential it signifies by falling back into the language of wifely obedience. In response to Orual's pleading for her to return to Glome, she replies, 'I am a wife now. It's no longer you that I must obey' (Lewis 1956: 127). Later, she explains her resistance to Orual's plan to come into the god's chamber with a lamp by confessing that she is 'afraid – no, I am ashamed – to disobey him' and that she is 'only his simple Psyche' (Lewis 1956: 163). This may be seen as another instance in which Lewis's clear impulse to depict a relationship to divinity that transgresses normative categories comes into conflict with both the limits of his imagination and the implications of absolute (patriarchal) sovereignty to which divinity is inextricably tied. Once again, however, Irigaray's analysis of women's complex navigations of silence and discourse, especially religious discourse, opens the text to alternative readings. Regarding Mary and other holy women, Irigaray expresses serious reservations about woman's ability to articulate her relationship to divinity according to a 'masculine' signifying structure, and so Mary remains silent in response to the angel. Likewise, the novel repeatedly emphasizes the inadequacy of Psyche's speech when it comes to describing her experiences, and thus it is not too far of a stretch to question whether the language of obedience she uses may be yet another effect of the patriarchal religious language at her disposal, which can only conceive of Psyche's relationship with the god in terms of mastery and devouring.[5]

Till We Have Faces is not the only instance in Lewis's writing in which divine incarnation or the eucatastrophic meeting of heaven and earth is understood in erotic and sexual terms. Most notably, *That Hideous Strength* concludes with Venus descending upon the house of St Anne's at midnight while animals noisily mate in the garden outside the house. Shortly thereafter, the protagonist Jane goes down to the small Lodge beyond the big house to reunite with her husband Mark. Importantly, however, *That Hideous Strength*'s sexual and spiritual imaginary is still organized according to a strict hierarchy, in which 'complementarian' divisions among genders are meant to evoke profane, 'feminine' humanity's need to submit to a transcendent and 'masculine' divine authority. The culmination of this is when Ransom instructs would-be scholar Jane to abandon her career ambitions and '[h]ave children instead' (Lewis [1945] 2005: 530), and the novel ends with her 'descending the ladder of humility' (Lewis [1945] 2005: 533) as she descends the hill to meet her husband and face her future as homemaker, the 'natural' order of things restored. *That Hideous Strength* thus inhabits a spiritual–sexual economy that can only conceive of female sexuality as the grounds for the role of motherhood and domesticity divinely preordained for all women, even to the point where, earlier in the novel, Ransom has to restrain an enraged Merlin from executing Jane for having used contraception. Irigaray points out that within such an economy, '[t]he mother [. . .] will have masked the woman' and '[t]he membrane used to wrap up the goods, both to assist and to hide the work of (re)production, must close off and conceal the inner prize of pleasure. The inner fires. The threat to every fetishistic economy' (Irigaray [1974] 1985: 117).

Till We Have Faces, by contrast, does not confine Psyche to a destiny of childbearing; in fact, Psyche does not speak of bearing children at all even if she does respond to Orual's protestations in such a way that, in Orual's words, '[y]ou would have thought she was my mother, not I (almost) hers' (Lewis 1956: 163).

Here, the mutual pleasure and love cultivated between Psyche and the god of the Mountain is an end in itself that not only resists assimilation into a reproductive economy, but for which reproduction is of no concern at all save in the Fox's imagination when he speculates that 'she'll be with child, no doubt, before we've time to look about us' (Lewis 1956: 145). Yet like Irigaray, Lewis simultaneously attempts to turn the roles and personifications assigned to women within a patriarchal order against that order, with mixed results. If Psyche does appear to Orual like a mother, it is in the sense that her divine becoming eludes Orual's infantilization and appropriation of her as a fetish object for Orual's own emotional gratification. This is made most clear late in the novel in which Orual, at her lowest point of despair, rereads her book to 'gorge [herself] with comfort, by reading over how [she] had cared for Psyche and taught her and tried to save her and wounded [herself] for [Psyche's] sake' (Lewis 1956: 285), with the language associated with devouring serving to undermine Orual's perception of her love for Psyche. Likewise, Psyche's 'disobedience' of the god can be interpreted less as a transgression of an authoritative command than a violation of what Irigaray calls the 'luminous shadow' in which she experiences 'a *touch* that opens the "soul" again to contact with divine force' (Irigaray [1974] 1985: 193) and an attempt to contain the pleasure cultivated in her erotic escapades within the rational patriarchal discourse in which she has been educated. Her exile which follows is thus not merely a banishment from the god's house but, as Orual later learns from the Essurian priest who worships Psyche, a severance from her own Divine Nature that can only be recovered once Psyche completes 'all manner of hard labours, things that seem impossible' (Lewis 1956: 246) assigned to her by Ungit.

Undoubtedly, this emphasis on partition-breaking pleasure as itself a cultivation of divinity provides some scope for challenging the patriarchal theological assumptions articulated within *That Hideous Strength*. Yet the fact that Psyche's divine becoming still appears alternatively as something *like* submission to a sovereign divine force on the one hand and 'matronly primness' (Lewis 1956: 162) on the other nonetheless leaves much to be desired in a novel devoid of alternatives to Psyche's particular expressions of divinity. The archetype of the divine woman as a nurturer, community-builder and healer, which Irigaray champions and Psyche embodies, easily slips back into patriarchal stereotypes and modes of representation even as they purport to turn them against themselves and towards woman's own pleasure. Psyche's assumption of the roles of wife and mother in her divine becoming is no less inevitable in the text for all that they may vary slightly from the usual manner in which they are prescribed within a patriarchal religious context.

This slippage becomes even more apparent towards the end of the novel, as the boundaries between Orual's and Psyche's subjectivities begin to blur and Psyche intercedes to tame the radical potential of Orual's suppressed femininity embodied in Ungit. When the god of the Mountain banishes Psyche into exile, he issues a decree to Orual as well, saying, 'You, woman, shall know yourself and your work. You also shall be Psyche' (Lewis 1956: 174). Initially, Orual takes this to mean that 'if [Psyche] went into exile and wandering, [Orual] must do the same' (Lewis 1956: 176), but in the novel's second part it becomes clear that this statement is tied to Orual's own ability to cultivate divinity within herself. Following her revelation that she 'is' Ungit and her despair of ever attaining spiritual beauty, Orual experiences other visions that disrupt her ordinary sense of time and space. From her vision of being trampled by the golden rams, discussed in the first chapter of this book, Orual takes the lesson that '[t]he Divine Nature wounds and perhaps destroys us merely by being what it is' (Lewis 1956: 284). As she is struck by this realization, she sees another woman standing in the field, gathering the golden wool left behind in the rams' joyous charge. Seeing this, Orual remarks, 'What I had sought in vain by meeting the joyous and terrible brutes, she took at her leisure. She won without effort what utmost effort would not win for me' (Lewis 1956: 284).

In another vision, Orual finds herself

> walking over burning sands, carrying an empty bowl. [. . .] I must find the spring that rises from the river that flows in the deadlands, and fill it with the water of death and bring it back without spilling a drop and give it to Ungit. For in this vision it was not I who was Ungit; I was Ungit's slave or prisoner, and if I did all the tasks she set me perhaps she would let me go free.
> (Lewis 1956: 285–6)

In the course of the vision, the bowl Orual carries becomes her book, and she is brought before the gods to make her complaint. What she reads out loud, however, is not the carefully reasoned case written in Greek which comprises the novel's first part but a much shorter piece full of anguish and scrawled in 'a vile scribble – each stroke mean and yet savage, like the snarl in my father's voice, like the ruinous faces one could make out in the Ungit stone' (Lewis 1956: 290). Orual realizes that 'this, at last, was [her] real voice' (Lewis 1956: 292) and that '[t]he complaint was the answer. To have heard [herself] making it was to be answered' (Lewis 1956: 294). After this, Orual is reunited with the Fox and taken down into the deadlands, where she is shown a series of murals painted on the walls of a pillared courtyard depicting Psyche gathering wool left behind by the golden rams, then toiling through the desert carrying the bowl for the water of death as in Orual's visions. The Fox explains that these were the tasks assigned to Psyche by Ungit in order to reclaim her godhood as in the Essurian priest's story, but that '[a]nother bore nearly all the anguish' (Lewis 1956: 300). It is at this point that Orual is reunited with Psyche, now made a goddess, yet when she looks down into the reflecting pool in the courtyard, she sees '[t]wo Psyches [. . .] both beautiful (if that mattered now) beyond all imagining' (Lewis 1956: 307–8). The vision ends as Orual hears a repetition of the god of the Mountain's prophecy: 'You also are Psyche' (Lewis 1956: 308). Orual and Psyche are thus revealed to be part of each other, with Psyche's journey towards godhood inextricably interwoven with Orual's own torturous path towards personal revelation and religious conversion.

The way in which Orual's 'becoming Psyche' (i.e. her cultivation of her *psyche* and becoming of her 'true' self) is bound up with Psyche's reclamation of her divinity can be interpreted in terms of Irigaray's insistence upon women's need for feminine incarnation in order to articulate themselves as sovereign subjects. Both of these visions are laden with imagery and concepts that invite comparison to the way in which Irigaray frames the arduous and often treacherous path that women under patriarchy must tread in order to uncover their divinity. The labours which both Psyche and Orual must perform in Psyche's exile are done in the service of Ungit, who, as I argued in the previous chapter, embodies a femininity that appears monstrous because it eludes or exceeds any patriarchal scheme of representation. The vast desert which Orual finds herself-as-Psyche traversing to the deadlands thus corresponds to Irigaray's assertion that 'the road [woman] will have to take in order to flee [patriarchal logic] is not nothing. Moreover, she doesn't know where she is going, and will have to wander randomly and in darkness' (Irigaray [1974] 1985: 193). It is particularly interesting that in Psyche's case this road leads her towards the 'sunless country' (Lewis 1956: 286) of the deadlands to retrieve the water of death for Ungit, a fertility goddess, since for Irigaray 'woman' haunts the transcendent divinity of patriarchal theology as a repressed reminder of birth, death and finitude. Although, as I discuss later, the novel's exact framing of this is problematic, to say that Orual bears the strife in Psyche's struggle to become divine is, in one way, to say that Orual's own redemption as woman necessitates that she journey into the unfamiliar, 'feminine' territories left unacknowledged by her education in Greek wisdom. As with Irigaray's woman in the process of becoming divine, Orual 'has become accustomed to obvious "truths" that will actually hide what she is seeking' (Irigaray [1974] 1985: 193) and which must be broken wide open or set ablaze as she becomes Psyche.

Interpreted in this way, the labours of Psyche and Orual thus represent the tension between a supposed 'essentially' feminine incarnation of divinity and the difficulty of embodying this divinity for women attempting to resist definition by a patriarchal culture. While Orual finds the path to the deadlands an inhospitable desert, 'a huge torture chamber' she must endure 'till [she] felt as if the flesh would be burned off [her] bones' (Lewis 1956: 286), Psyche is able to cross the apparent wasteland 'merry and in good heart' (Lewis 1956: 300) with a song on her lips. The suffering of Orual, which enables the ease with which Psyche crosses the desert, is strikingly evocative of the imagery which Irigaray uses to describe the experience of women who journey into the depths of erotic passion and divine love via *la mystérique*:

> The only possibility is to push onward into the night until it finally becomes a transverberating beam of light, a luminous shadow. Onward into a *touch* that opens the 'soul' again to contact with divine force, to the impact of searing light. She is cut to the quick within this shimmering underground fabric that she had always been herself, though she did not know it. And she will never know it or herself *clearly* as she takes fire, in a sweet confusion whose source cannot at first be apprehended. She is torn apart in pain, fear, cries, tears, and blood that go beyond any other feeling. The wound must come before the flame.
>
> (Irigaray [1974] 1985: 193)

The topography of Orual's conversion experience mimes the purgatorial process of transgressing consciousness, representation and patriarchal discourse outlined by Irigaray. It begins in the nocturnal temple of Ungit and dark caverns of her first vision in which she comes to identify herself with those earth-bound spaces, and follows her to the desert, in which the process of her redemption is underscored by the sensation of her flesh being set ablaze.

This wounding of Orual as a prelude to the 'flame' of spiritual revelation that aids Psyche's divine becoming is also present in the vision of the golden rams. Here, the divine rams' trampling of Orual is revealed not to be an expression of wrath but as a resistance to Orual's desire to possess their beauty by force. This challenges the reader to re-evaluate the scene of Psyche's banishment and the god's destruction of the valley. As in Irigaray's account of divinity, where the darkness of radical doubt gives way to a light that shatters every programme of optical representation devised by the patriarchal gaze, Orual's first face-to-face encounter with the god manifests as 'a lightning that endured [. . .] pale, dazzling', although '[her] glimpse of the face was as swift as a true flash of lightning. [She] could not bear it for longer' (Lewis 1956: 172). The lightning-flash of revelation in which Orual glimpses the god is also accompanied by a disruption in the stability of her vision; as she recounts,

> [i]t is strange that I cannot tell you its size. Its face was far above me, yet memory does not show the shape as a giant's. And I do not know whether it stood, or seemed to stand, on the far side of the water or on the water itself.
>
> (Lewis 1956: 172)

Admittedly, there are several key details in this scene which depart significantly from Irigaray's account of woman's initial, painful encounter with divinity, such as the fact that Orual describes the light as 'without warmth or comfort' (Lewis 1956: 172) and reads the god's gaze as one of 'passionless and measureless rejection' (Lewis 1956: 173) which directly contrasts Irigaray's association of divine light with overwhelming passion. However, to some extent, these can be attributed to Orual's unreliability as narrator. Her later revelation from her vision that the rams 'rushed over [her] in their joy' (Lewis 1956: 284), and that the Divine Nature behaves in a similar way, throws her previous narration of a coldly judgemental divinity into question and leads her towards a more intimate and dynamic relationship to divine incarnation.

There are many potentially subversive elements at work in both Irigaray's and Lewis's accounts of women undergoing initially painful transformations in their quests for a theology that will enable their liberation. Both of them take seriously the difficulty of escaping the traps laid by patriarchal theology and other phallogocentric modes of defining and imagining women. Notably, the answer which Orual had hoped to receive from the gods comes instead from her ability to finally tell her own story in front of them without wrapping it in the veil of Greek wisdom. It would not be difficult to imagine a version of *Till We Have Faces* in which this act alone would allow Orual to enter theology on her own terms and free Ungit from her characterizations within patriarchal theology.

Instead, in both *Till We Have Faces* and Irigaray's work, the reader is left with figurations of divine femininity that, while beginning their journeys in a position of Ungit-like disruptiveness, end up little altered from the forms of femininity appropriated by masculinity. Over the course of Irigaray's work, even the violently burning light that initially characterizes divine passion in *Speculum of the Other Woman* is eventually, in 'Toward a Divine in the Feminine', domesticated so that 'consenting to receiving divine bliss is not so remote from enjoying a ray of sun' (Irigaray 2009: 20). In Irigaray's theological imaginary, woman redeems herself by cultivating virtues – such as nurture, community and resistance to domination – traditionally devalued because of their association with femininity and motherhood. However, as I have already shown, Irigaray remains content to rehabilitate these qualities and take their relationship to femininity at face value rather than deconstructively work through them.

Orual's and Ungit's own redemption – their becoming-Psyche – manifests in a similar process of taming. As the Fox narrates Psyche's final task, 'Psyche must go down into the deadlands to get beauty in a casket from the Queen of the Deadlands, from death herself; and bring it back and give it to Ungit so that Ungit will become beautiful' (Lewis 1956: 301). It is telling here that the novel stops short of questioning Ungit's (and thus implicitly Orual's) supposed ugliness and the need for this ugliness to be corrected in order for her to become divine. It is strikingly similar to how Irigaray critiques the notion that '[f]emale beauty is always considered a *garment* ultimately designed to attract the other into the self' and instead insists that it be 'perceived as a manifestation of, an appearance by a phenomenon expressive of interiority' (Irigaray [1987] 1993: 65) but does not go on to further challenge the approved cultural scripts by which beauty is defined. It is these same standards at whose mercy Orual endures loneliness and countless abuses in the early passages of *Till We Have Faces*, but which the text ultimately fails to subvert.

Till We Have Faces attempts to present Psyche as a living, breathing divine woman in the process of becoming in contrast to the statue of Aphrodite in the temple, but the idealization of her 'divine' qualities produces much the same effect by the end of the text. However much Psyche may transgress the social niceties and religious doctrines of her culture in cultivating divinity, the text still idealizes her in positing her as divine and immobilizes her within predetermined definitions of femininity and divinity. The Fox, for instance, extols her in Platonic terms, saying that she is '"according to nature"; what every woman, or even every thing, ought to have been and meant to be, but had missed by some trip of chance' (Lewis 1956: 22). For all that the characterization of Psyche attempts to suggest the transgressive potential of qualities traditionally gendered as 'feminine', Lewis, like Irigaray, is too quick to re-inscribe a single definition of femininity as the ideal and universal standard.

Orual's divine becoming, then, is not a liberation of the dark femininity embodied by dragon-in-the-neighbourhood Ungit, which would threaten the entire phallogocentric structure in which the concepts of divinity, womanhood, beauty and desire are caught. Ungit must instead be purified and brought in line with the standards of divine femininity embodied by Psyche. It is true, as I demonstrated in Chapter 1, that Orual's redemption brings her to a new understanding of ethical and horizontal love for the other, in a manner analogous to Irigaray's claim that '[l]ove of neighbour is an ethical consequence of becoming divine' (Irigaray [1987] 1993: 68). Yet while the text attempts to show this love crossing social, political, sexual and theological boundaries throughout, it stops short of contesting cultural restrictions regarding in which types of (heterosexual and cisgender) femininity this love can be cultivated. The divinity, beauty and love emblematized by Psyche scandalously overwhelm the partitions placed around them by the patriarchal cultural and religious order she inhabits, but she embodies all these qualities in a manner still *legible* as divine, as beautiful, as loving within its discourse, even in excess. Reading Psyche in terms of Irigaray's ideals of divine womanhood thus underscores Joy's observation that '[Irigaray] still warns against accepting "feminine" stereotypes that are prescribed by the patriarchal tradition, but appears oblivious to the fact that her own descriptions are in similar need of discriminating evaluation' (Joy 2006: 159).

Yet although Psyche's characterization shares many of the same limitations and exclusions as Irigaray's attempt to construct a feminist religious imaginary, a careful reading can also create space to question this through attention to the novel's status as fantasy. By contending with the necessary provisionality of myths of divine womanhood and fairy stories of marital bliss, and by positioning itself as 'A Myth Retold' in its subtitle, *Till We Have Faces* implicitly acknowledges its own complicity in potentially reductive depictions of femininity. In Chapter 1 I already discussed how Psyche's fairy tale of her gold and amber palace simultaneously prefigures and obscures the form that her relationship with the god takes. I also noted how the traumatic rupture in her belief in the story as she is offered to the god mimes how moments of eucatastrophe in fantasy texts suggest the disruptive justice of the other. This pattern becomes a repetitive motif in the novel's treatment of depictions of women in myths, religious ceremonies and art. If, as I suggested in the first section of this chapter, depictions of sexuate divine becoming such as Irigaray's can also be understood in terms of a eucatastrophic opening of possibilities rather than a prescriptive programme, the supposed universality of the divine female archetypes they imagine can be deconstructed without undermining their value to feminist theologies.

Psyche's need to be stripped of the story of her gold and amber palace is paralleled by the stripping of her own ceremonial garb before she enters the god's bedchamber. While Orual assumes a veil of honorary masculinity to grant herself authority over her kingdom and neutralize the horror of her femininity, Psyche's face is much earlier covered over with the signifiers of ritual sacrifice and female subservience. When she is led to the Holy Tree on the morning of the Offering, her visage is 'painted and gilded and be-wigged [. . .] like [one of the] temple girl[s]' (Lewis 1956: 80) who also serve as the male priests' concubines. For Irigaray, the veil refers to 'the eternal female' imprisoned within the 'ideals and moral rules and self-reflective and self-representative gazes' (Irigaray [1974] 1985: 82) of patriarchy, and it is behind just such veils that the temple girls and Psyche are transformed into caricatures of women with 'huge flaxen wigs and their faces painted till they looked like wooden masks' (Lewis 1956: 42). In the 'veiling' of Psyche and the temple girls, Lewis demonstrates how even theologies that nominally seek to elevate the 'feminine' can attempt to neutralize divine femininity by confining women to ideals that ultimately serve patriarchal authorities, much as Lewis's own characterization of Psyche is equally suspect on these terms.

Once she is brought to the god's palace, Psyche is bathed by female spirits to wash away her mask before she enters his bedchamber. In one sense, this implies that Psyche's divine becoming demands that she approach the god with her 'true' face, calling to mind Irigaray's similar description of the woman's face in the sacred caress:

> Beloved, the female lover emerges from all disguises. No longer frozen in a deadly freedom but permitted growth, which is still possible, and a face without any habits, which lets itself be seen in order to be reborn beyond what has already appeared.
>
> (Irigaray [1993] 2001: 124)

Psyche must lose any figurations of divine or virtuous femininity either projected onto her by her culture or devised by her own mind before she is able to enter an erotic embrace with divinity. Because the text is constantly reminding its readers of its own status as a myth and of the inherent non-neutrality of mythmaking, however – chiefly through the use of unreliable narration and its emphasis on storytelling as theological imagination – this extends to the way in which the novel itself constructs Psyche as a character. The novel's ending suggests that one of the chief barriers to Psyche's divine becoming is the way in which others perceive her divinity. One of the murals Orual sees in the deadlands shows Psyche attempting to make her way towards the throne of Ungit, tempted by a crowd of people crying out, 'Istra! Princess! Ungit! [. . .] Stay with us. Be our goddess. Rule us. Speak oracles to us. Receive our sacrifices. Be our goddess' (Lewis 1956: 302). Psyche pays no attention to the crowd, but instead walks on.

That Psyche's divine becoming depends on her wariness towards any attempt to understand her as a goddess, and that most of her clearest moments of divine revelation are marked by darkness and textual silences, lends her journey a level of nuance not necessarily perceptible in how Irigaray characterizes divine womanhood. Notably, the courtyard in which Orual witnesses this story of Psyche's divine becoming and her own involvement in that process, and in which she is finally redeemed and reunited with Psyche, is enclosed by pillars, which I noted in Chapter 2 can be understood as a phallic motif representing patriarchal modes of thinking, writing and speaking. However inadvertently, this story of woman's redemption is still structured according to phallogocentric principles, and the femininity of Psyche, like that of the statue of Aphrodite, takes on a form still susceptible to assimilation within a patriarchal theological framework. As a fantasy text aware simultaneously of the transformative potential of mythmaking and of its severe limits, *Till We Have Faces* suggests the need for a deconstructive rather than prescriptive affirmation of feminist figurations of divinity.

Although the eucatastrophic revelation Orual experiences leads her to proclaim to Eros, 'I know now, Lord, why you utter no answer. You are yourself the answer' (Lewis 1956: 308), her story ends mid-sentence as she dies, with Arnom instructed to 'give up the book to any stranger who will take an oath to bring it into Greece' (Lewis 1956: 309). This final emphasis on the open-ended life of the book destabilizes the universalizing and essentializing tendencies the novel has shared with Irigaray's writing up to this point by drawing attention to its linguistic, discursive and cultural specificity, and emphasizes the text's openness to deconstruction and resistant interpretation by the reader. Thus, *Till We Have Faces* is, like Irigaray's quest for a feminine religious imaginary, frustratingly limited in its scope despite the numerous radical opportunities it creates, only managing to elude prescriptivism in readings attentive to fantasy's inherent provisionalit.

'Her own mythological artefact': *The Passion of New Eve* and the theatre of divine womanhood

While *Till We Have Faces*' characterization of Psyche shares many common impulses with Irigaray's quest for a feminine divinity, and examining the two together throws into sharp relief both the potential and limitations of their respective theological imaginations, it is the deconstruction of the very possibility of a universal female incarnation of the divine that concerns Angela Carter's *The Passion of New Eve*. Evelyn's journey into the desert, in which he is taken into the lair of the fertility goddess Mother and transformed into a second Eve destined to redeem the world, not only shares many narrative and topological parallels with Orual and Psyche's intertwined journey towards divine becoming but is also, at first glance, framed in almost identical conceptual terms to Irigaray's writing. Yet fantasy, in Carter's hands, is every bit as much a site of parody and subversion of mythopoetic and theological tropes and archetypes as it is a space for articulating a new theological imaginary. The goddesses, monsters and other mythic beings populating Carter's fantastical vision of the American West are revealed to be complicit in their own construction and in the worldbuilding of the landscape they inhabit. Thus, while the divine beings in *The Passion of New Eve* are often presented as generative fictions, they are still unavoidably *fictions*, not to be taken as universal or final. Carter's novel suggests that if we are to take up Irigaray's quest for a divine in the feminine, we do so at the peril of creating new prescriptions for women that are not so different from the patriarchal norms we wish to undo.

In much the same way as Orual's spiritual transformation begins in interior spaces – first in the close and pungent temple of Ungit and then in the cavernous space beneath the Pillar Room – so also Evelyn's transformation into Eve takes place in Beulah, a realm which 'lies in the interior, in the inward parts of the earth' (Carter [1977] 2012: 43). (Beulah takes its name from the King James translation of Isa. 64.2: 'thou shalt be called Hephzibah, and thy land Beulah: for the Lord delighteth in thee, and thy land shall be married' (KJV).) While Orual's visions can never quite escape the ubiquity of phallic pillars, '[Beulah's] emblem is a broken column' (Carter [1977] 2012: 43), and its entrance is marked by a towering column representing 'a stone cock with testicles [. . .] [b]ut the cock was broken off clean in the middle' (Carter [1977] 2012: 44). On this fractured pillar is inscribed a legend in Latin: 'INTROITE ET HIC DII SUNT [. . .] ENTER, FOR HERE THE GODS ARE' (Carter [1977] 2012: 44). This space is designated as the realm of the gods, over which the fertility goddess Mother presides, and thus its configuration evokes Irigaray's concept of the divine 'mother-matter' (Irigaray [1974] 1985: 162) as the ground and foundation of existence that threatens the transcendent unity of being represented by the phallus. Indeed, we are told that

> Mother built this underground town, she burrowed it out below the sand; Holy Mother whose fingers are scalpels excavated the concentric descending spheres of Beulah, unless, that is, she herself has always been there – a chthonic deity, a presence always present in the shaping structure of dream.
>
> (Carter [1977] 2012: 43)

Mother's seeming agelessness as implied by this passage, as well as the suggestion of her omnipresence in society's collective unconscious, further aligns Mother with Irigaray's first mat(t)er that is repressed and covered over in the positing of subjectivity within the patriarchal *logos*. Upon his capture, Evelyn is imprisoned within a 'warm, red place' that he eventually realizes 'was a simulacrum of the womb', with a chorus of women's voices intoning 'NOW YOU ARE AT THE PLACE OF BIRTH' (Carter [1977] 2012: 49) over a loudspeaker. In sharp contrast to patriarchal theologies that maintain the stability of their constructions by partitioning themselves off from 'the "body's" first resources' (Irigaray [1974] 1985: 164),[6] the configuration of Beulah and the theology ruling it all point back to the womb in a manner that ruptures Evelyn's masculinist world view and sense of self.

Although Mother's feminist mytho-/theological project departs from Irigaray's writing insofar as she aims to fashion a man into 'a perfect specimen of womanhood' (Carter [1977] 2012: 65) rather than cultivating feminine ideals in a subject assigned female at birth, the impulses underpinning both are nearly identical. The emblem of the broken pillar and Evelyn's eventual castration and transformation into Eve in the cavernous, womb-like depths of Beulah are both positioned to signify the threat that, in Irigaray's view, considerations of birth (and therefore of finitude and thus mortality) pose to patriarchal masculinity. Likewise, Mother, like Irigaray, seeks to bring about a feminist messianic age by rehabilitating archetypes of divine womanhood. She designates Evelyn as 'a new Eve [. . .] [a]nd the Virgin Mary too' (Carter [1977] 2012: 67) who will 'bring forth the Messiah of the Antithesis', for, as she explains matter-of-factly to Evelyn, 'Woman has been the antithesis in the dialectic of creation quite long enough' (Carter [1977] 2012: 64). Like the temple of Ungit and the house of the god of the Mountain, Beulah (another name for heaven), and Mother's rule over it, also suggests a transgression of the boundaries separating the sacred from the profane. In Evelyn/Eve's words, 'Beulah is a profane place' (Carter [1977] 2012: 46) and 'a place where contrarieties are equally true' (Carter [1977] 2012: 44). This description echoes Irigaray's declaration that 'woman [. . .] remains the simultaneous co-existence of opposites. She is *both one and the other*' (Irigaray [1974] 1985: 165).

Castration quite obviously figures heavily into Eve's formation as a female subject, and on one hand this may seem to deviate from Irigaray insofar as the latter's writing arises from an impulse to imagine woman in terms other than the lack of a phallus. On the other, in its violent transformation in the underground caverns of Beulah, Evelyn/Eve's body can be interpreted as a locus for both the patriarchal fear of contamination by femininity and the womb as detailed by Irigaray, as well as Irigaray's investment in a certain female exceptionalism for the messianic redemption of the world. Irigaray argues that for a subject defined in phallogocentric terms, 'access to the earth must be barred by developing an onto-theology at the very outset', otherwise '[being] might be seduced into returning to the womb of the mother-earth where the identity of being with itself is endangered, or at least problematic' (Irigaray [1974] 1985: 164). As in *Till We Have Faces*, the journey into the realm of the gods in *The Passion of New Eve* is narrated in terms of a return to the womb in which a self-identity that fears and rejects femininity is thrown into question and, especially in the latter's case, radically reconstituted.

From the moment of his arrival in Beulah, Evelyn feels both his masculinity and his sense of self profoundly under threat. Sitting in the red room in which he is first imprisoned, he experiences a moment of existential panic in which he is overwhelmed by a sense of materiality and his own embodiment:

> Beneath the earth, sweating as I was in its humid viscera, I felt the dull pressure of the desert, of the vast prairies, the grazing cattle, the corn; I felt upon me the whole heaviness of that entire continent with its cities and its coinage, its mines, its foundries, its wars and its mythologies imposing itself in all its immensity, like the night-mare, upon my breast. [. . .] My fear took on a new quality; not only the fear for my own safety, now, but dread of the immensity of the world about me.
>
> (Carter [1977] 2012: 49)

Later, when he is brought before Mother, Evelyn realizes that '[b]efore this overwhelming woman, the instrument that dangled from [his] belly was useless' (Carter [1977] 2012: 56–7), and that '[s]ince [he] had no notion how to approach her with it, she rendered it insignificant; [he] must deal with her on her own terms' (Carter [1977] 2012: 57). Mother is femininity in excess, 'a femaleness too vast, too gross for [Evelyn's] imagination to contain' (Carter [1977] 2012: 63) because she is a woman who resists appropriation as an object within a patriarchal sexual economy or incorporation into a masculine paradigm. Such an overwhelming presence, in Irigaray's view, serves 'to break down the walls around the (male) one who speaks, sees, thinks, and thereby now confers being upon himself, in a prison of self-sufficiency and a clarity made of the shadow of denial' (Irigaray [1974] 1985: 192). Or, to use Mother's own words to Evelyn, '[t]o be a man is not a given condition but a continuous effort' (Carter [1977] 2012: 60). To enter Mother's domain is, at least in Mother's own view, to be rendered vulnerable to the other and thus freed from the self-same prison of phallogocentric masculine subjectivity.

At first, however, Eve's sense of alienation from herself following her operation is only heightened, as she spends her early days as a woman lamenting that 'where [she] remembered [her] cock, was nothing. Only a void, an insistent absence, like a noisy silence' (Carter [1977] 2012: 71), at one point even reflecting that Mother has 'turned [her] into [her] own diminutive, Eve, the shortened form of Evelyn' (Carter [1977] 2012: 68). The image she sees when she looks in the mirror, which in Lacanian psychoanalysis is crucial to the formation of subjectivity, is one which she 'in no way could acknowledge as [herself]' (Carter [1977] 2012: 71).[7] Later, when Mother asks her, 'How do you find yourself?' she can only mournfully reply, 'I don't find myself at all' (Carter [1977] 2012: 72). While, as I discuss in Chapter 4, much of Eve's crisis of subjectivity can be understood as an experience associated with many queer coming-out and gender transition narratives, it is also possible to interpret her fractured sense of self in terms of the heterogeneity which Irigaray associates with feminine subjectivity. Because this point is so closely linked to anatomy for Irigaray (the phallus versus the two lips of the vagina), it would not be difficult to argue that Eve, having lost her phallus, has also lost the sovereignty of selfhood that man enjoys within a patriarchal order but has yet to cultivate the 'privileged place of self-affection for a woman' (Irigaray 2009: 18). She thus still experiences her new-found womanhood as a lack, and in place of a stable sense of self is, to use Irigaray's words again, a 'hysteria that a phallocratic culture has aroused in [women] by taking [them] away from [themselves]' (Irigaray 2009: 18). As I will detail further in the second half of this section and in the next chapter, however, the rest of the novel does much to problematize this anatomically deterministic view of subjectivity.

Evelyn's process of feminization as Eve in his journey into the womb of the earth literalizes and offers an extreme example of the loss of stability the masculine subject fears when his repressed origins in the womb are brought to light. After all, if, as Irigaray argues, patriarchy constructs man as a unified and sovereign subject above woman, who by contrast 'is never resolved by/in being' (Irigaray [1974] 1985: 165), then from this perspective any threat to a phallocentric unity of being is a feminization. Yet the text does not seem to be suggesting that women are inherently castrated subjects, only that they are constructed as such by a phallocentric logic and would be understood in those terms by someone used to operating within such a world view. Accordingly with Mother's title as the 'Castratrix of the Phallocentric Universe' (Carter [1977]

2012: 64), this patriarchal logic is repeatedly and openly challenged as part of Eve's psychological reconditioning. On the eve (no pun intended) of Evelyn's surgery, he pleads with Sophia, asking her 'why she should have chosen me for her mother's experiments, of what crime I had been guilty to deserve such a punishment', which she answers by simply posing him the question, 'Is it such a bad thing to become like me?' (Carter [1977] 2012: 65). Post-operation, Eve is subjected to an 'inscrutable video-tape composed of a variety of non-phallic imagery such as sea-anemones opening and closing; caves, with streams issuing from them; roses, opening to admit a bee; the sea, the moon' (Carter [1977] 2012: 69). Castration, for Mother and the inhabitants of Beulah, does not represent a universal condition of women's subjectivity as it does for the patriarchal psychoanalysts Irigaray seeks to refute but as part of a process of reconfiguring one's own subjectivity and the wider cultural theological and mythological imagination. As Sophia, Evelyn's caretaker, explains to him, 'Myth is more instructive than history' (Carter [1977] 2012: 65).

In Mother's hands, then, Eve's transformed body becomes a synecdoche for a wider project to redeem the earth through a feminization of America's repressed theological and mythological inheritances. This project to undo the violence of American history by resurrecting a divine ideal of womanhood is almost identical to the way in which Irigaray invokes archetypes of motherhood as a response to the Chernobyl accident and the Cold-War-era threat of nuclear warfare in *Thinking the Difference* (1989). In her words,

> [t]o re-establish elementary social justice, to save the earth from total subjugation to male values (which often give priority to violence, power, money), we must restore [. . .] the mother-daughter relationship and respect for female speech and virginity. This will require changes to symbolic codes, especially language, law and religion.
>
> (Irigaray [1989] 1994: 112)

Mother's agenda, like Irigaray's, is to turn back to the origin and reclaim the mythic ideal of a pre-lapsarian state of being which she feels has been denied woman, which she hopes to do by reinvesting power in religious archetypes and symbols of womanhood such as Eve and Mary. By doing so, she hopes to remake the American religious landscape into one defined by the 'female' values she cherishes, the future this would herald symbolized by the divine child Mother hopes to bring forth by impregnating Eve with the former Evelyn's sperm. In other words, Mother wishes to preordain Eve to birth divinity into the world by means of the other (gender) within herself, thus literalizing the privileged position woman occupies with regard to her ability to cultivate a relationship with the other in Irigaray's theological imaginary.

This would all seem to suggest that Evelyn's descent into Beulah and subsequent transformation into Eve are to be a re-inscription of the presumed eternal and universal attributes of divine womanhood championed by Irigaray. The novel's narration attributes the apocalyptic state of its dystopian America to the archetype of 'Old Adam', whose desire to purify himself of finitude and 'sewers of history' takes the 'clean, abstract lines, discrete blocks, geometric intersections' (Carter [1977] 2012: 12) of rationality as an alibi. The type of female exceptionalism espoused by Irigaray, in which (cisgender) women are uniquely equipped not just socially but also biologically and anatomically to birth divinity in the world by fostering a 'concern for the sensible, for the tangible and the natural environment, for intersubjectivity, for relations with the other gender, for the future, for being and doing-things together' (Irigaray 2004b: 156), pervades almost every aspect of the theological mythos that governs Beulah. Also prevalent in the prophetic utterances of Mother and her followers or 'daughters' is the essentialized rhetoric Irigaray employs to designate 'masculine' and 'feminine' ethics. Yet the seemingly harmonious theological imaginary that governs Beulah, and the matriarchal world order it is intended to bring forth, also sounds notes of dissonance, traces of its own artifice that reveal the contradictions inherent within, and even impossibility of realizing, its eschatological aims to redeem the world via divine womanhood. Mother, Sophia and the other women populating Beulah are all mythmakers and worldbuilders of a fantastical society whose essentializing configurations of gender, and specifically divine womanhood, are belied by the technological processes of its construction.

Among the inhabitants of Beulah, Mother fulfils the role not only of divine figurehead and object of worship but as 'the concrete essence of woman' (Carter [1977] 2012: 57), the universal, eternal and natural archetype of womanhood as old as the earth itself. When Evelyn is first brought before her, she ceremonially declares, 'The garden in which Adam was born lies between my thighs' (Carter [1977] 2012: 60), and even before this, Sophia hails her as the

> [i]neradicable vent of being, oracular mouth
>
> absolute beginning without which negation is impossible
>
> in one hand she holds the sun
> and the moon in the other

> she shakes stars off her shoulders
> when she yawns earthquakes
>
> (Carter [1977] 2012: 58)

before reciting a litany of goddesses and divine women from religions the world over. Contrary to what all this portentous ceremony suggests, however, Mother's divinity is not a natural property but one that has been self-imposed through Mother's ingenious technical skill at plastic surgery. As Evelyn describes her, Mother is a 'self-anointed, self-appointed prophetess, the self-created godhead that had assumed the flesh of its own prophecy' (Carter [1977] 2012: 55) and thus become

> her own mythological artefact; she had reconstructed her flesh painfully, with knives and with needles, into a transcendental form as an emblem, as an example, and flung a patchwork quilt stitched from her daughters' breasts over the cathedral of her interior, the cave within the cave.
>
> (Carter [1977] 2012: 57)

Mother mythologizes herself as an embodiment of supposedly eternal 'feminine' values, and her proclamation to Evelyn that 'to be a man is [. . .] a continuous effort' strongly implies that Evelyn's journey into Beulah and to Mother is a return to a more natural state of being, a quest to '[r]eintegrate the primal form' (Carter [1977] 2012: 61). Yet all this pomp and circumstance obscures the fact that Mother's own divine status is also achieved through a concerted and conscious effort.

Mother's self-creation demonstrates that while fantasy's investment in myths and tales of Faërie can uncover and give voice to 'others' who are repressed, rendered illegible or dismissed as 'unreal' within normative hegemonic structures, as I have argued throughout this book, this does not mean that fantasy is inherently closer to an ultimate, absolute truth. Myth, as Sophia declares to Evelyn, may well be more instructive than a patriarchal understanding of history when it comes to narrating the experiences of those silenced and abused by patriarchy, but Carter's text reminds the reader that both involve processes of construction and are open to deconstruction. The universal womanhood that Mother claims by virtue of her status as a goddess is achieved both by artificially reshaping her own bodily morphology and by cobbling together attributes from disparate sources, both metaphorically in terms of the goddesses from different cultures that Mother supposedly embodies, but also literally, as demonstrated by the many breasts from her followers that she sews onto her torso.

This sense of artifice extends to Evelyn's description of Beulah itself, which he characterizes as

> a triumph of science and hardly anything about it is natural, as if magic, there, masquerades as surgery in order to gain credence in a secular age. Yet now, when I think of Beulah, I am not sure I do exaggerate its technological marvels, either make too much of them – or else my fallible and shell-shocked memory has invented most of them, in order to soften the mythic vengeance on me there.
>
> (Carter [1977] 2012: 47)

Here, the text deliberately blurs boundaries between science and magic, and by extension generic boundaries between fantasy and science fiction, to emphasize both the limits of phallogocentric secular reason and the inherent constructedness of myth. Carter's text is not criticizing artificiality per se; Eve and Mother are no less 'real' in their womanhood than any other character in the text. Yet the text's persistent exposure of the non-essentiality of womanhood prompts interrogation regarding what form of divine womanhood Eve is destined to inhabit. The outlook is not encouraging. Upon looking in the mirror for the first time Eve finds that her captors

> had turned me into the *Playboy* center fold. I was the object of all the unfocused desires that had ever existed in my own head. I had become my own masturbatory fantasy. And – how can I put it – the cock in my head, still, twitched at the sight of myself.
>
> (Carter [1977] 2012: 71)

Mother and her followers have indeed fashioned Eve into an archetype of divine womanhood, but it is still a fetishized image of 'woman' as constructed on patriarchal and phallogocentric terms, replicated with clinical precision. This is foreshadowed earlier in Mother's operating theatre, where as Mother brandishes her obsidian scalpel, Evelyn notes that he is '[t]o be castrated with a phallic symbol! (But what else, says Mother, could do the trick?)' (Carter [1977] 2012: 67). There is in Mother's imagined reply to Evelyn's observation a deconstructive acknowledgement that any feminist project exists in relation to the phallogocentric structure of discourse. However, Mother's phallic scalpel also signals that the role prescribed for Eve is not sufficiently interrogated.

Eve is the perfect image of divine womanhood, but the attainment of this status immobilizes her in the gaze of a cultural imaginary in need of further deconstruction. Her psychological reconditioning takes the form of video sequences consisting mostly of archetypal images of motherhood and feminine suffering, including what Eve surmises must be 'every single Virgin and Child that had ever been painted in the entire history of Western European art' (Carter [1977] 2012: 69). Meanwhile, Sophia delivers lectures to Eve detailing 'the horrors my old sex had perpetrated on my new one' (Carter [1977] 2012: 70). Despite their nominally militant resistance to patriarchy, the womanhood that the inhabitants of Beulah would prescribe for Eve is one that would still confine her to a destiny of motherhood and suffering, with little in the way of alternatives offered. Nothing exists of her reshaped psyche but 'many Virgins with many Children, a mother vixen batting its cub affectionately about the ear with a maternal paw and brownish stills from old movies, any numbers of them, ghost of a face folded in sorrow' (Carter [1977] 2012: 74). Even after Eve rebels against Mother's plans and steals away on a motorized sand-sled the night before she is to be impregnated, her prospects are not much better. Roz Kaveney notes that '[w]hen Eve ceased to be a man, she ceased to be an agent in her own story – other women may actively pursue their own desires and needs, but the most she ever manages is to escape from one mess into another' (Kaveney [1994] 2007: 193).

Eve's status as a blank slate of a character without agency following her transformation in Beulah can be understood as a warning against overly narrow and prescriptive characterizations of divine womanhood. As seen in the abuses Eve suffers over the course of the novel, these often replicate the oppressions wrought by patriarchy and too uncritically reproduce its tropes of representation. Likewise, the totalitarian authority that Mother commands stands as a rebuke to the female exceptionalist tendencies displayed in feminist projects like Irigaray's. It turns out that divinity, as metaphysical sovereignty and authority, does not become less hierarchical or less violent simply because it is figured as a woman and associated with images of motherhood. Although Carter is far from condemning feminist variations on theological concepts, as the discussion in Chapter 4 makes clear, the fantasy of *The Passion of New Eve* consistently underscores that these incarnations are constructed and open to deconstruction. They do not grant privileged access to transcendence, and it takes more than a simple swapping of roles to unsettle patriarchal theology.

This point is further underscored by the final passages of *The Passion of New Eve*, which can be understood both as a parody of the idea of a universal divine womanhood and as a subversive variation on fantastic eucatastrophe. As civil war rages around her, Eve is led by Lilith, Mother's daughter, to a cave on the coast of California, where she 'must slide into the living rock all alone to rendezvous with [her] maker' (Carter [1977] 2012: 175). As she navigates the cavernous underground space, Eve seems, for a time, to be on a journey to regain wholeness. The walls of the cave become increasingly soft and womb-like until they are '[w]alls of meat and slimy velvet' (Carter [1977] 2012: 180), seeming to fulfil the reintegration of the primal form prophesied in Beulah. Time begins to run backward and for a moment it seems that Eve has achieved divine womanhood and fulfilled her quest to redeem the world. Yet the moment does not last; she is rejected by the womb-like cave as '[t]he walls of meat [expel her]' (Carter [1977] 2012: 182) and left alone in darkness crying for Mother with no answer. Eve reflects that 'Mother is a figure of speech' (Carter [1977] 2012: 180), a self-created fiction useful for some purposes but dangerous if adopted as an eternal symbol. In this way, the use of fantasy in *The Passion of New Eve* demonstrates the necessity of incarnations and Christologies that are more unsettled than that offered by Irigaray, as well as the perils of too readily embracing figurations that claim universality.

Conclusions

This chapter has engaged with the necessity of theological imaginaries that reconfigure incarnation on feminine terms. Luce Irigaray's contribution to this pursuit in feminist theology cannot be overlooked, but her project poses serious problems from a deconstructive standpoint because of its essentialist, overly prescriptive definition of 'woman' as well as its reliance on metaphysics and exceptionalist tendencies. Through my analysis of *Till We Have Faces* and *The Passion of New Eve*, I have shown that fantasy can confront these problems head-on. The character of Psyche in *Till We Have Faces* may signify a domestication of the more disruptive energy of Ungit, but the novel's overt concern with processes of mythmaking opens the text to a reading that takes the construction of divine femininity into account. *The Passion of New Eve*, meanwhile, uses its particular variant of self-aware fantasy to expose the fundamental instability, as well as the dangers, of messianic projects like Irigaray's. Nevertheless, the aim of Irigaray's project in searching for a sexual- and gender-marginalized theology of incarnation is a crucial one in which fantasy literature can play a vital role. The following chapter concerns itself with queer theologies of incarnation that, while broader in scope and more unsettled in their imaginations, arise out of the same impulses that motivate Irigaray's philosophy.

4

Drag(on) theology

The queer strangers of fantasy

So far, I have shown how fantasy literature is uniquely equipped to articulate a deconstructive position oriented towards alterity, or radical difference devalued and even rendered inarticulable, within theological discourse. I have detailed the argument put forth by Hélène Cixous and others that difference is always already gendered as feminine, and demonstrated that the strange and often monstrous figurations found in fantasy can be critically aligned with Cixous's aim to give voice, through her practice of *écriture féminine*, to 'feminine' imaginaries, desires and bodily experiences otherwise erased from discourse. In the previous chapter, I explored in more detail fantasy texts' ability to make feminist interventions into theology through readings of *Till We Have Faces* and *The Passion of New Eve*. These texts were considered in relation to Luce Irigaray's problematic but groundbreaking project to re-imagine a Christian theology of incarnation on feminist terms. I argued that fantasy texts are able to engage in feminist re-visionings of divinity incarnate, often in ways that are strikingly similar to Irigaray's own imaginative efforts, but that their tendency to foreground the provisionality of, and processes involved in, their own mythmaking and worldbuilding serves as a crucial counterpoint to Irigaray's gender essentialism and investment in metaphysical concepts of divinity. As I demonstrated, both of these latter tendencies in Irigaray end up reasserting the exclusionary and reductive definitions of womanhood they are intended to resist, and place her project at odds with the feminism espoused by Cixous, despite arising out of similarly deconstructive aims.

This chapter brings together the previous chapter's focus on representations of divinity with the more overtly deconstructive focus of the first two chapters, to highlight fantasy literature's potential to develop queer theological imaginaries. These imaginaries locate incarnations of God or gods at specific sites of gendered and sexual difference, at the same time as they break with essentialist and generalized concepts of alterity. As untenable as the full sweep of Irigaray's particular theological imaginary ultimately proves even for cisgender, heterosexual women not aligned with her standard of divine womanhood, let alone queer and transgender women, the claim central to her work – that incarnational theology is inherently articulated according to specifically gendered and sexuate forms of embodiment – is one that remains crucial to queer theology. As Linn Marie Tonstad argues,

> Irigaray's contention that sexual difference would be the salvation of our age if we thought it through is at best a vast overstatement, but her very making of the claim is a clue to the centrality of gender and sexual difference in our cultural moment[.]
>
> (Tonstad 2016: 224)

Gender identities and sexual orientations that deviate from heterosexual and cisgender norms – in other words, those that would be designated as 'queer' – dominate contemporary intra-religious debates in Christianity,[1] debates which often form the basis not just for ecclesiastical practices but also for public policies that seek to regulate and police the lives and bodies of queer and transgender people. This means that articulating theology from a queer position, and especially speaking queerly *about* theology, which forms the focus of this chapter, carries significant stakes not only for queer and transgender people of faith but for queer and transgender people more generally. Throughout this chapter, I will show that envisioning the incarnate God as the queerly embodied other at the margins of hetero- and cis-sexist theological structures has the potential not merely to safeguard the well-being of queer and trans individuals but to create transformative (and trans-formative) possibilities for how religion, gender and sexuality are enacted in society.

I will begin this chapter by detailing the embattled history of the term 'queer' and the particular challenges and possibilities queerness poses for theology. My summary will give particular attention to Marcella Althaus-Reid's project of Indecent Theology and, to a lesser extent, Tonstad's queer reading of resurrection and apocalypse as a resistance to theologies focused solely on the inclusion and affirmation of queer individuals. Tonstad's interpretation of the second coming of Christ overlaps significantly with the deconstructive reading of fantastic eucatastrophe I outlined in the first chapter, and thus it will provide a useful segue into discussing fantasy literature's particular potential for queering theology. Fantasy's creation of secondary worlds through imaginative play with elements of the primary world, I will argue, reveals discontinuities and alternative possibilities within the latter in a manner similar to Judith Butler's theorization of drag culture as a deconstructive play on normative presentations of gender. Fantasy literature can also imagine worlds in which lives that would be considered queer and marked by precarity and religious marginalization in the primary world are deeply entwined with the structure of religious life, and this can hold transformative rather than merely therapeutic or cathartic significance. Through queer theological readings of *The Passion of New Eve*, *The Left Hand of Darkness* and the *Earthsea* cycle, as well as detours through other fantasy texts, this chapter will draw attention to the radical possibilities and questions that emerge from claiming fantasy literature as an essential resource for queer theology.

Queer(ing) definitions

In the introduction to his widely influential edited volume *Fear of a Queer Planet*, Michael Warner notes that 'queer' is 'a term initially generated in the context of terror' (Warner 1993: xxvi). Long understood as a stigmatizing slur against gender and sexual deviants, 'queer' began to be reclaimed in the context of gay and lesbian solidarity during the AIDS crisis in the 1980s, most memorably in the slogan popularized by the lobby group ACT UP and its later outgrowth Queer Nation: 'We're here; we're queer; get used to it!'[2] The term 'queer theory' was coined for scholarly purposes by Teresa de Lauretis in 1991, as a way of contending with the increasingly niche and widely divergent strands of writing and scholarship that at that time were synthesized under the banner of 'gay and lesbian studies'. De Lauretis argued that

> our 'differences', such as they may be, are less represented by the discursive coupling of those two terms [. . .] than they are elided by most of the contexts in which the phrase is used; that is to say, differences are implied in it but then simply taken for granted or even covered over.
>
> (De Lauretis 1991: v–vi)

For de Lauretis 1991: the politically correct usage of the phrase 'gay and lesbian' ironically solidifies separations between various areas of discourse on gender and sexuality by either reifying or erasing them, a critique that may be extended to the current (as of this book's writing) prominence of 'LGBTQ+' and its attendant micro-discourses on identity.[3] By contrast, 'queer theory' signifies

> [an] effort to avoid all of these fine distinctions in our discursive protocols, not to adhere to any one of the given terms, not to assume their ideological liabilities, but instead to both transgress and transcend them – or at the very least problematize them.
>
> (De Lauretis 1991: v)

Put simply, the advent of 'queer theory' marks a deliberate bringing together of disparate strands of thought, connected by their naming of sites of deviance from hegemonic gendered and sexual norms but marked also by their distinctions from and discontinuities with each other. At stake for de Lauretis was the way in which '[a] common front or political alliance of gay men and lesbians [. . .] [was] made possible, and indeed necessary, in the United States [. . .] by the AIDS national emergency and the pervasive institutional backlash against queers of all sexes' (De Lauretis 1991: v). At its core, queer theory seeks to build alliances among the bodies of knowledge produced by gender and sexually marginalized people, marking out differences and speaking across them without being overwhelmed by them or treating them as fixed or absolute. In de Lauretis's era, as in our own, this is not merely a matter of scholarly interest but of survival.

In the years since its inception, queer theory has mutated and developed to encompass a broad range of positions, commitments and experiences. Donald E. Hall notes that 'there is no "queer theory" in the singular, only many different voices and sometimes overlapping, sometimes divergent perspectives that can be loosely called "queer theories"' (Hall 2003: 5). What 'queer' offers to scholarship on gender and sexuality is that in foregrounding difference as its primary focus – both difference from the heterosexual and cisgender mainstream of society and difference(s) within that difference – it allows discourse to become malleable and encompass a wide and ever-changing range of experiences, desires, political struggles and intersections of oppression. Gerard Loughlin comments that in one sense, this means that

> [q]ueer seeks to outwit identity. It serves those who find themselves and others to be other than the characters prescribed by an identity. It marks not by defining, but by taking up a distance from what is perceived as the normative. The term is deployed in order to mark, and to make, a difference, a divergence.
>
> (Loughlin 2007: 9)

Similarly to the discursive position of 'woman' outlined in Chapter 2, queer designates a potentially disruptive alterity that, in hetero- and cis-normative discourses, must be covered over and suppressed to maintain the stable identities of normative subjects and stability per se. Put another way, queerness threatens cultural imaginaries constructed on heterosexual and cisgender terms, both because it cannot be located at a fixed point within their schemes of representation and because it disrupts the possibility of fixing even the most normative (heterosexual and cisgender) identities. Its manifestations in culture (such as the gender play that Butler identifies in drag culture, to be discussed later in this chapter) transgress boundaries of gender and sexuality presumed to be stable, revealing them to be neither absolute, universal, inevitable, nor even at one with themselves.

Yet as elusive as queerness is in frustrating the possibility of paradigms of selfhood, whether it is the universal, transcendent subject of Enlightenment philosophy or the subject as defined within more recent identity politics, it cannot be regarded as a pure negation (or in theological terms, *kenosis* or emptying) of identity. To be 'queer' is not to reject identification wholesale but to, in Hall's words, 'abrade the classifications, to sit athwart conventional categories or traverse several' (Hall 2003: 13). Queer theory's preoccupation with deconstructively working through coherent points of identification in order to unsettle them can be most clearly seen in one of its most influential immediate precursors: Judith Butler's *Gender Trouble* (1990). Butler's text adopts a Derridean stance to show the ways in which most feminist discourses of their time served to re-inscribe a binary configuration of sex and gender that not only fails to account for how differences in race, culture and class influence gendered subjectivity and oppression but also 'requires both a stable and oppositional heterosexuality' (Butler [1990] 2007: 30–1). Butler demonstrates that gender and sex, 'man' and 'woman', are not coherent, universal categories of identification, nor can 'gender' as a social category be fully disentangled from a supposedly more stable, more natural 'sex'; on the contrary, '[g]ender is the repeated stylization of the body, a set of repeated acts within a highly rigid regulatory frame that congeal over time to produce the appearance of substance, of a natural sort of being' (Butler [1990] 2007: 45). Rather than attempt to build a feminist project on a shared sense of womanhood, *Gender Trouble* advocates disruptions and parodies of approved social codes in the hopes of creating 'a fluidity of identities that suggests an openness to recontextualization and resignification' (Butler [1990] 2007: 188). Butler's theory of gender – and their elaborations and refinements of it in later work – has come to be emblematic of a queer approach to identity, and their project will be revisited in more detail in relation to fantasy later in this chapter. While some of the texts cited as 'queer theory' in this study pre-date de Lauretis's classification of the discipline, as do most of the works of fantasy literature referenced in this chapter, they (and their characters) participate in this queer practice of exceeding and disrupting stable categories.

Queer, then, is both more and less than a designation of identities across the LGBTQ+ spectrum; it is an ethical, theoretical and political commitment to the deconstruction of normative gender categories as they coincide with violence against cis-hetero-patriarchal society's others. At the same time as it remains irreducible to whatever designations of sexual orientation or gender identity may be generally accepted in common parlance in any given time and place, it is nonetheless historically rooted in the oppression of LGBTQ+ people. Both this acronym and the term 'queer', however, contain within themselves many uneasy alliances, whose uneasiness must be taken into account if queerness is to be invoked responsibly. Of particular significance for this chapter's engagement with queer theory are the tensions that often emerge between queer's fascination with disrupting coherent gender and sexual identities by focusing on the points at which they break down, and the concern some trans theorists demonstrate for defending the social legitimacy of transgender identities beyond being symbols for queer subversion. While the field of transgender studies that has emerged over the course of the last three decades is by no means a monolith and comprises at least as diverse a range of theoretical and political positions as queer theory, an account of some of the discontinuities and points of divergence between queer and trans theory is necessary for the critical discussions undertaken in this chapter.[4]

Cáel M. Keegan has identified the relationship between queer theory and trans studies as one which has often been, in practice, appropriative, noting that 'queer studies has often moved to absorb trans* studies into its antinormative and deconstructive regimes without adequately inquiring after the consequences for transgender lives' (Keegan 2018: 391). In Keegan's analysis, queer theory's insistence on the instability and incoherence of sex and gender identity can find itself at odds with many (though certainly not all) transgender people's self-understanding. Where queer disruption may hold liberatory potential for people, both cis and trans, who find the heterosexual matrix of binary gender unliveable, it can also be a roadblock for transgender people for whom it is a political necessity to insist upon the reality of their genders as they experience them, to align aspects of their sexed embodiment with their gender identities and to make the legal and medical means of doing so more widely and readily accessible.[5] As Keegan notes,

> [b]ecause queer studies tends to understand gender, sexuality, and identity as effects of normative power, it can erode the bases by which trans* studies might

legitimately claim gender as felt or innately experienced, thereby replicating the denial of transgender experience also found in stigmatizing medical or political discourses. In valuing trans phenomena largely when they subvert gender norms, queer studies has historically sorted, cited, and disciplined some portions of trans into itself while rejecting others as retrograde and conformist (crossdressing, genderqueer, and androgyny are welcome; transsexuality is not).

(Keegan 2018: 391)

Queer theory often tends to take gender-nonconforming, genderqueer and non-binary people, who may experience their lives as transgressing, crossing and re-crossing, sitting athwart or even existing 'off the map' from binary gender, as queer signs of gender's inherent instability. Trans theorizing, meanwhile, may rely on a variety of critical frameworks in its aims to equip transgender people to tell stories about gender that can materially enrich and improve their livelihood, and to insist upon these as substantive in their own right. As Grace E. Lavery noted in a talk delivered to the Modernist Studies Association, later published in her newsletter, 'where queer theory establishes performativity as a general condition of gender expression, trans discourse distinguishes between different techniques as more or less efficacious in different circumstances' (Lavery 2019: 7 of 8 paras).

The points of conflict between 'queer' and 'trans' that Keegan identifies are by no means inevitabilities; his account is, by his own acknowledgement, more pragmatic and descriptive than universal (Keegan 2018: 386). Indeed, Lavery points out that '[t]rans studies [. . .] theorizes many non-binary and genderqueer positions whose relation to queer theory is one of belonging and fellow-travelling – and many (perhaps most; perhaps all) trans people are also, obviously, queer' (Lavery 2019: 3 of 8 paras). The discussions of queer theology and fantasy undertaken in this chapter and in the conclusion to this book intersect, at many points, with transgender, non-binary and genderqueer experiences of embodiment, many of them articulated by theorists, artists and fantasy writers – including Judith Butler, Jack Halberstam, Sasha Velour, Kai Cheng Thom and Neon Yang – who are both transgender and queer. Nevertheless, 'queer' and 'trans' are not synonyms for one another, and to the extent that 'trans' can be said to be included within 'queer', it is as part of an embodied, coalitional politics and not as a mere symptom of what 'queer' describes. Likewise, I cannot claim, in this chapter, to provide a full account of fantasy literature's theological potential, such as it may exist, from a transgender standpoint, even if at times fantasy's queer theological resonances may seem to overlap with such aims. In this area, I hope that my analysis points to openings for further study and critique by scholars who are thoroughly grounded in transgender experience, community and struggle.[6]

Queering theology

Queer's embrace of instability and incoherence when it comes to identity, its deconstructive ambivalence towards positive representation and its affirmation of structures of desire rendered illegible within totalizing systems of thought, all pose significant challenges for theology. For one thing, Tonstad notes that many church communities 'are concerned with faithful reproduction, which often takes two different forms: (1) faithfulness to established doctrine and (2) a concern for purity that expresses itself by determining who is allowed to approach the eucharistic table and how' (Tonstad 2018: 124). Within such communities, queer theory's rejection of purity discourses, and its demonstration of the contingency of cultural and institutional practices, especially those related to gender and sexuality, may appear as a threat to the foundations of their religious identities (and in many ways, this is not wholly incorrect). For another, as the discussion of Indecent Theology in this section will show, queer criticism has a habit of unearthing inextricable links between sexual desire, gender norms, religious doctrines, familial orders and socio-economic structures where no such connection may have been presumed to exist. In practice, this means that even those religious communities that nominally affirm LGBTQ+ identities and relationships and acknowledge the non-finality of any of their language and metaphors for God are subject to queer scrutiny and critique when it comes to the traditions they reproduce. While this chapter will be unable to provide an exhaustive account of how queer theologies have contended with these issues, an overview of some notable approaches to queer theology is necessary for understanding what fantasy literature and queer theology can offer to each other.

In this endeavour, Althaus-Reid's groundbreaking project of Indecent Theology and Tonstad's more recent queer intervention into trinitarian theology are both indispensable resources. Both theologians emphasize, again and again, theology's need not merely to be revised or expanded but to be re-imagined, and both of them acknowledge the deconstructive attention that must be paid to existing theological structures and religious institutions in order to construct alternative imaginaries that pave the way for a liberatory praxis. Both are also concerned with how queer theology can engage with alterity as simultaneously religious, ethical and political. What follows in the remainder of this section is an account of the particular theological strategies outlined by Althaus-Reid and Tonstad, which I will draw on and reference in my examination of fantasy's relationship to queer theology. This discussion will also include references to two fantasy short stories, Samuel R. Delany's 'The Tale of Potters and Dragons' (1979) and Kai Cheng Thom's 'i shall remain' (2019), in order to demonstrate how Althaus-Reid and Tonstad's strategies for queering theology can be embodied in literature.

Undressing orthodoxy: Althaus-Reid's Indecent Theology

Marcella Althaus-Reid has famously described her particular queer theological project as 'theology without underwear', drawing on the image of an indigenous woman in Althaus-Reid's native Argentina who goes without underwear as she sells lemons so that 'her musky smell may be confused with that of her basket of lemons, in a metaphor that brings together sexuality and economics' (Althaus-Reid 2000: 1–2). Aside from the scandalous image such a metaphor conjures in the context of religious life, it is also intended to provoke an interrogation of how poverty and sexual marginality are inseparably co-implicated with one another as well as with theological systems. Rather than a widening of the pool of religious inclusion, queer theology for Althaus-Reid consists of a deconstructive 'undressing' (Althaus-Reid 2000: 18) of hegemonic theological imaginaries to reveal incoherences, discontinuities and exclusions inherent both in their constructions of gender and sexuality, and in the distribution of power within religious communities and in God–human relations. Such uncoverings are indecent because they expose the inevitable non-neutrality of theological constructions. They demonstrate that the way 'religious Grand Narratives displace sexual discourses according to the criteria of capital and production [...] confers propriety, decorum, decency to our theological discourses' (Althaus-Reid 2000: 18). This opens up a space for reclaiming the body, its desires and its sexual acts – particularly when those bodies are queer, transgender, female or colonized, and particularly when they exist at intersections of the above – as the loci for theological re-invention.

This practice of theological undressing is crucially distinct from the normative and rehabilitative positions that discourses of inclusivity tend to privilege. Theological undressing is not simply a matter of stripping back the garments of doctrine to demonstrate that God, Christianity, the Bible or the sacraments were always 'really' queer all along. On the contrary, it reveals that heteronormativity and the Christian theological tradition cannot be easily disentangled from one another, that, for instance, '[t]here is no pure, incorruptible and unique, coherent Jesus beyond the law of sexual regulation of heterosexual Systematic Theology' (Althaus-Reid 2000: 110). Yet as Althaus-Reid also shows, '[e]very discourse of religious and political authority hides under its skirts suppressed knowledge in exile, which is marginal and indirect speech', articulated through 'religious and political counter symbols and mythological contradictions of the official versions' (Althaus-Reid 2000: 20). In Derridean fashion, these queer counter-narratives point 'not to a beginning of sexual resistance fixed in time' nor to an ultimate transcendence of gender and sexuality, 'but to the several openings which were suppressed or calmed down in the process of the hegemonisation of meaning' (Althaus-Reid 2000: 20). Indecent Theology, in other words, undresses precisely by dressing itself in the often piecemeal and mismatched garb unceremoniously cast aside by heterosexual theology, unsettling the latter's presumed inevitability while revealing alternate possibilities.

In searching for subversive ways of inhabiting theology, Althaus-Reid is often drawn to indigenous spiritual practices suppressed by the Christian orthodoxy of settler colonialism, many of which have persisted in hybrid forms among poor communities in Latin America. While Althaus-Reid is under no illusion that pre-colonial traditions constituted a pure space devoid of gendered and sexual oppression, they heavily inform the thought experiments she deploys in her writing to map out potentially liberating sites of theological reflection. If there is a literary mode that this practice closely resembles, it is fantasy fiction. Though it is not always necessarily tied to postcolonial critical activity, and should not be conflated with real indigenous practices in the primary world, fantasy, too, is invested in creating hybrids.[7] Fantasy specializes in displacing and recombining religious and mythic figures, characters and symbols into new configurations and contexts. Whether their relationship to Western Christian orthodoxy is overt as in *The Passion of New Eve*, implicit like much of Le Guin's fiction or somewhere in between, such as N. K. Jemisin's *Inheritance* trilogy (2010–11), numerous fantasy texts undress theological concepts by giving them unfamiliar forms and placing them in unfamiliar gendered and sexual contexts. I will return to this point later to show how fantasy can be understood as theology in drag, extending the queer theological project Althaus-Reid undertakes. A further account of that project is needed, however, before such an argument can be made.

Chief among the disrobings performed by Indecent Theology is its revelation that matters of the 'spirit', as distanced from and diametrically opposed to the 'body' in Western hetero-patriarchal theologies, are in fact always already matters of the body. To this extent, Althaus-Reid's theological project broadly arises out of Irigaray's demonstration that all theology is unavoidably incarnational and sexual, as well as her interrogation of whose bodies are granted representation and legitimacy within a theological paradigm, and furthermore whose bodily desires and pleasure structure the prevailing theological imaginaries in the West. Yet Althaus-Reid goes further than Irigaray in her subversive play on the morphology of divine and human bodies and the sexual positions they assume in relation to each other. Rejecting both the universal heterosexual configuration prescribed by Irigaray and the transcendent platitudes espoused by her peers in queer theology, Althaus-Reid's glimpses underneath the skirts of theology prompt questions such as, 'Why not God the faggot? Why not Mary the Queer of Heaven?' (Althaus-Reid 2000: 67–8). Taking incarnation seriously within theology, as understood by Althaus-Reid, involves not only interrogating the gendered construction of divinity but also recognizing that 'we need a Christ in a lesbian love story, or homosexual or bisexual, even among the transsexual people of our society' (Althaus-Reid 2004: 94).

Fantasy's potential to re-imagine biblical narratives through a sexually subversive emphasis on the body and gender play in this way can be observed in Samuel R. Delany's short story 'The Tale of Potters and Dragons' (1979), part of his *Return to Nevèrÿon* cycle (1976–94). As Jes Battis has noted, the world of Nevèrÿon is one in which 'Delany juxtaposes the grammar of capitalist production, as seen from multiple perspectives, against the difficult and sometimes impossible conjugation of fetishes and desires, in order to expose the embeddedness of the market within the motions of sexuality (and vice-versa)' (Battis 2009: 478). For this reason, the entire series can already be understood as 'indecent' in the way that Althaus-Reid deploys the term, but 'The Tale of Potters and Dragons' explicitly situates theology in the midst of the conflicting economies of desire its characters must navigate. The tale follows three characters whose paths cross as they travel to the remote Garth Peninsula on business with the mysterious Lord Aldamir: Bayle and Norema, who are competing mercantile apprentices each hoping to secure a trade deal with the fabled lord, and Raven, a foreign mercenary hired by another noble to assassinate him. During their ship's journey from the port city of Kolhari, the sailors entreat Raven, who hails from the matriarchal society of the Western Crevasse, to 'tell [. . .] the tale – of how your western god made the world and the trees and flowers and men and women' (Delany [1979] 1988: 225). After initially refusing, tauntingly insisting that 'it is not a man's story. It is for women' (Delany [1979] 1988: 226), Raven finally relents after Norema asks her to tell the story.

Raven's tale is immediately recognizable to readers as a gender-inverted variation on the biblical narratives of Creation and Fall from the first three chapters of Genesis, with language that also riffs on the first chapter of John's Gospel. God here is gendered as female, and rather than John's logocentric proclamation that '[i]n the beginning was the Word, and the Word was with God, and the Word was God' (Jn 1.1, NRSV), Raven begins her story by saying, 'In the beginning was the act [. . .] and the act was within the womb of god' (Delany [1979] 1988: 227). Likewise, god's act of creating the world is narrated with startlingly visceral bodily imagery:

> Then she breathed the winds from her nostrils and voided her bowels and bladder to make the bitter soil and the salt seas. And she vomited her bile, green and brown, out upon the water and upon the land, and the shapes in which it fell became models for the animals and trees and fish and flying and crawling insects and birds and worms and mollusks that live about the earth and water and air. And god modelled the animals all from the flesh of her body.
>
> (Delany [1979] 1988: 227)

Instead of the first man and woman, Adam and Eve, of the biblical creation narrative, the god of Raven's tale creates two women, Jevim and Eif'h (the latter of which is phonetically reminiscent of 'Eve'). Although, as in Genesis, the Fall of humanity in Raven's story is caused by an act of disobedience to god, her tale makes clear that this disobedience manifests in a failure to recognize that 'the act is always manifest in diversity, difference, and distinction' (Delany [1979] 1988: 229). Rather than praise god by honouring difference in creation, Eif'h searches for the 'pure and unpolluted essence of the act' (Delany [1979] 1988: 229) and sits in adoration of the sun and stars, admonishing Jevim to '[e]at not of the apple nor the pomegranate nor the mango nor the peach. Rather, worship the act only in its purest manifestation' (Delany [1979] 1988: 230–1).

Whereas the biblical narrative of the Fall positions sin as a consequence of Adam and Eve's reliance on their own wisdom rather than God's in their eating of the fruit from the Tree of the Knowledge of Good and Evil, Raven's story inverts this motif to suggest that Eif'h and Jevim's original sin is their neglect of the fruit, which signifies their failure to attend to the embodied communion with difference that is the driving impulse of god's creation. The fullness of god's being, in this story, is not to be found in unblemished purity but in the impure chaos of embodied existence and to suggest otherwise is idolatry. Rather than end the story with the woman Eve bearing the blame for humanity's descent into sinful nature, Raven's tale ends with god beating Eif'h until her body bears signifiers of masculinity:

> And where god beat her on the face, coarse hairs sprouted; and where god beat her on the throat, her voice roughened and went deep; and where god beat her about the breasts, the very flesh and organs were torn away so that she could no longer suckle her daughters; and where god beat her about the groin, her womb was broken and collapsed on itself, and rags of flesh fell, dangling, from her loins, so that when they healed, her womb was forever sealed and useless, and the rags of flesh hanging between her legs were forever sore and sensitive, so that Eif'h was forever touching and ministering to them, whereupon they would leak their infectious pus.
>
> (Delany [1979] 1988: 232)

Whereas the consequence of the Christian reading of the creation narrative from Genesis has historically been that women and femininity have been stigmatized and denigrated, Raven's story not only displaces this stigma onto the (cisgender) male body but places the very emergence of masculinity (and, by extension, heterosexuality) at the moment of humanity's fall. The very word 'man', when spoken by Raven, is styled as ''man, to indicate that in the language of the Western Crevasse, the word for 'man' is a diminutive that translates as 'broken woman' (Delany [1979] 1988: 232). The subversion of scripture that this story signifies is also a double-subversion, as Raven implies that what we are reading is not a revisionist writing of primary-world scripture but a covered-over original, saying that 'the 'men in this strange and terrible land will try to take even this tale and turn it to their own, distorted purposes, be it Eif'h's name or Jevim's apple' (Delany [1979] 1988: 234–5).

Although Raven's story hints at the deconstruction of gender and sexuality at points, privileging lesbian affection and de-coupling childbearing from heterosexual intimacy, taken on its own it often reads more like the essentialist feminist myths of origin parodied by Carter in *The Passion of New Eve*. The story's preoccupation with an original, its implicit anatomical determinism regarding gender and naturalization of certain structures of relation and its simple inversion of patriarchal hierarchies are at first glance difficult to square with the deconstructive queering of scripture that Althaus-Reid advocates. What allows this narrative to become not simply an inversion of the Genesis creation story's motifs but a queer undressing of its sexual politics are the layers of ambivalence and metafiction in which Delany shrouds the tale. Upon hearing it, Norema is horrified, saying to Raven, 'But what must a story like that do to your men? [. . .]

[I]t seems as if it tries to cut them down at every turn' (Delany [1979] 1988: 236). To this, Raven replies that 'our way is the natural way ordained by god herself, whereas I have no idea whose set of social accidents and economic anomalies have contoured the ways of your odd and awkward land' (Delany [1979] 1988: 236). By staging a theological dialogue between these two women that is an inverted mirror image (a common motif in the Nevèrÿon series) of the patriarchal and heterosexual assumptions of doctrine in the primary world, Delany unsettles the very notion of divinely ordained norms of gender and sexuality themselves. Raven's statement that the patriarchal norms taken to be divinely mandated in our world are in fact caught in the web of capital and social relations reveals more than she intends; it threatens to unravel the bodily politics and economics hidden under the skirts of all invocations of divine law, including Raven's own. To the queer reader, this may prove a balm similar to the eerie calm Bayle experiences, unable to reconcile his conscious discomfort with his bodily sense that 'somehow the tenseness the tale had produced in him had settled his whole insides [. . .] as though the tale had been a healing spell!' (Delany [1979] 1988: 235).

Delany also crucially casts the finality of this 'undressing' – the implication that Raven's tale is an original of which our biblical creation myth is a co-opted copy – into further uncertainty, thanks to the meta-fictional conceit of Nevèrÿon itself. The text of Delany's series is regularly interrupted with scholarly asides by S. L. Kermit and K. Leslie Steiner (both avatars of Delany himself), explaining that the tales are ostensibly adaptations of an immeasurably ancient text known as 'the Culhar' Fragment' (Delany [1979] 1988: 11) which is thought to be one of the oldest known pieces of written text. The Fragment is, however, an entirely fictional fabrication in the text, which frustrates any claims to antiquity present within Delany's text, whose setting likewise seems fluid and unstable in terms of its relatability to any primary-world location or historical period. Even the name Nevèrÿon underscores the text's awareness of itself as a fantasy. Kermit comments on a place name in the Culhar' Fragment that could be variously translated as 'across never', 'across when', 'a distant once', 'far never' or 'far when' (Delany [1979] 1988: 323), and the name Nevèrÿon phonetically sounds like *never yon*, all of these names evoking a distant time or place that never existed: in other words, a fantastic secondary world. The space Raven's tale occupies in the text of *Return to Nevèrÿon* thus lifts the skirts of theological storytelling not to reveal a hidden 'truth' underneath but to point to the deferral of theology's claims to ultimacy as contingent on the organization of bodies within relations of society and capital.

Similarly, while Althaus-Reid insists on the necessary particularity of queer readings of scripture and church tradition, they are never to be taken as settled or final. On the contrary, the practical framework in which Indecent Theology is undertaken is both bisexual and polyamorous; that is, 'independently of the sexual identity of the theologian as an individual' (Althaus-Reid 2003: 15), Indecent Theology is bisexual insofar as its desires and imagination regarding loving relations between humanity and God extend in a variety of directions and thus 'cannot be pinned down in a stable or fixed way' (Althaus-Reid 2003: 16). It is also polyamorous in its capacity to hold together and negotiate between multiple, discontinuous configurations of theological imaginaries and/as sexual positions at once, in the process 'permanently introducing "unsuitable" new partners in theology' (Althaus-Reid 2003: 17). Althaus-Reid does not mean here that bisexuals and people who practise polyamory are necessarily more adept at relating to multiplicity and plurality than those who do not or that the theologian's own sex life should necessarily include these things; however, as metaphors for an unsettled, sexual theology, bisexuality and polyamory are fruitful. A bisexual, polyamorous approach to theology means that God, church tradition, sexual desire, sacramental ritual, scripture and embodied gender all occupy the same space (whether that space be a church, a nightclub, a slum, a drag show or a sex dungeon) and are not abstract unities to be faithfully reproduced. Rather, they are fluidly and performatively enacted in the everyday lives of queer people. This is theology for

> sexual dissenters whose theological community is made up of the gathering of those who go to gay bars with rosaries in their pockets, or who make camp chapels of their living rooms simply because there is a cry in their lives, and a theological cry, which refuses to fit life into different compartments.
>
> (Althaus-Reid 2003: 2)

Queer theology as envisioned by Althaus-Reid is a theology in which people's chaotic, everyday sexual lives are the starting point for reflection on God incarnate and Christian ethics and not the other way around. Its resistance to the prescriptiveness of a heterosexual, cisgender, male incarnation means that the images of God it posits are as restless, contingent and unpredictable as the desires of its subjects.

To the practitioner of Indecent Theology, then, the body of Christ (referring both to Christ as an embodied figuration of God and to the church as Christ's body on earth) is an irreducible multitude of bodies that touch and brush up against each other in unexpected ways in a virtually inexhaustible variety of loving embraces, although the theological implications of such exchanges need to be thought through at every stage.[8] Bodies' positions in relation to each other, after all, are where gendered and sexual notions of divine authority, and the hierarchies they serve to structure within religious institutions, are made manifest. Althaus-Reid notes that a ritual gesture such as kneeling at the Eucharist can lead to reflection on 'positions of subordination and sites of possible homo- and hetero-seductions, because these are theologically distributed around the axis of the priesthood's male genitalia' (Althaus-Reid 2003: 11). In this instance, the position assumed by communicants in relation to the priest's penis is a literalization of the phal(logo)centric construction of divine knowledge within the church, to say nothing of the by now exhaustively documented instances of sexual abuse in the global Catholic Church that it calls to mind. Indecent Theology acknowledges that Christianity as an institution has historically favoured organizations of bodies (to give two more examples, reproductive sex and the heterosexual nuclear family) that serve to reaffirm industrial capitalistic regimes, and sacralized them to the exclusion and subjugation of alternative socio-sexual orders in an effort to maintain colonial and class hegemony. Its energies are thus concerned with affirming the unique sacredness of bodies in non-(re)productive rebellion that refuse to stay put or abide by preordained moral codes.

Althaus-Reid's practice of theology without underwear is 'not the improvement of a current theology through some addenda such as gender and sexual equality, but a theology with a serious Queer materialist revision of its methods and doctrines' (Althaus-Reid 2003: 148). Such a pursuit is 'costly: it is neither a fashionable game nor an occasional transgressive sexual distraction', but asks the theologian always to consider that '[t]here are real bodies present in our discourses and these are bodies of economic suffering and sexual oppression' (Althaus-Reid 2003: 110). Indecent Theology's demand that its practitioners dismantle patriarchal, hetero- and cis-sexist constructions of God and the authoritative understandings of scripture and church doctrine that accompany them means, in one sense, that the indecent theologian is a nomadic wanderer without a home or a lover whose appetites are never fully satisfied. In another, however, it allows us to consider what queer religion without the expectation of assimilation into dominant structures might entail, and the possibilities this offers, contingent though they are, are also potentially liberating and joyous for those already consigned to the closet or forced into exile and alienation by religious authorities. By betraying the patriarchal God of heterosexuality and leaving the confines of his church, Indecent Theology endeavours to liberate 'God as the sexual stranger at the gates of theology' (Althaus-Reid 2003: 60). For Althaus-Reid, the God of queer theology is a god encountered in communities of the sexually oppressed, theology's 'others', whose holiness resides in the disorganization of religious and political systems that place restrictions on people's sexual lives.

Theology of failure: Tonstad's queer messianism

If Althaus-Reid's Indecent Theology demonstrates the role fantastic invention may play in envisioning theologies that threaten heteronormative constructions of reality, Linn Marie Tonstad's queer account of resurrection and apocalypse offers a vision of what this could mean for eucatastrophe in fantasy. As I demonstrated in Chapter 1, Tolkien's investment in eucatastrophe as a feature of fantasy is heavily informed by a Christian hope in the second coming of Christ and shares the anticipatory structure of deconstruction in its provisional figuration of an unlooked-for transformation in the face of the other. Tonstad's theology of the second coming is an attempt to think through a disruptive ethical relation with God-as-other for queer people, particularly queer women. It therefore also carries implications for the role of fantastic eucatastrophe both in deconstructing heterosexual and cisgender norms of desire, relationships and embodiment, and in dramatizing that deconstructive movement. The queer theology Tonstad articulates shares Althaus-Reid's commitment to radically re-visioning theology from a sexually marginalized standpoint, rather than simply reforming or expanding it to be (nominally) more inclusive. Her recent interventions into trinitarian theology have served to demonstrate 'the unexpected ways divine difference gets gendered and sexed, grounding the ultimacy of heterosexuality in the Christian imaginary' (Tonstad 2016: 11). Tonstad follows Althaus-Reid's argument that relations among divine and human persons are understood as sexual positions, and thus theological imaginaries, even those apparently unrelated to gender and sexuality, have material consequences for which forms of love are designated as holy and which bodies are privileged in religious contexts. While her critiques of gendered and sexed representations of the Trinity, particularly the crucified Christ, will be pertinent to this chapter's later discussion of *The Passion of New Eve*, it is her vision for resurrection, the Eucharist and apocalypse that I wish to highlight here.

Tonstad advocates a queer theology premised on 'the apocalyptic logic of nonreproductive trinitarian temporality' (Tonstad 2016: 3); that is, a deconstructive eschatology, premised on neither the simplistic negation nor faithful repetition of identity but instead on the unforeseeable transformation of relationships in bodily communion with God-as-other. In her view, 'the resurrection symbolizes the outcome of [Christ's] entire ministry: the final transformation of human persons through their rematerialization' (Tonstad 2016: 244). The body of the risen Christ prefigures Christianity's eucatastrophic hope of redemption, in which 'God comes close in love to transform human difference from its seemingly inevitable, sinful tendency to turn into competition necessitating self-sacrifice into the possibility of table fellowship in friendship with each other and Jesus' (Tonstad 2016: 238). Importantly for Tonstad, however, '[r]esurrection *disallows* the simple extrapolation of the whole-healed subject', since 'the church has no direct access to Christ's body, for Christ is not only resurrected; he is also ascended' (Tonstad 2016: 263). This leads Tonstad to conclude that '[r]esurrection's representational register requires apophasis and disidentification rather than identification' (Tonstad 2016: 263). Acknowledging its discontinuity with the resurrection and its constant state of anticipation with regard to the transformation of apocalypse allows the church to refuse the reproductive logic that prescribes identity categories and distinguishes between decent and indecent sexual and spiritual practices. Tonstad is clear, however, that 'new creation does not undo the conditions of creation as it was' (Tonstad 2016: 242). Christ's risen body retains the scars of crucifixion, and 'has not become ethereal or vaporous – he eats and drinks, he can be touched' (Tonstad 2016: 243).

In deconstructive terms, we might therefore say that Tonstad figures the apocalyptic second coming of Christ as the advent of the radically other that transforms the current order and initiates a new relation; in her words, '[w]e do not yet know what we shall be; we see through a glass darkly; we live in the time of the already-not-yet' (Tonstad 2016: 242). Christ as the stranger at the gates exceeds any conceivable system of representation and is thus without proper pre-figuration, but in deconstructive fashion the queer church '[figures] the uncontrollability (and free gift-giving) of the other Christ not by abjuring positive claims for itself [. . .] but in its free distribution of the sign of what it neither is nor has: the body of Christ' (Tonstad 2016: 271). In most Christian traditions, this distribution is situated around the banquet table of the Eucharist, in which members of the church enter into communion with the body of Christ (and with each other as fellow members of Christ's body) by partaking of sacramental bread and wine. The Eucharist is a particularly fruitful site of queer theological reflection for Tonstad because of the shifting and expanding bodily borders involved; in her figuration Christ's body does not replace bread and wine, but its boundaries expand to include them, and similarly the body of Christ distributed in the Eucharist also infinitely multiplies to co-inhere in the bodies of communicant worshippers. As she puts it,

> [t]he transformation of materiality signalized in the eucharist, and extending behind the cross in Jesus' statement, 'This *is* my body', signals that multitudes may be present in the same space. The transformation of the body here works with the body's limits to make visible relation without spatialized womb-wounds or penetration. The body's limits do not disappear, but spatial location becomes coinhabitable, and the colocality of different bodies – presence in the same place at the same time – transforms the nature of relationality and community beyond their deformation. One need not move aside to make room for the other, for there is enough space for all.
>
> (Tonstad 2016: 239)

The queer erotics of the Eucharist figured by Tonstad is one in which a relation with God as *tout autre* takes the form of coming-close in pleasurable surface-touches and loving coinhabitance. Yet again, we can see an extension of Irigaray's theological project, but one that is far less prescriptive and certain about the forms taken and spaces occupied by bodies in sacred communion than Irigaray.

Taking up Tonstad's theology of apocalypse as part of a queer theological understanding of fantasy means that, similarly to my discussion of fantastic applications of Irigaray in Chapter 3, eucatastrophe becomes associated with the body and its desires. In the same way that Tonstad's queer church distributes the sign of the resurrected body that it does not possess in the advent of Christ's coming, fantasy literature distributes (and provokes longing for) figurations of an other to which it cannot provide direct, unmediated access in pre-figuration of a transformative communion. From this perspective, the unpredictable transformation of bodily relations that Tonstad envisions finds provisional representation in a variety of fantastic figurations, visions of embodiment commonly understood as impossible in the primary world. One of these is the arrival of the dragon-women, and the transformation of mortality that accompanies them, in the *Earthsea* series, which I discuss in the next section. Another is the psychic orgy scenes in the speculative television series *Sense8* (2015–18) created by Lana and Lilly Wachowski and J. Michael Straczynski, in which eight individuals whose lives span different continents become empathically linked to form a hybrid consciousness known as a 'cluster'. In their sexual encounters with one another and even with those outside their cluster, these sensates' bodily borders become permeable, sharing experiences of pleasure; national borders and global distances dissolve while sites of intimacy become infinitely coinhabitable, and sexual orientations and gender identities become fluid and mutable.

One short story which encapsulates both Althaus-Reid's emphasis on the need to venture outside the gates of normative theology, and Tonstad's investment in a bodily sacrament that resists Christian triumphalism, is Kai Cheng Thom's 'i shall remain' (2019). The story follows a monstrously incarnated goddess exiled from the heavenly 'Shining City' (Cheng 2019: 98) as she tends the wounds of a diseased warlord who comes to her temple offering tribute. The narrative indecently brings together notions of sacrament, sexuality and economy as the nature of the unnamed goddess' healing power invites parallels to the labour of a transgender sex worker. Though in all other respects the goddess' appearance, such as her 'shining scales and head-tails', marks her as other than human, her 'bare breasts and phallus' (Cheng 2019: 99) code her as transfeminine (an identification shared by Cheng herself). The tribute offered by the warlord consists of 'a jangle of metal coins and jewels and computer circuitry' in a gesture that the goddess describes as 'the most ancient of sacraments': 'something that is given up for something granted in return' (Cheng 2019: 100). Furthermore, the goddess states that 'the gift of [her] Divinity is delivered through touch' (Cheng 2019: 102), healing the warlord in an overtly sexualized ritual that 'must always begin, with intimacy. with trust. with sacred exchange' (Cheng 2019: 103), and in which the goddess (with the help of Selen, her gorgon) has to carefully assert her own autonomy against the warlord's attempts to wrest her Divinity from her by force. This healing sacrament is narrated by the goddess as a form of bodily co-inherence as 'deeper and deeper into his body [she dives]' (Cheng 2019: 103), and at the moment of climax, she is transported to the heavenly city from which she is exiled:

> and for a single instant, i am there in the place where i was made. i smell its perfumed air. i see its skies, blue and free of the smog that chokes the Below. i hear its music, taste the sweetness of ambrosia. i soar among the vaulted arches and spires wrought in architecture so glorious that the memory of them still makes me long to weep.
>
> (Cheng 2019: 105)

In this way, Cheng provocatively re-figures communion with Divinity as sexual co-inhabitation as experienced by those most intimately aware of religion's and sexuality's mutual embeddedness within economies of exchange.

Much like Tonstad's figuration of the Eucharist, however, Divinity as possessed and experienced by the goddess is distanced from a triumphalist and hierarchical exercise of divine power that would reproduce patriarchal and heterosexual dynamics. Interspersed with the goddess' account of the healing sacrament in her temple are her reminiscences of her former days as 'Best Beloved, Daddy's Delight, preferred child of the Shining Father by whose Divinity we are all called into Being' (Cheng 2019: 99) and her subsequent exile from that privileged place by her own choice. 'Shining Daddy' (Cheng 2019: 98) is a figuration of divine sovereignty as constructed by patriarchal and heterosexual Christian metaphysics, a lofty and increasingly distant deity who gradually abandons the world Below to a fate of implied climate collapse. When the goddess makes the choice to depart the Shining City to dwell with those Below, Shining Daddy's admonishment that *'you do this by choice, and by choice alone. my love is infinite and unending and you are the one who spurns it'* echoes some Christian understandings of free will, salvation and damnation, with Shining Daddy declaring that *'you need only repent, and you may return to me'* (Cheng 2019: 104). The goddess' departure from heaven provocatively positions her as both Christ and Lucifer, descending to earth to bring salvation and healing to those outside the Shining City's gates at the same time as she is cast out due to her opposition to Shining Daddy's rule. Yet Cheng also complicates this theological re-visioning even further, as the goddess relinquishes her initial aim to enforce her powers of healing and transformation on earth unilaterally. Where once she dreamed of healing humanity by imposing the splendour of her divinity upon the world, she now realizes that this is because Shining Daddy's coercive love has

> found a home in my heart and tried to remake me in His image. i would have ruled the Below with His hand, in His Design, and thought myself free. but i know this now:
> love that you cannot leave is not love.
>
> (Cheng 2019: 106)

In sacrificing her impulse to rule, the unnamed goddess of Cheng's story resists any attempt to straightforwardly read her as a Christ figure per se and paradoxically calls into question the limitations of a love that is limitless in its claims. Likewise, the sacrament the story describes differs from Tonstad's reading of the Eucharist; this is not necessarily a free distribution of the sign of the body but an intimate encounter between bodies mediated by an economy of exchange.

Yet compromised and ambivalent though their encounter is, the goddess and warlord in the story come to embody salvific roles for one another, the goddess in her healing of the warlord's wounds and the warlord in the way this ritual revivifies the goddess with his essence. The warlord, like the goddess, is himself a stranger outside the gates of his society at the same time as he appears to be 'the greatest warlord in the region' (Cheng 2019: 98), his body marked as 'other' by illness and his devotion to the goddess heavily implied to be taboo. Though her status seems to fluidly shift at various points in the story between deity, demon and mortal, the goddess, by the end of the story, seems to embody Tonstad's vision of the church which enables the strangers outside the gates of orthodoxy to embody the promise of divine healing and transformation for one another through its very failure and weakness under the conditions of this world. Although both Cheng and Tonstad share an apocalyptic vision based on an embrace of failure and rejection of mastery, however, Tonstad's formulation carries this further than the ambivalent conclusion of Cheng's story, in which the goddess reaffirms her decision to live among mortals and share their doom with no hope of salvation. Tonstad's queer figuration of the Eucharist, though by no means a 'liturgical magic' (Tonstad 2016: 257) that can guarantee a good relation in advance, is nonetheless a eucatastrophic heralding of the approach of the other and an anticipation of 'banquets without borders' (Tonstad 2016: 239) in the yet-to-come.

Drag(on) theology: Queer incarnations and fantastic embodiment

What might theological undressing entail in fantastic secondary worlds? As the previous chapter in this book showed, fantasy is equipped to offer incarnations other than those prescribed by a patriarchal logic, often deconstructively provoking more radical challenges to hierarchies between masculine and feminine embodiment than may seem readily available within traditional philosophical and theological structures. As I have already hinted, this continues to be the case in queer imaginaries where identity and its relationship to embodiment are self-consciously unstable or in constant flux. Tonstad has commented that, similarly to feminist theology, 'queer theology is often done in and through engagement with artistic and cultural forms', and that 'much of the most interesting work in queer theology takes shape in relation to resources irreducible to the usual theological texts and traditions' (Tonstad 2018: 126). The project of undressing theology is by no means a strictly negative one. Queer theological figurations de-naturalize heterosexual theology by opening possibilities rather than foreclosing them. This section will argue that the distance that fantasy takes up from primary-world structures and institutions can serve to make these possibilities more apparent. Some of the forms of embodiment depicted in fantasy, whether monstrous, marvellous or some combination of both, also have the peculiar ability to perform the fluidity, contingency and liminality of queer figurations, religious or otherwise. In this way, fantasy's relationship to theology can be understood as analogous to that between cis-hetero-normative structures of identification and one of the most long-standing institutions of queer culture: drag. Insofar as fantasy texts dress up theological concepts and personas in strange and often outsized garb in order to deconstruct their relationship to heterosexual and cisgender realities, fantasy literature is theology in drag.

While there currently exists a rich and varied field of scholarship surrounding drag and drag culture, it is necessary to revisit Judith Butler's seminal writing on the topic in order to understand fantasy as a site of theological drag. As stated earlier, Butler argues that gender is not an inherent attribute determined by an internal essence, but rather the effect of 'acts and gestures, articulated and enacted desires [that] create the illusion of an interior and organizing gender core [. . .] for the purposes of the regulation of sexuality within the obligatory frame of reproductive heterosexuality' (Butler [1990] 2007: 185–6). For this reason, Butler claims that 'the gendered body is performative' (Butler [1990] 2007: 185), not in the sense that gender presentation is a conscious *performance* that can be altered at will but in the sense that the entire social framework of gender is constituted by the surface-level attributes and behaviours that purport to be its mere expressions. Butler is not suggesting that gender is a mere falsehood to be discarded wholesale in favour of a more essentially 'true' existence; following Derrida and Cixous, they acknowledge the impossibility of simply leaping outside of or beyond cultural constructions as they exist at present. For them, 'the critical task [. . .] is not to establish a point of view outside of constructed identities' but 'to locate strategies of subversive repetition enabled by those constructions, to affirm the local possibilities of intervention through participating in precisely those practices of repetition that constitute identity and, therefore, present the immanent possibility of contesting them' (Butler [1990] 2007: 201). Butler identifies many different facets of queer culture(s), including 'drag, cross-dressing, and the sexual stylization of butch/femme identities' (Butler [1990] 2007: 187) that offer variations on, alternatives to and parodies of the male–

female configuration of gender, but their primary point of focus in *Gender Trouble* is drag.

Butler elaborates that

> [t]he performance of drag plays upon the distinction between the anatomy of the performer and the gender that is being performed. But we are actually in the presence of three contingent dimensions of significant corporeality: anatomical sex, gender identity, and gender performance. If the anatomy of the performer is already distinct from the gender of the performer, and both of those are distinct from the gender of the performance, then the performance suggests a dissonance not only between sex and performance, but sex and gender, and gender and performance. [. . .] *In imitating gender, drag implicitly reveals the imitative structure of gender itself – as well as its contingency.*
>
> (Butler [1990] 2007: 187)

While drag often gives the appearance, at least at first glance, of a harmonious rehearsal of normative gender, it also has a tendency to draw attention to its own artifice through the disharmonious conjunctions of sexed and gendered signifiers inscribed on the body of the performer. The self-consciously fictive nature of the drag performer's gender presentation provokes reflection on the fictitiousness of all forms of gender identity, opening onto possibilities for thinking gender otherwise than in the highly regulated, essentialist, binary construction prescribed within hetero-patriarchal society. While Butler's later work, most notably *Undoing Gender* (2004), elaborates on and complicates this formulation in articulating the tensions between drag culture, transgender embodiment and intersex struggles for bodily autonomy, they maintain that in all of these instances, 'more important than any presupposition about the plasticity of identity or indeed its retrograde status is queer theory's claim to be opposed to the unwanted legislation of identity' (Butler 2004: 7). The often parodic, often grotesque gender play of drag performances, taken on its own, is indeed an inadequate framework for fully understanding the myriad forms of embodiment and identification arising from transgender, non-binary, genderqueer and intersex experiences. The mainstream popularity and hyper-capitalism of *RuPaul's Drag Race* should also caution us against taking the radically subversive potential of drag as inevitable. Nonetheless, by mocking, subverting and destabilizing the idea of an original or essential gender as well as the norms that solidify around it, drag is able to challenge universalizing social scripts and open onto these other, more wide-ranging and fluid configurations of identity.

Indeed, it becomes clear in Butler's more recent work that what makes drag such a productive site of gender disruption for them is the way its unsettling of prescribed identity categories coincides with its imaginative articulation of new forms of embodiment in relation to gendered norms. What drag shares in common with trans, non-binary, genderqueer and intersex identities is that they 'make us not only question what is real, and what "must" be, but they also show us how the norms that govern contemporary notions of reality can be questioned and how new modes of reality can become instituted' (Butler 2004: 29). Drag does this as a conscious site of slippage that draws attention to the sites of slippage in all gender presentation where such questioning can start. Characterized by surface play as it is, drag has wide-ranging and transformative implications for how gendered embodiment is understood. Butler describes this potential transformation as 'the work of fantasy when we understand fantasy as taking the body as a point of departure for an articulation that is not always constrained by the body as it is' (Butler 2004: 28). Butler's use of 'fantasy' here derives from the psychoanalytic understanding of fantasy as the articulation of an unspoken or otherwise unspeakable desire, extending it into a world-making political stance. Following from the discussion of fantasy *literature*'s potential relationship to marginalized desires outlined in Chapter 2, however, it is also possible to use this formulation as a starting point for examining how fantasy texts might participate in the fluid and imaginative approach to embodiment Butler advocates. In that chapter, I detailed how Cixous draws on the vocabulary of fairy stories and worldbuilding to foster new relations to the embodiment of marginalized subjects, and also to the 'body' as a marginalized and neglected term in theology. What distinguishes fantasy as a literary genre, however, is its creation of new figurations of embodiment, accompanied by their own forms of desire and identification, that exceed what is prescribed as possible in the primary world.

As it dismantles, recombines and reconstitutes elements of the primary world in precisely such a way that throws their fixity and ultimacy into question, fantasy can be understood as theology in drag. Similarly, fantastical hermeneutics might equally be transposed to gender performance; Attebery's definition of the fantastic as 'creative and disruptive play with representations of the real world' (Attebery 2014: 32) could very well be applied to drag. Drag demonstrates that '[g]ender is the mechanism by which notions of masculine and feminine are produced and naturalized, but gender might very well be the apparatus by which such terms are deconstructed and denaturalized' (Butler 2004: 42). The stage of a live drag performance creates parameters in which gender can be turned against itself, in an arguably analogous strategy to the displacement of religious imaginaries into fantastic secondary worlds. Fantasy worlds provide a staging ground in which theological concepts can be dressed in strange garb that de-naturalizes the cisgender and heterosexual inheritances of religious traditions in the primary world. Borrowing theology's mythic register, iconography and concepts, fantasy rearranges them into forms that, in our own world, would be considered at the very least heterodox. In this way, fantasy is able to engage in the mythopoetic activity of religious imagination without being beholden to the prohibitions, decency mechanisms and universalizing tendencies that limit many religious institutions and ensnare their members in endless debates over whose bodies should or should not be included. In secondary worlds, theological figurations can come out of their closets, not to counterpose a fictive exclusionary order against a self-congratulatory queer 'reality', but in Butler's words, 'to challenge the contingent limits of what will and will not be called reality' (Butler 2004: 29). Fantasy, like drag, offers self-consciously unreal figurations of the body, such as the shapeshifting dragons of Earthsea or the similarly fluidly embodied inhabitants of Gethen in *The Left Hand of Darkness*, and in so doing it reveals the contingency of gender prescriptions thought to be absolute in dominant theological orders.

In its drag embodiment of theology, then, fantasy offers radical possibilities for challenging normative identities grounded in theological prescriptions, but the queer imaginaries and figurations it presents are by no means strictly utopian. For all that they trouble the boundary between possible and impossible (or, to borrow Butler's terminology, legible and illegible) embodiment, fantasy, drag and queer theology take as starting points embodied subjects *as they are*, rather than transcending or overwriting them. These are often bodies under threat and subjectivities fractured by internalized homophobia, trauma, frustrated desire and isolation. Butler notes that to be queer 'is to become the other against whom (or against which) the human is made. It is the inhuman, the beyond the human, the less than human, the border that secures the human in its ostensible reality' (Butler 2004: 30). It is thus no surprise that so much of the gender play in contemporary drag is also accompanied by flirtations with the fantastic and the monstrous. This is seen on full display in a 2017 performance by the drag queen Sasha Velour, in which Velour assumes the persona of Gollum as depicted in Peter Jackson's 2001–3 film adaptations of *The Lord of the Rings* while lip-syncing to Kate Bush's 1978 hit song 'Wuthering Heights'.[9] Such a performance highlights how fantastic discourses can be invoked to heighten drag's subversive play on identity and embodiment. As Velour's Gollum first emerges onstage, the performer pantomimes over an audio recording of Andy Serkis's performance of the character in Jackson's films. Immediately a struggle is re-enacted between Gollum's fractured identities: the well-intentioned but timid Sméagol on one hand and the abject creature of greed and malice manifesting the One Ring's power working both over and through Gollum on the other. By inhabiting these plural but antagonistic personas, Velour's performance dramatizes not only the inherent disharmony of identity that all drag enacts but also the heightened sense of disunity experienced by subjects confined to the closet and rendered illegible within the cis-hetero-patriarchal order.

In *The Lord of the Rings*, the One Ring is created by Sauron, a figure associated with monolithic, technocratic control and panoptical surveillance, and usually represented as a single eye atop a tower. While the Ring is on the one hand a manifestation of an external evil, its power primarily manifests by working within the psyches of those who wield it. The Ring also has the power to render its wearer invisible to most people, but with the cost of making them hyper-visible to the Eye of Sauron and placing them further within his control. When Sam puts on the Ring to hide himself from orcs, for instance, he '[feels] afresh, but now more strong and urgent than ever, the malice of the Eye of Mordor' (Tolkien [1954] 2011: 898). Elsewhere, Sauron's gaze is described as 'that growing sense of a hostile will that strove with great power to pierce all shadows of cloud, and earth, and flesh, to see you: to pin you under its deadly gaze, naked, immovable' (Tolkien [1954] 2011: 630). This is experienced by many characters throughout the novel and films, but five hundred years' worth of internalization of the Ring's influence, and of existing under the dominant gaze of Sauron, permanently transforms Sméagol from a hobbit into a monstrous hybrid subject, with the greed for the Ring reigning supreme over Gollum's consciousness.[10]

By displacing this struggle into her drag performance, Sasha Velour provokes comparisons between the violent fracturing of Gollum's subjectivity and the experiences of subjects grappling with the sway that homophobia and transphobia hold over their own presentation. In Velour's hands, the negotiations between invisibility and hyper-visibility experienced by the Ring-bearers invite comparison to '[t]he double-edged potential for injury in the scene of gay coming out' (Sedgwick 1990: 81) identified by Eve Kosofsky Sedgwick. For Sedgwick, the closet is 'that curious space that is both internal and marginal to the culture: centrally representative of its motivating passions and contradictions, even while marginalized by its orthodoxies' (Sedgwick 1990: 56). Like the Ring, it is a tool of hegemony (Sauron in the case of the Ring, compulsory heterosexuality in the case of the closet), offering invisibility and shelter from immediate threat, at the cost of reasserting itself as the structuring force around which identity is organized and negotiated in social spaces. Moreover, the closet's unique status as an articulation of heteronormativity through silences and non-disclosures means that coming out cannot simply happen once. Rather, in Sedgwick's words, 'every encounter [...] erects new closets whose fraught and characteristic laws of optics and physics exact from at least gay people new surveys, new calculations, new draughts and requisitions of secrecy or disclosure' (Sedgwick 1990: 68).

Velour's embodiment of Gollum's split identity can be seen to enact the incoherences and discontinuities revealed in these negotiations of the closet. This subtext is made even more apparent by an awareness of the performer's identity as a genderqueer person whose drag is actually embodied by two alter egos, the feminine Velour and a masculine persona named Alexander Velvet. The voice clips Velour pantomimes occur at a pivotal point in Gollum's internal struggle in the films. As Velour emerges from behind the umbrella that just barely conceals her transformation, Gollum's malevolent side insists, 'We survived because of *me*.' Here, as recontextualized by Velour, the voice of internalized cis-hetero-normativity speaks to urge the queer subject back into the closet for the purposes of survival and self-preservation. The performance segues into the Kate Bush lip-sync after Sméagol, brought back to the fore by the compassion and care of Frodo, attempts to banish the influence of the Ring from his consciousness, commanding it to '[l]eave now and never come back'. Following this (temporary) moment of triumph, the monstrous body of Gollum becomes the site of articulation for the violent and disruptive desires of Emily Brontë's heroine Catherine Earnshaw from *Wuthering Heights*. Subversive play on gender is an integral aspect of this act, but the monstrousness of its embodiment also deliberately takes on the grotesque discourses of representation produced by heteronormativity and binary gender and flaunts them in a transgressive manner. Velour's performance thus shows how fantastic reference points can be used to add even further layers and complexities to the dance between identification and disidentification Butler draws attention to within drag culture.

Double drag: Sacred parody in *The Passion of New Eve*

In the context of theology and fantasy literature, Sasha Velour's use of fantasy in her drag act can lead us to consider how fantasy can offer new ways of envisioning sacred incarnations and desires, without covering over the violence enacted by normative theological constructions. *The Passion of New Eve*, as I argued in Chapter 3, is also concerned with revealing such violence, in this case the violence of theological projects that treat 'woman' as a natural and unified category and restrict women's existence according to the norms of that identity. However, while Carter's fantasy is hostile to any attempt to articulate a theology that stakes claims as to its absolute reality, it does not denigrate the project of theology altogether. Of all the characters in the novel, the Hollywood starlet Tristessa de St Ange comes closest to embodying a type of divine womanhood, and she does so with the self-conscious artificiality of drag. If *The Passion of New Eve* laughs in the face of endeavours to sacralize supposedly 'natural' archetypes of gender, it also affirms embracing the unreality and incoherence of one's own gender and sexuality as a kind of sacred, creative act. Although Tristessa's self-conscious performance of gender cannot offer her, or anyone else, transcendence from the material conditions of oppression, and indeed can even serve to reaffirm them, it also allows her dexterity in navigating the complex web of power relations bound within gender and enables her to find sacredness in their midst.

From the novel's opening, Tristessa is associated with a type of queer sainthood. We learn that she has dedicated her acting career to performing feminine suffering and self-abnegation 'just as a medieval saint points to the wounds of his martyrdom' (Carter [1977] 2012: 2). The ambivalence of this act is also signalled early on, as Tristessa's performed suffering is established as the locus of both heterosexual male fetishization and queer longing. In the novel's opening scene, Evelyn receives fellatio during a screening of Tristessa's *Wuthering Heights*, and this image is juxtaposed with the cinema crowd of 'sentimental queers who, hand in hand, had come to pay homage to the one woman in the world who most perfectly expressed a particular pain as deeply as, more deeply than, any woman' (Carter [1977] 2012: 1). However saintly, though, Tristessa's existence is never anything but fantastical; Evelyn describes her as 'a piece of pure mystification [. . .] as beautiful as only things that don't exist can be' (Carter [1977] 2012: 4). Like Mother, she is a self-created fiction, having made herself into an ephemeral being of light and celluloid. She is, in Evelyn's words, 'the dream made flesh though the flesh I knew her in was not flesh itself but only a moving picture of flesh, real but not substantial' (Carter [1977] 2012: 4). Unlike Mother, however, Tristessa's embodiment of divine womanhood, while it plays a role in shaping Eve's own femininity, makes no claims as to its absoluteness and never presents itself as anything other than a holy fiction. This does not mean that Tristessa's performance of tragic womanhood cannot do harm, and indeed her films are used by Mother to condition Eve into her passive state of femininity, recalling Tonstad's critique of the place of suffering in Christology.[11] Eve's eventual relationship with Tristessa, however, proves to be a fleeting but transformative sacred encounter.

Eve encounters Tristessa in the flesh while kidnapped by the diabolical, aggressively misogynistic poet Zero. Kaveney has described Zero as 'an unholy cross between the macho littérateur and Charles Manson', and argues that 'life in Zero's ménage is a nightmare representation of male desire and [. . .] complicity in one's own oppression' (Kaveney [1994] 2007: 194). He keeps a harem of seven girls who worship him unquestioningly amid his constant sexual and physical abuse of them; Eve observes that '[t]heir seven faces had the unused and blinded look of nuns, all postulants in the church of Zero' (Carter [1977] 2012: 84). Zero, with his violent sexual appetites and mythologization of his own genius, is the embodiment of patriarchal, heterosexual theology taken to ludicrous and darkly parodic extremes. Having just escaped the clutches of Mother, Eve is quick to note that Zero, also, has fashioned himself into an image of godhood, so that 'the ranch-house was Solomon's Temple; the ghost town was the New Jerusalem; the helicopter his chariot of fire, his prick his bow of burning gold, etc etc etc' (Carter [1977] 2012: 97). Zero is on a mission to seek out and destroy Tristessa, whom he accuses of being 'this ultimate dyke' (Carter [1977] 2012: 88) who has 'blasted his seed because he was Masculinity incarnate' and 'magicked away his reproductive capacity via the medium of the cinema screen' (Carter [1977] 2012: 101). Where Tristessa's image of female suffering, fixed by the movie camera's gaze, is revered as a fetishistic object by the male Evelyn and later employed to condition Eve into an ideal of passive womanhood, in Zero's perception she is the queer other who gazes back. Her hyperfemininity and unreality paradoxically threaten to upend the reproductive and masculinist order of his harem.

Coming upon Tristessa's palace of crystal and glass in the desert, in which she has shut herself away in a deep sleep like a fairy-tale heroine, Eve, Zero and the rest of the girls discover that Tristessa possesses a penis when Zero attempts to rape her. This revelation is a troubled one in terms of its treatment in the novel, though this trouble is likely deliberate on Carter's part. Tristessa does not easily map onto any specific gender identity, and in any case, Carter seems less interested in such distinctions than in the way Tristessa's very existence exposes any rigid framework of gender as fictive and unstable, referring to the starlet using masculine and feminine pronouns interchangeably. As Eve reflects,

> [i]f a woman is indeed beautiful only in so far as she incarnates most completely the secret aspirations of man, no wonder Tristessa had been able to become

the most beautiful woman in the world, an unbegotten woman who made no concessions to humanity.

(Carter [1977] 2012: 125)

While it may be tempting to read this statement in essentializing terms, implying that Tristessa's transvestism suggests that s/he enacts male fantasies of archetypal womanhood, I would like to resist this in favour of suggesting that the womanhood that s/he enacts is always already a site of profound dislocation and discontinuity. While Kaveney describes Tristessa as 'the perfect mimic of endured female suffering' (Kaveney [1994] 2007: 195), I would argue that the revelation of Tristessa in the flesh more fundamentally displaces the origins of woman-as-passivity, woman-as-fetish-object and womanhood-as-suffering. Her portrayal as transvestite or drag artist indefinitely suspends the question as to whether the saintly suffering she embodies, already presented to the reader with an alienated distance, originates with her gender presentation or with the violent notions of gender with which multiple characters presume to speak for her. At the very least, Tristessa is no less 'real' than any other woman in the text; Eve's transformation makes clear that in the world of Carter's novel, the real and the synthetic are not mutually exclusive. Yet whereas in the first half of the novel Tristessa exists as an archetypal, if unattainable, ideal of womanhood, towards the end of the text s/he signals the incoherence of 'woman' as a category.

As if literalizing the dissolution of identity categories that Tristessa's presence in the novel signifies, Zero's girls begin laying waste to her palace and staging a forced, demented wedding ceremony between Eve and Tristessa, with Eve dressed in a suit and Tristessa in a white gown. Eve notes the peculiarity of the 'double drag' in which she is dressed thus:

This young buck, this Baudelairean dandy so elegant and trim in his evening clothes – it seemed, at first glance, I had become my old self again in the inverted world of the mirrors. But this masquerade was more than skin deep. Under the mask of maleness I wore another mask of femaleness but a mask that now I never would be able to remove, no matter how hard I tried, although I was a boy disguised as a girl and now disguised as a girl again[.]

(Carter [1977] 2012: 129)

The multiple layers of 'masks' that Eve notes on herself, with no sign of an original, call to mind the multiple levels of identity subversion that Butler identifies in any drag performance. In both cases, the question of 'reality' regarding gender becomes displaced and rendered, if not irrelevant, then at least beside the point. Indeed, as Jordan notes, Butler's deconstruction of 'the opposition between what is "natural" and what is "artificial"' is 'already implicit and explored in Carter's writing' (Jordan [1994] 2007: 202). In *The Passion of New Eve*, artifice is ultimately what creates and shapes the real. Likewise, while there may be scope to critique Tristessa's deployment in the text as a symbol of queer disruption, the overall narrative arc of Carter's text suggests that people cannot help but enact, even if by way of deconstruction, the ideals and archetypes that proliferate in the world they inhabit. Tristessa may serve as the text's most overt instance of gender subversion (as opposed to Eve's forced gender transition), but as Kaveney argues, the scene of double drag demonstrates that 'three-piece suits are drag as much as sequin frocks' (Kaveney [1994] 2007: 195).

For this reason, the ubiquity of artifice in the text does not preclude the ethical encounter with the other, nor the experience of the sacred within such an encounter. Eventually, Eve and Tristessa manage to escape Zero and his harem, stealing away into the middle of the desert, where they enter into a sexual embrace that evokes the collusion of bodies that characterizes Tonstad's reading of the Eucharist. Here, in the heart of the desert, words and forms dissolve for Eve as she asks, 'How can I find words the equivalent of this mute speech of flesh as we folded ourselves within a single self in the desert, under our dappled canopy, on our bed of filthy cushions?' (Carter [1977] 2012: 144). Dressed in the drag that constitutes both their identities, the two lovers initiate a sacramental, mutually transforming relation of unbecoming. This particular moment of transcendence is not an escape from the parade of carnivalesque disguises and larger-than-life personas that populate the rest of the novel; it is in fact enabled by them. The crossing and re-crossing of gender boundaries that Eve and Tristessa perform within their own identities find their culmination in this moment, as Eve wonders that

> what the nature of masculine and the nature of feminine might be, whether they involve male and female, if they have anything to do with Tristessa's so long neglected apparatus or my own factory fresh incision and engine-turned breasts, that I do not know. Though I have been both man and woman, still I do not know the answer to these questions. Still they bewilder me.
> (Carter [1977] 2012: 146)

In the conscious performance of the fantasy of gender, and in their seeming ability to inhabit multiple forms at once, Eve and Tristessa enter into sacred communion with one another in the midst of their marginalization. The moment does not last; soon after, Tristessa is killed by the evangelical child soldiers I discussed in Chapter 1. This suggests that, while the imagination of Carter's text may be a queer one, the novel also retains a real sense of the precarity and threat of violence that mark queer existences in the primary world – something that will also be discussed later in this chapter as it relates to the *Earthsea* series. Yet in this way, Tristessa comes to embody Althaus-Reid's notion of the queer saint as 'an outsider to society, not in the sense of failing to participate actively in the political life of her community, but due to her dissenting role' (Althaus-Reid 2003: 160). Such dissent in 'the sainthood of the Other gives rise to stories Christian theology cannot hear without modifying or editing' (Althaus-Reid 2003: 161), in the same way that Tristessa's gender dissidence has been covered over and tamed into an image of beatific sexual submission in her films. *The Passion of New Eve* offers a glimpse, however fleeting, of how embracing queer multiplicity and disharmony can open onto loving relations outside the gates of decency.

Queer failure in/as worldbuilding: Mystical perversions in *The Left Hand of Darkness*

While *The Passion of New Eve* depicts literal instances of drag to dramatize its characters' embattled relationship with normative gender and sexuality, *The Left Hand of Darkness* undertakes the much more ambitious pursuit of constructing an entire world whose configurations of gender and sexuality disrupt those of the primary world, exceeding even the categories and norms that solidify around queer discourses. It would be tempting to read the text's invention of a world without binary gender as itself queer and end the analysis there. To be sure, there is plenty of discussion to be had about how the genderfluid societies on Gethen de-naturalize dimorphic understandings of sex and gender, and, to a lesser extent, heterosexuality. This section will partly serve as an examination of how the fictional religious orders of Gethen, the Handdara and the Yomesh cult provide a fruitful illustration of how fantastic worldbuilding can function as a re-visioning of theology without binary gender or compulsory heterosexuality. Moreover, this potential for re-visioning is not only present in the concrete gender and sexually different aspects of society in Karhide and Orgoreyn; the text's own failures of language surrounding gender and sexuality also prove to be productive sites of queer disruption and re-invention. However, I also argue that *The Left Hand of Darkness* goes even further than this to trouble the designations of 'normative' and 'queer' themselves, showing how secondary worlds can destabilize and even invert where these terms are located in their social orders.

Social and sexual practices, body morphologies and presentations that may well read as queer in the primary world constitute the basic customs that govern everyday life on Gethen. Conversely, experiences of gender and sexuality considered normative in our world are defamiliarized as perversely queer in Le Guin's novel. Yet, as I will also show in my analysis, *The Left Hand of Darkness*' theological imagination enables and even demands an openness to perversion as a crucial facet of religious life, although how this manifests in Gethenian religious practices themselves is treated with considerable ambivalence.

A reading of Gethen as a queer secondary world is most obviously enabled by the novel's positioning of Genly Ai, who hails from Terra (or Earth), as its primary narrator. As I note in previous chapters, Genly's narrative voice provides the text with its audience surrogate for whom the Gethenians are inscrutably other, and nowhere is this more apparent than in the text's approach to gender. While my analysis in Chapter 2 focused primarily on how Genly tends to read anything unfamiliar to him about the Gethenians as 'feminine' (according to patriarchal definitions of femininity similar to those identified by Cixous), I want to make a slightly different point here. Genly's narration also highlights how the Gethenians' gender difference eludes conceptual and linguistic categories present in the primary world. He comments early on in the novel that although he has been on Gethen for two years, he is still unable to understand Gethenians on their own terms, instead 'self-consciously seeing a Gethenian first as a man, then as a woman, forcing [them] into those categories so irrelevant to [their] nature and so essential to my own' (Le Guin [1969] 2010: 12). Genly's remarks here closely parallel Alder's inability to see both of Tehanu's 'faces' at once in *The Other Wind*, which will be discussed in the next section, and they invite consideration of how the Gethenians' gender identities and sexual practices sit athwart designations familiar to Le Guin, her readers and her narrator. While I have deliberately chosen, in keeping with Le Guin's criticism of her own text, to use singular 'they/them' pronouns to refer to Gethenians in most of my quotations of the novel, it is an unavoidable fact that much of Genly's narration cannot help but fall back on references to primary-world, binary gender attributes. As a result, the novel contains numerous instances of what could be called linguistic drag. Genly's narration locates various Gethenian people at multiple, disparate sites of cis-hetero-normative gender identification at once, and in doing this it draws attention to the contingency, discontinuity and ultimate inadequacy of such associations. At one point, for instance, Genly refers to his 'landlady, a voluble man' (Le Guin [1969] 2010: 49) who is 'so feminine in looks and manner that I once asked [them] how many children [they] had' (Le Guin [1969] 2010:

50). The 'landlady' replies that '[they] had never born any. [They] had, however, sired four' (Le Guin [1969] 2010: 50). Elsewhere, in one of the most iconic lines from the novel, Genly declares, matter-of-factly, 'The king was pregnant' (Le Guin [1969] 2010: 106). The androgynous, fluid embodiment shaping Gethenian existence, while familiar and commonplace to Gethenians, reads as a series of transgressions of gender categories and subversions of expectations when narrated by the Terran Genly.

Of course, many of the gender transgressions Genly inscribes onto his portrait of Gethenian life do, when taken in isolation, have parallels in the primary world. There are, for instance, trans men (as well as masculine-presenting cisgender women and non-binary people) who become pregnant and bear children, and people who read as feminine (including trans women, as well as femme-presenting cisgender men and non-binary people) who 'sire' them. Yet what is striking about the genderqueer society Le Guin constructs is that the embodied lives of her subjects, when taken as a whole, frustrate any attempt to map them directly onto primary-world LGBTQ+ identities, including those that have come into common usage in the years since *The Left Hand of Darkness* was first published in 1969. The Gethenians' monthly cycles of kemmer, which are the only periods in which they experience sexual desire, and the unpredictable shifts in their anatomical features during sexual intimacy, are fantastical inventions that disrupt configurations of the body familiar to most readers. While aspects of the novel's worldbuilding may hold applicability for the experiences of many trans, non-binary, genderqueer and intersex people, the text is less interested in providing direct representational analogues to these identities than, in Butlerian fashion, challenging more wide-ranging systems of representation of gender and embodiment themselves.

A dissonance is thus created in the text, between its ambition to envision both a secondary world without the construction of gender present in the primary world and new forms of embodiment on the one hand, and the impossibility of transcending a language and cultural paradigm that is inescapably gendered along cis-hetero-patriarchal lines on the other. As seen earlier, the novel is able partially to navigate the latter by dramatizing this impasse through Genly's narration, but there are still textual slips in which heteronormativity and sexual dimorphism creep into its language and worldbuilding. As one example, the novel takes its title from Tormer's Lay, a Handdara song recited by Therem Harth rem ir Estraven as they travel across the Gobrin Ice with Genly:

Light is the left hand of darkness
and darkness the right hand of light.

> *Two are one, life and death, lying*
> *together like lovers in kemmer,*
> *like hands joined together,*
> *like the end and the way.*
>
> (Le Guin [1969] 2010: 252)

These lines of verse articulate the foundational Handdara principle of encounter with the irreducibly other, which I read with reference to a deconstructive reading of Emmanuel Levinas's theological ethics in Chapter 1. The novel also genders this theology of alterity as one explicitly related to sexual difference – specifically, the sexual difference within the 'same' of Gethenian identity. Much later on their journey, Genly draws the symbol of a yin–yang to illustrate the verse, saying, 'Light, dark. Fear, courage. Cold, warmth. Female, male. It is yourself, Therem. Both and one. A shadow on snow' (Le Guin [1969] 2010: 287). Le Guin employs this yin–yang formulation as a way both of preserving alterity without assimilation or mastery in the face-to-face encounter and in relating to the heterogeneity inherent in all subjectivity. While it is offered as a more confluent and fluid relationship to alterity than rigid, binary configurations of self and other, it still installs a dualistic model of gender into the Gethenians' identities, at a moment in the text when Genly should be coming to a less reductive understanding of them. This is, from one perspective, exacerbated by the implicit dimorphism of the Gethenians' sexual encounters in the novel. As the anthropologist Ong Tot Oppong states in her field notes, when a Gethenian finds a partner in kemmer,

> [t]he genitals engorge or shrink accordingly, foreplay intensifies, and the partner, triggered by the change, takes on the other sexual role (? without exception? If there are exceptions, resulting in kemmer-partners of the same sex, they are so rare as to be ignored).
>
> (Le Guin [1969] 2010: 96)

Le Guin herself acknowledges in revisiting her text that this detail of worldbuilding 'unnecessarily locked the Gethenians into heterosexuality', and that '[i]n any kemmerhouse homosexual practice would, of course, be possible and acceptable and welcomed' (Le Guin, [1981] 1989: 14).

A queer reading of *The Left Hand of Darkness* may rightly identify these shortcomings in the novel's language and worldbuilding as failures of imagination. And yet, as Jack Halberstam's theoretical work has served to demonstrate, queer readers need not be confined to culturally dominant modes of approaching such failures – that is, as something to be discarded, written off or else covered over in favour of more successful, (re)productive endeavours. In his words,

> [u]nder certain circumstances failing, losing, forgetting, unmaking, undoing, unbecoming, not knowing may in fact offer more creative, more cooperative, more surprising ways of being in the world. [. . .] In fact if success requires so much effort, then maybe failure is easier in the long run and offers different rewards.
>
> (Halberstam 2011: 3)

For Halberstam, failure is particularly generative in queer and feminist contexts because it 'allows us to escape the punishing norms that discipline behaviour and manage human development with the goal of delivering us from unruly childhoods to orderly and predictable adulthoods' (Halberstam 2011: 3). For instance, 'gender failure often means being relieved of the pressure to measure up to patriarchal ideals' (Halberstam 2011: 4). Failure, in other words, marks a deliberate refusal of what Althaus-Reid has termed the 'decency mechanisms' (Althaus-Reid 2000: 92) of normative society, which subordinate the chaotically embodied lives of subjects to abstract standards whereby success is measured. As Halberstam elaborates,

> [h]eteronormative common sense leads to the equation of success with advancement, capital accumulation, family, ethical conduct, and hope. Other subordinate, queer, or counterhegemonic modes of common sense lead to the association of failure with nonconformity, anticapitalist practices, nonreproductive lifestyles, negativity, and critique.
>
> (Halberstam 2011: 89)

As a framework for queer reading, particularly in a queer theological context, failure allows us to more fully embrace indecency as a way of locating sites of resistance in cultural imaginaries marked by histories of violence, oppression and exclusion. A hermeneutic of failure looks for what un- or even counter-(re)productive excesses of a text might have to say to people already set up to fail by a cis-hetero-normative culture. The excesses of drag, for instance, point to and celebrate the failure of all gender identities as coherent categories. Concurrently with this, failure demands a refusal of purity discourses in queer resistance to cis-hetero-normativity. As Halberstam notes, 'failure recognizes that alternatives are embedded already with the dominant' (Halberstam 2011: 88) but, in deconstructive fashion, inhabits them with openness to their disruption.

With Halberstam as a guide, we can read the failures of representing a world without binary gender in *The Left Hand of Darkness* as enabling its fantastical critique of gender rather than inhibiting it. For instance, the slippages in Genly's language regarding his 'landlady' make palpable the disruption that Gethenian society poses to Genly's notions of stable gender identity. In the oscillations between gender designations that it performs, we may consider the applicability of Genly's description alternately to men who can bear children and women who can sire them, in addition to genderqueer and genderfluid people. Another instance in the novel in which the failure of gendered language opens onto a multitude of unsettled associations is in the text's depiction of sex and romance. Although Le Guin is critical of her own heteronormative depiction of sexuality in the novel, this is itself given homoerotic undertones by the fact that all the Gethenian characters are referred to as 'he'. Crucially, as in Judith Butler's drag show, it is precisely the dissonances created between pronoun usage and character gender identity that safeguard against a settled reading that would make a one-to-one comparison between gender as it exists on Gethen and categories of gender and sexuality as they exist in the primary world.

Indeed, *The Left Hand of Darkness* also de-naturalizes primary-world genders and sexualities by portraying them as perverse and queer by Gethenian standards. Gethenians who, in the primary world, would be gendered as either male or female do exist, and they are in a perpetual state of kemmer as humans are. Genly notes that 'they are tolerated with some disdain, as homosexuals are in many bisexual societies' (Le Guin [1969] 2010: 67). The only area of society in which these 'perverts' serve a crucial purpose is in the Handdara ritual of Foretelling, and their role seems to be linked to the necessary presence of a person in full kemmer. During the ritual Genly notes that the Pervert 'paid no heed to anyone but the one next to him, the kemmerer, whose increasingly active sexuality would be further roused and finally stimulated into full, female sexual capacity by the insistent, exaggerated maleness of the Pervert' (Le Guin [1969] 2010: 67). This scene is far from utopian; over the course of the ritual the kemmerer becomes visibly uncomfortable with the Pervert's caresses. Yet in the sense that it is a gathering of differently sexualized bodies, from the Pervert to the kemmerer to the celibates that are also part of the ritual, as well as in the heavy erotic atmosphere of the ritual, the Handdara Foretelling embodies Althaus-Reid's ideal of a religious community forming in gatherings and encounters that, to the sensibilities of primary-world religious establishments, may be seen as unholy. In the Handdara, that which is profane and perverse plays an essential role in the sacred, a motif which is echoed in the less overtly religious context of the truck of political prisoners in Orgoreyn, and again in the love shared between Genly and Estraven in their little tent on the Gobrin Ice.

The queer theology articulated by *The Left Hand of Darkness* is perhaps best understood as a theology of failure. Genly himself describes the Ekumen's attempt to unify the mystical and the political as 'mostly a failure; but its failure has done more good for humanity so far than the successes of its predecessors' (Le Guin [1969] 2010: 146). In this, Genly has much in common with both Halberstam and Tonstad, as do the Handdara principles that inform much of Karhidish culture. As I have noted, Handdara privileges the unravelling of sovereign identity in the face of the other, and this tendency towards relationality and hesitancy to universalize is associated with shadows and darkness. Even *shifgrethor*, which Genly describes as 'the untranslatable and all-important principle of social authority in Karhide' (Le Guin [1969] 2010: 14), is later revealed by Estraven to originate from an 'old word for *shadow*' (Le Guin [1969] 2010: 266). Handdara is, in this way, very close to what Halberstam describes as 'shadow feminisms', which 'take the form not of becoming, being, and doing but of shady, murky modes of undoing, unbecoming, and violating' (Halberstam 2011: 4). A queer extension of deconstructive feminist projects such as those of Cixous and Butler shadows feminism 'issues [...] from a refusal to be or to become woman as she has been defined and imagined within Western philosophy' (Halberstam 2011: 124).

As a novel in which characters' genders and sexualities refuse the terms of any language that could be used to describe them, *The Left Hand of Darkness* certainly can be seen to participate in shadow feminism. So, too, can its polyvocal narrative structure, a literary equivalent of collage, which Halberstam identifies as an art form that 'refuses to respect the boundaries that usually delineate self from other' (Halberstam 2011: 136). While by the time of the novel's setting, the term *shifgrethor* is deployed ambivalently in Karhidish society, its initial meaning and resonance with Handdara motifs are sympathetic with Halberstam's radically queer vision. The Handdara also privilege a 'singular "ignorance" [...] expressed in the word *nusuth*', which roughly translates to 'no matter' (Le Guin [1969] 2010: 63). Among the Handdarata, the highest honour is given to those who are attentive to their shadows: to those devoted to unlearning, failure and unbecoming. Such importance is also placed on failure in Tonstad's queer messianism; in her words, '[t]he failure, rather than the success, of the church is the means of its symbolic pointing toward the body of Christ that lies outside the walls in whomever the church understands as its others' (Tonstad 2016: 271). Failure of theological language signals that the other *is other*, and when acknowledged can save theology from narratives of dominance and triumphalism. *The Left Hand of Darkness* demonstrates the potential of fantastic worldbuilding *as* a failure for queer theology. For Le Guin, Halberstam and Tonstad, failure is the rule of non-assimilation of the other.

Walking the Dragons' Way: Sacred multiplicity in *Earthsea*

Where both *The Left Hand of Darkness* and *The Passion of New Eve* dress theology in textual drag, the dragons of *Earthsea* dramatize this movement within the text itself. The shapeshifting dragons that appear in the final two novels, *Tehanu* (1990) and *The Other Wind* (2001), provoke imaginative reflections on embodied subjectivity that suggest a potential to unbuild the walls set up by binary gender and liberate subjects from the violence it legitimizes. In doing so, they also disrupt previously established mythological and theological knowledge in the series. In the opening of *Tehanu*, Tenar tells a story in which the wizard Ogion encounters a fisherwoman who appears to him as a dragon for an instant, '[t]hen that was gone, and he saw no dragon, but an old woman standing there in the doorway, a bit stooped, a tall old fisherwoman with big hands' (Le Guin 1993: 491). The dragon-woman invites Ogion inside, and as they eat and talk Ogion remarks, 'When I first saw you I saw your true being. This woman who sits across the hearth from me is no more than the dress she wears' (Le Guin 1993: 493). The woman, however, 'shook her head and laughed, and all she would say was, "If only it were that simple!"' (Le Guin 1993: 493). Ogion's encounter with the dragon-woman disrupts the essentialist logic that has characterized the magical lore of the series up to this point. While the art magic practised by the all-male wizards on Roke stems from the knowledge of 'true names', which promises direct access to the essences of natural phenomena as well as human subjects, the dragon-woman disturbs the possibility of this notion. I have already discussed, in Chapter 2, how the figure of the dragon in *Tehanu* is routinely associated with women in rebellion, especially in relation to the character Tenar. However, in both *Tehanu* and *The Other Wind*, the ambivalent embodiment of dragons also goes further to destabilize the notion of a fixed and unitary essence with regard to gendered subjectivity and bodily borders. This provokes a radical reimagination not only of theologically prescribed conceptions of embodied subjectivity in our own world but also of lore held to be sacred in the world of *Earthsea* itself.

The story of the fisherwoman of Kemay can be understood as fantastic drag because it fundamentally disturbs the distinctions between appearance and essence that Butler critiques in *Gender Trouble*. Shapeshifters are no stranger to earlier texts set in Earthsea, since wizards can transform into animals for short periods of time, but transformation through the art magic operates in a deterministic fashion; maintaining the transformation for too long makes the change permanent so that the subjectivity of the wizard is utterly overtaken by that of the animal. Ogion's encounter with the fisherwoman places him in an altogether different, queerer territory in which he is confronted with an irreducibly heterogeneous identity that eludes representation within the logic of his training as a wizard. As Tenar recounts, 'Ogion said [the woman's embodiment] was beyond all shape-changing he knew, because it was about being two things, two beings, at once, and in the same form, and he said that this is beyond the power of wizards' (Le Guin 1993: 490). More than simply refusing to retain a single shape over time, the body of the dragon-woman displays such a discontinuity with itself that she cannot be coherently perceived as either 'truly' woman or 'truly' dragon; to identify either of these presentations as a mere disguise and the other as her true being only elicits laughter on her part. As with drag in the primary world, however, the dragon-woman's story also points to modes of embodiment not present within the previous three novels. As she eats and talks with Ogion, she sings a song telling that 'in the beginning, dragon and human were all one' (Le Guin 1993: 492) before they separated, the dragons choosing the freedom of the skies and humans choosing to stockpile wealth and knowledge, losing their wings in the process. Her song also relates that 'there are those among us who know they once were dragons, and among the dragons there are some who know their kinship with us' (Le Guin 1993: 493).

It is no accident that the creation myth told by the woman of Kemay, which is not present in the lore of the wizards on Roke, is presented at the beginning of a novel that radically revises the *Earthsea* series' prior worldbuilding and politics in other respects as well. Where the previous novel, *The Farthest Shore* (1973), concluded with the restoration of balance to the world and the installation of a new king, Lebannen, on the throne in Havnor, *Tehanu* disturbs this supposed happy ending with an emphasis on the violence and alienation experienced by gender-marginalized subjects, even after Lebannen takes the throne. The novel's title character is introduced as a young girl who is sexually trafficked by her father and uncle, who then burn her in their campfire and leave her for dead until she is found and taken in by Tenar. This traumatic ordeal leaves her with severe facial scarring that renders her appearance monstrous to the other villagers in Re Albi.

When met with the sight of Tehanu's disfigured face, the superstitious villagers 'make the sign to avert evil', believing that 'the rich and strong have virtue; one to whom evil has been done must be bad, and may rightly be punished' (Le Guin 1993: 630). Besides Tenar, only Aunty Moss, the village witch, is willing to take Tehanu under her wing. Tenar speculates that Moss's is 'a dark, wild, queer heart' that is 'drawn to [Tehanu] not only by kindness but by [Tehanu's] hurt, by the violence that had been done to her: by violence, by fire' (Le Guin 1993: 512). 'Queer' is used in the archaic sense meaning 'strange' here, but it accrues other connotations by *The Other Wind*, which gives more detail on the sexual lives of witches:

> Though seldom celibate, witches seldom kept company more than a night or two with any man, and it was a rare thing for a witch to marry a man. Far more often two of them lived their lives together, and that was called witch marriage or she-troth.
>
> (Le Guin [2001] 2002: 14–15)

Witches in Earthsea embody sexual and social practices that are non-normative in their own society and would be labelled as 'queer' within our own. Although they often do bear children, their sexual, familial and child-rearing practices tend to be outside the heteronormative community organization of society at large. For this reason, witches are designated as monstrously queer people on the margins of society, even as the people of Earthsea venerate the male-dominated magical arts of Roke. This marking as queer often coincides with literal birthmarks or other differences of appearance, as '[m]any women and men with such a blemish or difference about them become witches or sorcerers perforce' (Le Guin [2001] 2002: 14). While Tehanu does not ultimately become a witch herself, her facial scarring draws Moss to her and thus also provokes a reading of her as a queer subject.

Tehanu's marginality within regular society – her queerness – also coincides with a multiplicity of identity as both human and dragon. At the end of *Tehanu*, she summons Kalessin, the Eldest of the dragons, to rescue Ged and Tenar from captivity, and the dragon addresses her as 'my child' (Le Guin 1993: 689). *The Other Wind*, meanwhile, concludes as Tehanu, now a young woman, transforms into a dragon and joins her 'sister' Orm Irian and Kalessin in flight: '[f]ire ran along her hands, her arms, into her hair, into her face and body, flamed up into great wings above her head, and lifted her into the air, a creature all fire, blazing, beautiful' (Le Guin [2001] 2002: 238). Tehanu's existence as a dragon-woman is consistently aligned with her monstrously perceived appearance throughout both novels. As Alder the sorcerer reflects at one point in *The Other Wind*, '[h]er disfigurement made it seem that she had two faces. He could not see them both at one time, only one or the other' (Le Guin [2001] 2002: 143). Tehanu's scars are frequently described as hardened and rigid, calling to mind dragons' scales, and her voice, raspy and hoarse from fire damage, evokes the abrasive voices of dragons, described as 'a whisper of steel sliding on steel' (Le Guin 1993: 516). There is a danger, in reading these descriptions, of reifying suffering and trauma as necessary prerequisites for queer fluidity and multiplicity or, just as worryingly, of pathologizing it as the result of such suffering. I would argue, however, that the conflation of Tehanu's scars with her hybrid identity as woman and dragon demonstrates both the threat of exposure that queer forms of embodiment pose to an inherently hierarchical and violent system of gender norms, and the further social marginalization many queer subjects experience within such a system because of that threat. As Butler notes,

> [i]f a person opposes norms of binary gender not just by having a critical point of view about them, but by incorporating norms critically, and that stylized opposition is legible, then it seems that violence emerges precisely as the demand to undo that legibility, to question its possibility, to render it unreal and impossible.
>
> (Butler 2004: 35)

Tehanu's facial scarring is associated with her disruptive embodiment and the multiplicity of her identity not because suffering is an inherent condition of queerness (even if it is a present reality for many) but because in it is something akin to the Derridean notion of the trace. It is a mark bearing witness to the gendered violence (and, indeed, to the violence inherent in gender) that society at large would prefer to cover over. In so doing, it points to the multiplicity of all identity and confronts the world of Earthsea with its silenced others.

Through the figure of the dragon, Le Guin enacts a re-visioning of her own secondary world that parallels the theological undressing practices outlined by Althaus-Reid. For all that dragons are held in distant, in some cases religious, reverence by the various human cultures of Earthsea, dragon lore rears its head as the return of a suppressed counter-discourse that disorganizes human doctrines and logics. This is shown clearly in the case of Seserakh, a princess from the island of Hur-at-Hur, where dragons are held to be sacred. Recounting a dream in which she finds herself treading on the holy ground reserved for dragons in her culture's religious rituals, she confesses to Azver, the Master Patterner of Roke, '[L]ast night I broke taboo! [. . .] I walked on the Dragons'

Way!' (Le Guin [2001] 2002: 217). To this, the Patterner replies, 'I think we're all walking on the Dragons' Way. And all taboos may well be shaken or broken. Not only in dream' (Le Guin [2001] 2002: 217). Ogion, too, prophesies this on his deathbed as, glimpsing Tehanu, he gasps out, 'The dragon – ' and then, 'All changed!' (Le Guin 1993: 502). In the novels, this change manifests in transgressions of boundaries and the unravelling of old institutions, especially those related to gender. Even as early as *The Farthest Shore*, Kalessin is presented as a creature so ineffable as to have no discernible gender; in Ged's words, 'I say "he", but I do not even know that' (Le Guin 1993: 436). Shortly after, in *Tehanu*, the wizards cloistered in the Great House on Roke find their quasi-monastic order at an impasse in their inability to choose a new Archmage after Ged loses his powers and returns to his home island of Gont. In the midst of their interminable debating, Azver cryptically prophesies about '*[a] woman on Gont*' (Le Guin 1993: 612). Shortly after, a young woman comes to Roke as a stranger at its gates, demanding to be instructed in the art magic. During a contest of magic in which the Master Summoner attempts to control her by calling her true name, Irian, she declares, 'I am not only Irian' and changes form so that the wizards 'didn't know whether [they] saw a woman that burned like a fire, or a winged beast' (Le Guin [2001] 2002: 99).

Dragons serve as a dramatization of theology in drag because they appear in the final two novels in the *Earthsea* series as subjects both marginalized within and positioned to disorganize the social orders in which they are nominally esteemed as sacred. The people of Hur-at-Hur are not the only ones for whom dragons are holy; the wizards of the Archipelago, too, derive their art magic, which they bar women like Irian from practising, from the language of the dragons. Like the queer God of Indecent Theology, the dragon-women are strangers erased from, and denied access to, the privileged discourses of which they are ostensibly the centre. In this way, *Tehanu* and *The Other Wind* also hold the worldbuilding of *Earthsea*, as a textual construction, accountable for its re-inscription of hegemonic norms and covering over of alterity. This is most clearly dramatized when Tenar admires a decorative fan in the weaver's shop, which depicts a scene of daily life in Havnor Great Port, but when held to the light reveals a flip side ordinarily hidden from view:

> Dragons moved as the folds of the fan moved. Painted faint and fine on the yellowed silk, dragons of pale red, blue, green moved and grouped, as the figures on the other side were grouped, among clouds and mountain peaks. [...] [She] saw the two sides, the two paintings, made one by the light flowing through the

silk, so that the clouds and peaks were the towers of the city, and the men and women were winged, and the dragons looked with human eyes.

(Le Guin 1993: 577)

Tenar's viewing of the fan in *Tehanu* prefigures the revelations in worldbuilding that characterize *The Other Wind*; it dramatizes how the dragons' appearance, like drag, makes visible the possibilities that are covered over in the textual construction of the body. As is implied by the sweeping vista of the scene depicted on the fan, this carries more than merely individualistic implications.

The appearance of the dragon-women heralds the eucatastrophic conclusion of the *Earthsea* cycle, which is ultimately not the restoration of equilibrium seen in *The Farthest Shore* but a fundamental shift in the world order in the face of the other. The changes can be wide-ranging, as seen in Irian's breaking of gender barriers on Roke, as well as intimate. The clearest instance of the latter can be seen in the familial bonds shared by the dragons. Though born to different human families, Tehanu and Irian call each other 'sister', and both are called 'daughter' by Kalessin. The non-essentialist, affective reconfiguration of the family this creates is strikingly parallel to the 'found families' that often emerge in queer communities, such as the drag houses that have emerged in Black and Latinx queer communities in New York since the 1960s. Butler has described these drag families as 'a cultural life of fantasy that not only organizes the material conditions of life, but which also produces sustaining bonds of community where recognition becomes possible, and which works as well to ward off violence, racism, homophobia, and transphobia' (Butler 2004: 216). Tehanu's journey from an abusive biological family to found families, first with Tenar and Ged, and later with Irian and Kalessin, parallels the experiences of many queer people for whom a return to the biological family means the threat of violence and alienation. As Butler also makes clear, however, the 'fantasy' of queer families carries the potential to be not only consolatory but transformative. While the creation narrative recited by the woman of Kemay, and the similar but nonetheless distinct myth relayed by Seserakh, provides crucial touchstones for the dragon-women's reconfiguration of the world, it is clear that they are not undifferentiated, pre-lapsarian unities to which any return is possible or even desirable. At the end of *The Other Wind*, Tehanu, Irian, Alder and the wizards come together to dismantle the partitions around the Dry Land, a piece of ground that the wizards stole from the dragons in a failed attempt to conquer death and create an eternal afterlife.

This conclusion signals a resistance to a heterosexual, patriarchal theological order that seeks to subordinate mortal, bodily concerns to ostensibly transcendent prescriptions and abstract matters of the spirit. That the wizards' quest for immortality coincides with their colonization of the dragons' land is revealing when the queer embodiment of the dragons is read in relation to primary-world theological orders. As Althaus-Reid's critique of heterosexual theology makes clear, the desire for immortality, of the theological subject as well as of heterosexual theology's concepts and symbols, is inextricable from theology's difference-suppressing, colonizing impulses and its tendency to act as border police for who is granted access to transcendence and who is not. The unbuilding of the wall separating the world of the living from the Dry Land can be read both as an indecent disruption of a colonizing heterosexual order and as a transformation of finitude similar to that articulated in Tonstad's theology of the Eucharist and resurrection. For Tonstad the Eucharist multiplies the body of Christ to co-inhere with wheat, fruit and the bodies of communicants, prefiguring an eventual transformation of all relations. Similarly, in Earthsea to die comes to mean a transformation in which subjects neither achieve immortality, nor are they obliterated. Rather, as Tehanu says,

> I think [. . .] that when I die, I can breathe back the breath that made me live. I can give back to the world all that I didn't do. All that I might have been and couldn't be. All the choices I didn't make. All the things I lost and spent and wasted. I can give them back to the world. To the lives that haven't been lived yet.
> (Le Guin [2001] 2002: 231)

For Le Guin, as for Tonstad, death and resurrection are not opposites but, in a queer variation on Emmanuel Levinas's ethics of alterity, inescapably bound up with each other as transformations of embodied existence in relation to others.

The unbuilding of walls with which *The Other Wind* concludes is crucially not a dissolution into an undifferentiated universalism. Rather, it is a deconstruction of barriers that preserves difference rather than erase or subsume it; in Azver's words, '[w]hat was built is broken. What was broken was made whole' (Le Guin [2001] 2002: 240). The dragons depart to fly on the other wind, and the humans remain in Earthsea. Yet while only a few individuals demonstrate the disruptive multiplicity of identity that the dragon-women do, the change that they herald is one that affects all of life on Earthsea. While social systems are not obliterated, they are fundamentally transformed; the school on Roke remains standing but only, as Azver says, '[s]o long as the wind can blow through the windows' (Le Guin [2001] 2002: 232). Implicit in this is a deconstructive imperative for existing structures to remain open to the approach of the other and to allow themselves fluidity and transformation. The *Earthsea* series demonstrates that a theology in drag is a theology that walks the Dragon's Way, able to break taboos and disrupt normative regimes, not to assimilate the other into the order of the same but to proliferate sites of subversion from originary difference. Like the people of Earthsea who are both woman and dragon, queer theology points to a fully God, fully human Christ who makes trouble with these categories of identity and is encountered wherever bodies are in rebellion.

Conclusions

In this chapter, I have argued for an understanding of fantasy as theology dressed in drag. Implicit in this pursuit has been a need to take queer theology beyond debates about the inclusion of LGBTQ+ people in the church and a need to broaden our theological imagination regarding loving relationships with the other. By inhabiting fictional secondary worlds and embracing the fabulous and monstrous figurations of embodiment that become thinkable within fantasy literature, I have argued, queer theologians are better able to deconstruct hetero- and cis-normative prescriptions of embodiment embedded within faith traditions. Fantasy literature enables theologians to provisionally imagine the alterity of Christ as incarnated across a spectrum of specific marginalized bodies. At the same time, fantasy as theology in drag does not merely serve to therapeutically affirm existing LGBTQ+ identity categories; like the drag show, fantasy can disorganize existing schemes of categorization and representation and open onto other forms of embodiment. In this way, fantasy opens theology to trans-figurations in its images of incarnation and challenges us to imagine God, ourselves and our relationships with God and each other in new and unsettled ways.

In the Indecent Theology professed by Althaus-Reid and the queer messianism espoused by Tonstad, the sacred is to be encountered in unholy and 'indecent' assemblages of bodies on the margins of cis-hetero-patriarchal society. While the practices of theological undressing that these theologies entail do not aim for an ultimate and settled 'reality' of God or the body, they open onto a remaking of the world in the face of a queer God, who appears as the stranger at the gates of theological discourse to transform bodily relations. These theological practices can be located within the fantasy texts I have examined in this chapter. In *Tehanu* and *The Other Wind*, the presence of subjects who exist simultaneously as woman and dragon disrupts the sacred knowledge of the wizards of Earthsea and initiates a transformation of finitude that parallels Tonstad's queer reading of the Eucharist. The multiplicity of identity presented within the *Earthsea* novels is also present in the complex web of gender subversions and transformations that Eve and Tristessa undergo in *The Passion of New Eve*. In particular, their sacramental sexual encounter in the desert affirms the possibility of glimpsing the sacred in the midst of, rather than transcending, disharmony and artifice. Meanwhile, I have shown that the linguistic failures of *The Left Hand of Darkness* can be read as a kind of textual drag that unsettles its depiction of gender in ways that are productive for theological reflection. Understood in conversation with Halberstam and Tonstad, the Handdara in *The Left Hand of Darkness* presents itself as a theology in which failure enables a politics founded on loving relations with the other. In all of these texts, the queer God-as-other announces Godself in the midst of the unholy, unreal, unclean and monstrous.

Monstrous messianisms

Conclusions

I have argued, in this book, that fantasy literature is singularly equipped to deconstruct and reconfigure theology from a variety of queer and feminist standpoints. Resisting a view of fantasy as an exercise in religious apologetics that reaffirms exclusionary and oppressive orthodox positions, I have instead developed a theory of fantasy that is deconstructive and oriented towards an encounter with the radically other. Viewed as a homologous structure to the deconstructive philosophy of Jacques Derrida and the ethical philosophy of Emmanuel Levinas, the messianic consolation of fantasy that Tolkien calls 'eucatastrophe' is an event that can disrupt the theological figurations offered within fantasy, in addition to theology in the primary world. This textual openness apparent in the structures of fantasy can also cultivate in readers an openness to encountering the other, and to understanding and embracing the other in ourselves. In the face of theologies and religious institutions that locate salvation in the faithful reproduction of structures of cisgender masculinity and heterosexuality, fantasy literature's willingness to break with the rules of possibility in the primary world makes it a counter-discourse capable of identifying the sacred in the profane, monstrous and 'different-than'. While the Christian doctrine of the incarnation and the life of Christ promise good news and liberation for all, Luce Irigaray and Marcella Althaus-Reid have shown that this can only be good news for gender and sexually marginalized people if we are willing to take seriously the role that gender, sexuality and bodily desire play in our theological storytelling. Fantasy literature's disruption of consensus reality can transgress the limits of primary-world theologies' conceptions of incarnation, religious life, gender and sexuality. In the strange figurations of fantasy, Christ may appear as the sexual stranger at the gates or as a dragon in the neighbourhood of normative theology, demanding not merely inclusion in but a wholesale transformation of theological constructions of reality.

Although *Till We Have Faces*, *The Left Hand of Darkness*, *The Passion of New Eve* and the other texts I have discussed in this study embody widely divergent approaches to fantasy, worldbuilding and theological deconstruction, what they share in common is their tireless commitment to navigating this ambivalent territory. Feminist and queer theological projects that resist sovereign subjectivity and inhabit self-consciously unstable positions of otherness are difficult undertakings, if necessary for re-visioning theology from the margins. As these texts show, however, the provisional figurations of fantasy are more than suited to wedding the need for specificity in marginal projects to the recognition of the absence of a unified subject. Over the course of this book, they have enabled me to explore fantasy's potential to write theology from the body and its desires by way of Cixous's theory of *écriture féminine* and opened a critical discussion on both the subversive potential and overly prescriptive nature of Irigaray's quest for a feminine incarnation of the divine. Finally, these texts point to fantasy's potential to undress theology by, paradoxically, dressing it in drag, giving fabulous new forms to theological figures and concepts that can transform relations between God and humanity not in spite of but precisely because of their artificiality and embrace of their own failure.

For the remainder of this study, I wish to briefly identify some horizons of further inquiry suggested by the discussions I have undertaken in this volume, as well as outline some of the approaches to theological re-visioning being taken by fantasy texts of the twenty-first century. The potential for deconstructive feminist and queer theological readings of fantasy is by no means limited to the texts I have used as case studies in this book. On the contrary, fantasy's interest in radically rethinking the norms established by primary-world religious structures seems to have been reinvigorated over the past decade. Beginning in the early 2010s, there has been a massive influx of works in the fantasy genre, including texts as distinct from one another as N. K. Jemisin's *Inheritance* trilogy (2010–11), Ann Leckie's *The Raven Tower* (2019) and Neon Yang's *Tensorate* series (2017–19), that participate in gender-disruptive exercises in theological imagination similar to the texts I have examined here, though with some significant differences. Contemporary fantasy literature of the twenty-first century expands on the subversive experiments in worldbuilding and theological storytelling found in twentieth-century texts. However, these newer texts also necessarily enter into a dialogue with a liberal politics of LGBTQ+ inclusion and identity categorization that was nowhere near as culturally dominant in the late twentieth century as it is today, with the *Tensorate* series navigating this territory with considerably more success than *The Raven Tower*. As I noted in this book's Introduction, the emergence of these texts has coincided with a growing scholarly interest in both the affordances and limitations of fantasy for representing marginal subjects or articulating alternative social and political visions. At the same time, it is necessary to reiterate that this current work is less a product of a linear progression in social attitudes on the part of authors and scholars than it is simply the most recent incarnation of a long-standing tradition of contending with alterity and marginality in fantastic literature. The fantasy works of Leckie, Yang and Jemisin, for the most part, can be understood as engaged in the same theological and political processes of deconstruction as the twentieth-century texts I have already discussed, even as they broaden and deepen the scope of theological inquiry and gesture towards new potential areas of study.

Divine speech and matter: Ann Leckie's *The Raven Tower*

Ann Leckie is primarily a science fiction author whose experimentation with gendered language and speculative embodiment is a defining aspect of her work. Her Hugo-winning Imperial Radch trilogy (2013–15) is notable for its exploration of artificial consciousnesses inhabiting human bodies, its creation of distinctive alien theologies and religious practices, and its subversion of gendered pronoun conventions by having its narrator, Breq, refer to all characters as 'she'. Even more experimental is her 2019 novel *The Raven Tower*, which attempts to carry similar thematic fixations over into the fantasy genre, with mixed results. *The Raven Tower* is a tale of revenge, its narrative not only overtly riffing on the plot of William Shakespeare's *Hamlet* but gradually unveiling a longer revenge plot centuries in the making. Set in a world in which gods inhabit aspects of nature, the novel tells the story of the kingdom of Iraden, which has long been granted protection and prosperity by a god known as the Raven, in exchange for the regular sacrifice of a person appointed to the office of the Raven's Lease each time 'the Raven's Instrument – the bird embodying the god that called itself the Raven' (Leckie 2019: 16) – dies. When Mawat, the heir to the office of Lease, rides to the holy city of Vastai with his aide, Eolo, for his father's sacrifice and his own instalment as Lease, he arrives to find the Instrument already dead, his father missing and his uncle acting as Lease, and immediately suspects foul play. Mawat's challenge to his uncle's claim to the office of Lease and Eolo's endeavours to uncover the truth are observed by the Strength and Patience of the Hill, a mysterious god inhabiting a large boulder who comments on the novel's events to Eolo in the second person while concurrently giving an account of their own history and how it ties into that of the Raven.

While the religious landscape of *The Raven Tower* bears little resemblance to Christianity, the theological, sociological and political questions it raises are nonetheless pertinent to the themes I have explored elsewhere in this book. Through the narrative voice of the Strength and Patience of the Hill, Leckie not only allows the reader access to a fantastic approximation of a non-human alterity's consciousness but also provokes critical reflection on the act of theological mythmaking similar to that undertaken by Lewis in *Till We Have Faces*. As Strength and Patience explains,

> [s]tories can be risky for someone like me. What I say must be true, or it will be made true, and if it cannot be made true – if I don't have the power, or if what I have said is an impossibility – then I will pay the price. [. . .] It's safer for me to speak of what I know. Or to speak only in the safest of generalities. Or else to say plainly at the beginning, 'Here is a story I have heard,' placing the burden of truth or not on the teller whose words I am merely accurately reporting.
>
> (Leckie 2019: 18–19)

For gods in this secondary world, *all* speech acts carry the potential to be performative and to bring about what they purport to merely describe. Thus, much of Strength and Patience's storytelling is couched in qualifiers and caveats to cast uncertainty on the events being described, which heightens the reader's awareness that the text they are reading is a carefully constructed narrative. As Liz Bourke notes in her review of the novel, '[a]s the *you* of the narrative cannot reveal Eolo's interiority, except through his actions, we become aware in parallel that there are things the *I* of the narrative is definitely not saying' (Bourke 2019: 4 of 9 paras). In explicitly drawing attention to this, Leckie's text takes full advantage of fantasy's ability to highlight the non-finality of, and deconstructive processes at work within, religious narratives, as well as the dangers of treating these narratives as the final word.

This is especially brought to the fore towards the end of the novel, as Strength and Patience recounts the nationalist myth of Iraden's conquest of the religiously and culturally pluralistic port city of Ard Vusktia with the help of the Raven, which contrasts sharply with their own narration of the same events earlier in the novel:

> Only a story, though if you have been listening to me, and have understood me so far, you know that it is a story built around a particular selection of facts, twisted to particular ends. This version of events is widely repeated and believed all through Iraden, but it is rarely told in Ard Vusktia, and then only by Iradeni. People who pass on a different account of the events of that day generally don't do so within earshot of their Iradeni conquerors.
>
> (Leckie 2019: 336)

As this passage suggests, *The Raven Tower* is also concerned with theology and religion as functions of national, cultural and political economy, and Leckie is especially attentive to the relationship between religious observance and the flow of natural and economic resources. The conflict between Iraden and Ard Vusktia is initiated when the Raven lays claim to the strait between Ard Vusktia and Vastai, disrupting a complex network of trade facilitated by an agreement over driftwood between the gods of the north and the gods of the south. Strength and Patience is convinced to join the gods' war effort against the Raven when the shortage of resources resulting from this disruption leads a neighbouring tribe to violently raid the Kaluet, the band of nomadic hunter-gatherers who worship Strength and Patience.

The network of economic relations that Strength and Patience encounters upon their arrival in Ard Vusktia even extends to the gods themselves, as they quickly learn that the more powerful gods with religious establishments are appropriating the power of more minor gods in their service, which has had its own devastating impact on the surrounding landscape. In turn, once the Raven overpowers Ard Vusktia, the Raven exploits a loophole in Strength and Patience's agreement with Oissen, the god of medicine, to enslave Strength and Patience for the protection of Iraden, placing the stone they inhabit at the base of the Raven Tower in Vastai. The god's-eye view of theology, economics and ecology that the novel's narrative perspective affords also makes clear that the priorities of gods are not the same as the priorities of humans. In the novel's present, Mawat's uncle Hibal slaughters the Raven's Instrument and secretly imprisons Mawat's father, leaving the Raven vulnerable in order to curry favour with a foreign power and their god. This petty political scheming, and Mawat's plot for revenge against his uncle, pale in comparison to the vengeance against the Raven and Iraden that these events enable for Strength and Patience, whose allegiance to humans is highly selective. The weakening of the Raven unleashes plagues on Vastai that are reminiscent of the plagues of Egypt from the book of Exodus, and although Strength and Patience spares Eolo, few of the novel's other characters fare well in the retribution that ensues.

Because of Strength and Patience's long view of history, Leckie is able to depict human religious life as caught within an intricate web of material relations, similar to the Marxist analysis involved in Indecent Theology. Because of this, and its fascination with humanity's existence alongside the gods and the non-human bodies they inhabit, her novel is also deeply concerned with the ecological implications of theology that have been outside the scope of this study, but that are of ever-increasing relevance and urgency in the twenty-first century given widespread cultural awareness of ecological exploitation and climate collapse. Yet while *The Raven Tower* attempts, at points, to link gender and sexuality to this impressive portrait of global ecology and economy in its theological storytelling, these aspects of the text are among the most underdeveloped. Most notably, the novel's human protagonist, Eolo, is a transgender man, and there are moments in which his interactions with other characters hint at how the text's religious landscape intersects with his experience of gender. Although there are indications that trans people are similarly marginalized in Iraden as they are in our world, the devout Mawat unreservedly offers to petition the Raven 'to make it so [Eolo] could [. . .] be who [he is]' (Leckie 2019: 4). Eolo, however, replies, 'I already am who I am' (Leckie 2019: 4) and expresses uncertainty over whether he even wants to modify his body. Later, when the Lady Tikaz discovers Eolo's gender identity, she recalls hearing that in the more religiously diverse Ard Vusktia, 'they think such things are normal', and that 'way up north, where it's cold and icy all the time, the gods' favourite priests are all [. . .] like you' (Leckie 2019: 266). Though it is never explicitly stated in the text, this could be a hint as to why Strength and Patience, who hails from the north, is drawn to Eolo without realizing it.

These would be compelling aspects of the characters, their world and its myriad theologies for the novel to address, but they are given no further exploration beyond these exchanges, nor are they shown in action in the text. While this is perhaps understandable given that the text's narrator is a god who has only ever inhabited a stone, it also gives the impression that Leckie has merely imported gender and sexual identity categories wholesale from our world into her secondary one. In a world where the entirety of human society is organized around a complex network of relations with transcorporeal gods, there seems to be little reason why gender and sexuality should be understood as they are in the primary world. This is not to say that Eolo needs a narrative 'reason' or justification for being trans (an all-too-common complaint levied at fantasy texts featuring LGBTQ+ characters) or even that his gender identity should be a primary thematic concern for the novel. But, partly due to the lack of interiority he is granted and partly due to the way the narrative isolates him from any other named trans characters, his representation is divorced from a meaningful sense of queer or trans life and politics. For all of *The Raven Tower*'s intricate examination of systems of theology, ecology and political economy, it demonstrates a distinct lack of insight into gender as a structure tied to these systems. As a result, the queer and trans representation that is present in the text tends to come across as somewhat perfunctory, if not tokenistic; its surface-level diversity inadvertently highlights the normative assumptions and values imported into the text's secondary world. Still, despite its shortcomings in this area, *The Raven Tower*'s formal experimentation and the inventiveness of its fictional religious practices make it a theologically rich text.

Swimming against the tides: Neon Yang's *Tensorate* series

While *The Raven Tower* inadvertently exposes some of the pitfalls of surface-level queer and transgender representation in a fantastic setting, Neon Yang's *Tensorate* series (2017–19) queers primary-world gender and sexuality categories in much more satisfying and elegant ways while resisting simplistic utopianism in doing so. In this regard, it is comparable to the fantastic gender-queering experiment undertaken in *The Left Hand of Darkness*. Although the overarching plot of the four novellas comprising the series involves a class struggle over the control and distribution of magical knowledge and technologies, Yang mostly uses this as a backdrop for loosely connected vignettes meditating on desire and kinship. Similarly to N. K. Jemisin's *Inheritance* novels discussed further, Yang's novellas explore the ways in which sexual desire, love and familial ties messily intersect with structures of class oppression and empire. The first two novellas, *The Black Tides of Heaven* (2017) and *The Red Threads of Fortune* (2017), follow the magically adept Sanao twins, Akeha and Mokoya, as they abandon lives of privilege and comfort to join the Machinist rebellion against their mother's empire. *The Descent of Monsters* (2018) details the rebel Rider's search for their long-lost twin who has been imprisoned and experimented on by the magical authorities of the Tensorate. Finally, *The Ascent to Godhood* (2019) delves into the violent history of romance and betrayal between the Machinist leader Lady Han and Protector Sanao Hekate.

One of the most effective and intriguing aspects of Yang's worldbuilding is its unique treatment of gender. In the *Tensorate* novellas, children are not assigned a gender at birth; instead, they are allowed to choose their gender later in life, sometimes but not always undergoing magic-aided surgical procedures to confirm their gender. Notably, there is also no prescribed age at which this must happen, and it is strongly implied that many people spend a couple years experimenting with their gender presentation before they become confirmed (Yang 2017a: 74). Puberty is even magically halted until a person arrives at their chosen gender; the text explains that '[u]ntil a young person confirmed their gender, the masters of forest-nature kept the markers of adulthood at bay' (Yang

2017a: 117). By creating a secondary world in which virtually *everyone*'s gender is achieved via processes of transition, Yang, who is non-binary, unravels the tangle of associations and norms that constitute gender in our world and provocatively alerts the reader to the decisions (both conscious and unconscious) and sociocultural processes by which gender is established and enforced. Characters change pronouns, sometimes more than once, as readers follow their journeys through the text, suggesting a fluid understanding of identity and the forces that shape it (for this reason, I have endeavoured to reflect this in my discussions of characters here). This brings the *Tensorate* texts in line with Butler's quest for a non-coercive relationship to gender in *Undoing Gender* and demonstrates the possibilities that fantastic secondary worlds afford not only to queer imaginaries but to transgender ones as well. While it would be tempting to interpret this in utopian terms, Yang's narrative treatment of this subject matter is decidedly ambivalent, demonstrating a variety of ways of relating to gender and presenting several characters who still find themselves on the periphery of their world's gender system.

When Mokoya announces their plans to be confirmed as female on the twins' seventeenth birthday, for instance, Akeha becomes baffled by the choice. While Mokoya explains that she has 'always felt like one. A girl' (Yang 2017a: 81), Akeha still finds themself attached to a childhood vow 'never to get confirmed' (Yang 2017a: 74) and unable to articulate their own gendered desires: 'Ideas and feelings bubbled up as though their mind were boiling over. None of it lined up into coherent, defensible thought' (Yang 2017a: 82). Through Akeha's ambivalence about gender, Yang is also able to take up a nuanced exploration of the relationship between identity and desire. Akeha's eventual decision to be confirmed as a man emerges concurrently with the discovery of their own sexual attraction to men, and they seem to have difficulty clearly delineating where their sexual desire ends and their sense of self begins. Having grown up largely apart from men, they reflect that '[m]en were creatures of distant fascination, with their broad backs and tanned cheeks, and Akeha had never considered that they might be one of them' (Yang 2017a: 118–19). Trying to envision themself dressed as a man, Akeha realizes that '[i]t felt different. Not *right*, exactly, but there was something there', their mental litany of '*I want. I want*' gradually being replaced with '*I am*' (Yang 2017a: 119). Although this discovery is still fragile and provisional, with Akeha even resolving to 'tell Mother [. . .] before I change my mind', he finds that this nonetheless enables '[n]ew possibilities, new understandings, new ways of being' (Yang 2017a: 119). By the time of *The Descent of Monsters*, however, Akeha is once again referred to as 'they' (Yang 2018: 110), suggesting that Akeha has arrived at a sense of self more fundamentally inarticulable and queer even in relation to the gender system of the secondary world. The *Tensorate* series depicts gender transition as a revelatory but provisional and sometimes lifelong process, not just queering primary-world binary gender but also destabilizing the norms shored up by its own experimentation with gender.

While religion and theology are not primary thematic concerns for the *Tensorate* novellas, they are often key background details that inform characters' choices and outlooks. The religious landscape of the *Tensorate* novellas also demonstrates the affordances of fantasy for theological storytelling and re-visioning for theologies beyond Christianity, with potential points of connection with Vincent's (2012) work on secondary-world fantasy as an avenue for interreligious dialogue. The setting reflects the religious plurality of the primary-world pan-Asian cultures on which it is based, including Yang's native Singapore: the Grand Monastery where Akeha and Mokoya are raised and trained in Slackcraft (the series' form of magic) is broadly evocative of Zen Buddhist traditions, and there are references to mosques in several settings. The novellas are also interested in religion as a site for political and cultural dissidence, sometimes coinciding with a queer and deconstructive relationship to orthodoxy. Akeha's involvement with the Machinist rebellion begins when he rescues the Machinist Yongcheow from Tensorate soldiers and the two quickly become lovers. Yongcheow is a devotee of Obedience, a loose amalgam of Islam and Christianity, and his choice to join the rebellion is rooted in his understanding of its theology. As he puts it, '[t]he Almighty decides our circumstances. He doesn't decide our actions. It's what He gave us free will for' (Yang 2017a: 165). Later, he remarks that '[t]he saying goes, "The black tides of heaven direct the courses of human lives." To which a wise teacher said, "But as with all waters, one can swim against the tide"' (Yang 2017a: 166). If the first novella in the *Tensorate* series is primarily concerned with the forces that shape people's lives and identities, Yongcheow offers to Akeha a theological means of navigating his own desires in relation to these forces. Not only does Akeha become a convert to Obedience when he joins his lover in the rebellion, choosing to swim against the tides of class oppression and empire, but later novellas also suggest that they have found a way of swimming against the tides of gendered social pressures. In Yongcheow's view, political and gendered dissidence do not preclude obedience to the will of God, but are rather acts of participation in God's creation.

The Red Threads of Fortune sees Mokoya coming to similar realizations, framed not in terms of the will of God but in terms of fate and the ontological make-up of the world itself. Similarly to Le Guin's *The Other Wind*, this novella treats eucatastrophe not only as an unlooked-for moment of grace but also as a destabilizing moment that queers the text's worldbuilding and magic. This text follows Mokoya's abortive attempts to recover from the sudden death of her young daughter and her haunting by flashbacks of past traumas and prophetic visions whose outcome she seemingly cannot change. *The Red Threads of Fortune* also introduces Rider, a foreigner from the Quarterlands who is described as genderqueer and occupies an arguably queer relationship to spatiality, travelling from place to place by folding the Slack, the substance of the world that Tensors manipulate for their magic. While at the start of the novella, Mokoya regularly recites to herself a litany concerning the Five Natures of the Slack from her training at the monastery, her close relationship with Rider teaches her that '[t]he Slack was not just divided into five natures – that was the Tensorate way of thinking – but infinitely malleable' (Yang 2017b: 189).

Plagued by a vision in which Rider dies in a battle with a naga and desperate for a way to avoid such an outcome, Mokoya meditates, and as she does so, her dogmatic understanding of the Slack and the Fortunes unravels along with her sense of self:

> Dissolve the trappings of Monastery training. Discard the frameworks of Tensor study.
>
> Dissolve memory, dissolve personhood. She was no longer Mokoya, yet she remained unchanged. A collection of occurrences in space and time, mathematical possibilities intersecting and colliding, not a living thing but a coalescence of possibilities.
>
> (Yang 2017b: 189)

As in its treatment of gender, the text here queers the principles of its own worldbuilding, recalling Halberstam's notion of queer knowledge gained from unlearning and failure. From this revelation, Mokoya comes to the realization that her 'visions, born from her unconscious mind, were her uncontrolled attempts to rearrange the patterns in the Slack', and that '[f]or a prophecy to be undone, the prophet herself had to be undone' (Yang 2017b: 190). When Mokoya sacrifices herself to defeat the naga and save Rider, freeing them from the threads of fortune to which her vision inadvertently tied them, she embodies the surrender of the sovereign subject for the sake of the other, literally unravelling the fabric of the text's world to enable its eucatastrophic conclusion. There is resurrection in this ending as well, as Rider uses their alien Slackcraft to save Mokoya's life. The *Tensorate* series demonstrates that like Le Guin, Neon

Yang is an author whose fantastic worldbuilding is attuned to the instability of its own construction, rewriting the limits of possibility according to the dogmas not just of our world but of its own fictional society as well.

Gods and seduction: N. K. Jemisin's *Inheritance* trilogy

Among the twenty-first-century fantastic texts that most thoroughly embody fantasy's potential for queer, feminist theological re-visioning are the novels in N. K. Jemisin's *Inheritance* trilogy (2010–11). Similarly to Delany's Nevèrÿon, Jemisin's secondary world of the Hundred Thousand Kingdoms serves as a staging ground for 'indecent' explorations of sexual longing and desire, gender, global economics, race, colonization and slavery. Jemisin's trilogy is distinct, however, for its consistent foregrounding of theology and metaphysics in its sustained engagement with this web of power relations. Although the novels inhabit a polytheistic cosmology in which gods, demigods (or 'godlings') and humans directly interact with each other – and in which the gods are every bit as flawed as the humans who worship them – the worldbuilding and narrative provoke complex imaginative reflections on Christian metaphysics, fleshly incarnation and god(s)-as-other. Moreover, Jemisin continually depicts the relationship between these cosmic themes and the more quotidian human politics with which they are bound up primarily through the lens of the erotic.

The trilogy's first volume, *The Hundred Thousand Kingdoms* (2010), establishes the global politics of its setting as the product of a millennia-spanning family conflict between the gods known as the Three: Bright Itempas, the god of light and order, Nahadoth, the god of darkness and chaos, and Enefa, 'the goddess of twilight and dawn', a 'balance' between the first two (Jemisin 2010a: 6). The novel begins at the tail end of a two-thousand-year period of relative peace and prosperity known as 'the Bright' (Jemisin 2010a: 45) overseen by a central ruling family, the Arameri, who derive their power from their devotion to Itempas. The Arameri's rule, however, is quickly established as an imperial theocracy, as the worship of any god other than Itempas is outlawed in every land, and heresy is brutally punished by torture and death. The Arameri have also enslaved Nahadoth and several of his godling offspring, imprisoned in flesh, as punishment for their war against Itempas following Enefa's death by Itempas's hand. Entering this familial and political drama is Yeine, a young warrior queen from the 'uncivilized', barbarian nation of Darr, whose late mother was an estranged heir to the Arameri throne. As Yeine finds herself in the midst of a power struggle for a throne she does not want, she also becomes a bargaining chip in the enslaved gods' quest for liberation while she begins to piece together the true story of the Gods' War that has been covered over by official doctrine.

The narrative arc of the *Inheritance* trilogy strikingly dramatizes and enacts Althaus-Reid's methods of undressing theology in the face of imperial and hegemonic power. Much of Yeine's new knowledge of the gods following her arrival in Sky is bodily and erotic in nature, as she finds herself overcome with desire for Nahadoth and, later, discovers that her body houses a fragment of the fallen Enefa's soul. While the priests in the Order of Itempas propagate the belief that in the time of the Three, Nahadoth was 'pure evil' (Jemisin 2010a: 25), Yeine uncovers that before the Gods' War, the Three were polyamorous lovers. The relationship of this cosmological figuration to primary-world Christianity is complex. While his association with a monotheistic religious institution and colonial rule make it tempting to read Bright Itempas as a straightforward allegory for the Christian God, and Jemisin clearly draws significant influences from Christian theology and practice for the religious landscape of her secondary world, the resemblances are more suggestive and evocative than deterministic. Although they are Three, Itempas, Nahadoth and Enefa do not map cleanly onto the persons of the Trinity in Christian theology; rather, they periodically evoke contentious figurations, facets of or ways of understanding God, Christ or Christian theology in general. In particular, the varying shades of light and darkness that the Three are said to inhabit, and the theological, metaphysical and ethical values these represent, are broadly consistent with the theological treatment of light and darkness in *Till We Have Faces* and *The Left Hand of Darkness*. While the polyamorous desires and relationship patterns the Three and their godling offspring display throughout the trilogy enacts a fluidity and openness similar to what Althaus-Reid desires from a polyamorous approach to theology, this is often frustrated by both divine and human hierarchies of power in the texts' narrative.

As the bright Skyfather, Itempas embodies the 'light' of reason, sovereignty, visibility and order that tend to characterize the God of heterosexual, patriarchal, Western metaphysics. He is also obsessed with the metaphysics of *logos*, since 'to name a thing is to give it order and purpose' (Jemisin 2010a: 143), and multiple references are made to the power of his gaze. As the archetypal representation of order and sameness, Itempas is (or at least seems to be) an ideal figure for legitimizing the Arameri's imposition of their will upon all of the Hundred Thousand Kingdoms. Similarly to the Shining Daddy of Cheng's 'i shall remain', Itempas's relationships with Enefa, Yeine, Oree and Nahadoth raise provocative questions regarding the limits of the love of a god whose will is absolute. While *The Broken Kingdoms* and *The Kingdom of Gods* (2011) add nuance to Itempas's motivations, depicting him as an anguished lover, the novels make clear that the possessive and controlling nature of this love must be redeemed and transformed in order for the Three to be fully restored.

Nahadoth and Enefa, by contrast – and Yeine, once she ascends to godhood and assumes Enefa's former place among the Three – embody different figurations of godhood as disordered, fleshly alterity that, in the view of the Arameri and the Order of Itempas, corrupt and pollute the purity of the Bright Father's will. From a Christian standpoint, they evoke the 'sexual chaos and the chaos of death' that, in Althaus-Reid's words, 'are the two suppressed forces of Christianity although paradoxically they constitute the Christian paradigm' (Althaus-Reid 2000: 68). In Jemisin's depictions of Enefa and Yeine, there are shades of an Irigarayan reclamation of the tropes of woman-as-earth and woman-as-mortality; they are both goddesses of creation with dominion over life and death, without whom mortal life could not exist. Like Irigaray's divine woman, they inhabit the site of difference between Itempas's order and Nahadoth's chaos. Yeine's ascension to godhood at the first novel's conclusion is also described using feminine-coded language associated with childbirth.

Nahadoth, meanwhile, can be read as a figure of monstrous drag evoking a fluid understanding of gender and sexuality as well as a more generalized ethical alterity simultaneously shaped by and constantly eluding the gaze of the subject. Like the swirling Maelstrom that birthed him, and in a manner similar to the trace of deconstruction, his chaotic existence simultaneously makes possible and also threatens the stability and coherence of the universe. As the god of night, he also represents seduction and insatiable sexual appetites that are simultaneously dangerous and alluring to humans, functioning as both a receptacle and amplifier for the repressed desires of mortals. Although all the gods in the trilogy have attributes which render them monstrous and 'other' in the eyes of humans, Nahadoth owes much of his unique monstrosity, his potent sexuality and the fluidity of his gendered appearance to what others project onto him. The extent to which this renders him a figure of marginal alterity in the trilogy's first volume stems from his status as a slave to the Arameri. As he explains to Yeine, '[a]ll your terrors, all your needs [. . .] push and pull at me, silent commands' (Jemisin 2010a: 292). Although it is Nahadoth's nature to be shaped by the desires of mortals, however, he is not reducible to any form the mortal gaze may give him. Even the visible forms he inhabits are in constant flux, with shifting facial features and gendered attributes. In the temple of Sarenna-nem in Yeine's home city of Arrebaia, Nahadoth takes on a woman's face before transforming into something altogether more alien, and in *The Kingdom of Gods* he assumes a motherly form to comfort his firstborn Sieh, the god of childhood and trickery. In contrast to Itempas, who according to Sieh 'has always and only been male' (Jemisin 2011: 7), Nahadoth, though '[labelled] as male for the sake of convenience if not completeness' (Jemisin 2011: 6), is fluidly gendered in a way that points to the ultimate arbitrariness of human identity categories. Nahadoth's darkness and chaos therefore position him as a figuration of godhood as simultaneously sexual, gendered and ethical alterity.

Though gender fluidity is most pronounced in Nahadoth, it is by no means limited to him; in Sieh's words, gender 'is only a game for us, an affectation, like names and flesh. We employ such things because you need them, not because we do' (Jemisin 2011: 100). Sami Schalk has noted that Jemisin's treatment of godly embodiment in the context of erotic relationships destabilizes even ostensibly 'queer' primary-world sexual categories, since 'if god/godlings have no sex or gender and their mortal realm gender presentation is chosen and mutable, then their sexuality cannot be described in gendered-attraction sexuality terms such as hetero-, homo-, or bisexual' (Schalk 2018: 132). Furthermore, Schalk argues that the gods' alien forms of embodiment and the mystery of their divinity mean that 'the possibilities for sexual pleasure get expanded beyond normative conceptions of sex through, literally, magic' (Schalk 2018: 133). In Jemisin's world, godhood, incarnated in mortal flesh or otherwise, is queer in relation to primary-world norms for embodiment, as well as the norms that are established for what can be thought of as holy according to the 'official' doctrines and religious narratives in the texts' secondary world. Similar to Althaus-Reid's claim that 'we can know God better through a radical negation of the way of closeted knowing found in the tradition of the church and theology' (Althaus-Reid 2003: 171), Jemisin's gods transgress both bodily and doctrinal norms in a variety of ways.

The theology of Jemisin's *Inheritance* trilogy is, primarily, a sexual theology in which the restless erotics of the relationships between gods and humans collide with the distribution and regulation of spiritual, material and cultural goods. This especially becomes noticeable in *The Broken Kingdoms*, as Yeine becomes the new goddess, Nahadoth is liberated and Itempas is bound in mortal flesh, all of which alters the power balance of the cosmos and literally rearranges the map of Sky. The novel's narrative focus also shifts to Oree Shoth, a commoner in Sky-in-Shadow, who observes the rapid transformations in the city's religious make-up as godlings return to the mortal realm, new cults spring up in their honour and the Order of Itempas, newly powerless to curb the proliferation of these heresies, struggles to maintain what authority it has left. Things become even more fragmented by *The Kingdom of Gods*, as the consolidation of power between the Arameri and the Order of Itempas has almost fully dissolved and a growing secularist movement known as the 'primortalists' (Jemisin 2011: 105) is on the rise (with the Arameri eventually shifting their allegiance to Yeine). Additionally, where *The Hundred Thousand Kingdoms* establishes that magic consists of the language of the gods, heavily controlled by a handful of elites in the Order of Itempas, Oree describes her world as one in which

> we all used a little magic now and again in secret. Every woman knew the sigil to prevent pregnancy, and every neighborhood had someone who could draw the scripts for minor healing or hiding valuables in plain sight.
> (Jemisin 2010b: 40)

Like the subversive spiritual practices Althaus-Reid identifies among the working poor of Latin America, the common people of Sky-in-Shadow practice everyday acts of resistance not just through their heterodox religious observances but through their reclamation of divine knowledge for their own purposes and mutual aid.

Whereas the only mouthpieces the reader gets for Itempas in *The Hundred Thousand Kingdoms* are the Order and the Arameri, *The Broken Kingdoms* and *The Kingdom of Gods* divorce the will of Itempas from the doctrines of the Order. Itempas spends the remainder of the series incarnated in mortal flesh as a servant, living among the city's poor and outcasts and sleeping in the streets until he is taken in by Oree. Where most of the Order's depictions of Itempas 'made him slimmer, thin-featured, like an Amn' (Jemisin 2010a: 137), the white-coded race of the Arameri, his actual mortal form is that of a Maroneh, a dark-skinned minority race of the Senm continent. *The Broken Kingdoms* especially wrings significant dramatic irony from Itempas's followers' failure to recognize their god, and at several points he even comes under threat from them. This invites parallels to the theological claim made in John's Gospel that Christ 'came to what was his own, and his own people did not accept him' (Jn 1.11, NRSV). The fact that Itempas's tenure as a mortal is penance for his sins against Enefa, rather than a voluntary act of humility and solidarity, admittedly makes it difficult to fully align him with a Christ figure in a literal sense. In another sense, however, through the mortal form of Itempas Jemisin's novels offer a figuration of Christ as the stranger at the gates of hegemonic theology transforming and redeeming the transcendent Christ of triumphalist and colonial Christianity.

While the theological imaginaries of *The Left Hand of Darkness*, the *Earthsea* series and *The Passion of New Eve* offer a few fleeting glimpses of the intersections between sexual, gendered, racial and cultural alterity, in Jemisin's series these connections are explored in much more nuanced and detailed ways. The novels are highly attentive to the erotic and gendered dimensions of the theological, colonial, racial and class dynamics present in their secondary world. The sexual theological nature of Jemisin's worldbuilding culminates in *The Kingdom of Gods*, which chronicles Sieh's sudden transformation into a mortal on his way to achieving full godhood and his complicated romantic relationships with two Arameri twins, Shahar and Deka, amid the dissolution of the Arameri's empire. The novel concludes with Shahar renouncing the Arameri's power and distributing their resources among the people of the Hundred Thousand Kingdoms. Earlier in the novel, Shahar had walked in on her brother Deka and Sieh as they christened the altar at the temple of the new palace of Echo with their lovemaking. Now, as she addresses the gathered delegation from throughout the world, she '[stands] where [her] brother and best friend had shown [her] how to love' (Jemisin 2011: 531). Just as the trilogy's overarching conflict demonstrates the points where religious conflict, colonial politics and sexual desire intersect, so the eucatastrophic emergence of a new and hopefully more just society is heralded by an act of queer eroticism located at the heart of religious observance in its secondary world, possessive jealousy and greed giving way to the sovereign subject's surrender to the other. Jemisin's *Inheritance* trilogy is not for the faint of heart, and even its eucatastrophic conclusion places heavy emphasis on the 'catastrophic'. It is an uncompromising example of fantasy's unique potential as a sphere of postcolonial and sexual theological re-visioning for the twenty-first century.

Awaiting eucatastrophe

Taken together, the works of Ann Leckie, Neon Yang and N. K. Jemisin suggest several avenues for future studies of fantasy literature and the margins of theology. First, they highlight key differences between an understanding of queerness as a coalitional politics and queerness as an essentialist identity category. The twenty-first-century rise of liberal, 'born-this-way' LGBTQ+ politics in the Anglophone world, which has focused primarily on gaining access and inclusion for LGBTQ+ people within existing institutions such as marriage and political office, has resulted in a view of (largely white, largely middle-class) LGBTQ+ people as a marketing demographic within the corporate world and popular media. In fantasy fiction, this has often manifested in fiction whose representation of primary-world genders and sexualities is inclusive, and therefore perceived as marketable to LGBTQ+ readers, but not necessarily transformative in its aims. While Leckie's science fiction novels manage to deftly avoid this pitfall, *The Raven Tower*'s surface-level attempt at diversity is jarring alongside its otherwise nuanced treatment of theological signifying structures and economic systems. Fantasy fiction that seeks merely to validate whatever gender and sexual identity categories exist in the author's particular culture at a particular moment in time is dangerously comparable to the self-congratulatory practices of church inclusion that Tonstad associates with a 'refusal of radically alternative social imaginaries' (Tonstad 2016: 256). In both cases, the imaginative and interpretive work of queer communities risks being reduced to a form of social capital that legitimates the owner's claim to progressivism and correct thinking, instead of seeking to enrich the lives of actual queer people.[1] Fantastic endeavours to queerly re-vision theology in the twenty-first century must take care that they do not inadvertently reaffirm and naturalize the gendered and sexual norms they claim to be subverting by importing them wholesale into a secondary world where the rules of our world need not apply.

By contrast, Jemisin's and Yang's respective works both indicate that deconstructively undressing normative theology, and its prescriptions for sexuality and gender, remains relevant and urgent in the twenty-first century. For both authors, queer theological storytelling is a project whose racial and postcolonial dimensions are every bit as urgent as, and inextricably linked to, their gendered and sexual ones. Jemisin's *Inheritance* trilogy, especially, conclusively establishes the practices of Indecent Theology, and fantasy's ability to articulate them, as being of continued relevance in the twenty-first century. Yet Leckie, Jemisin and Yang also highlight sites of theological re-visioning in fantasy that are in need of further critical attention. Leckie's *The Raven Tower* opens a space to consider fantasy's relationship to eco-theology and non-human alterity, while the pluralistic religious landscape of Yang's novellas invites theological criticism of fantasy literature from outside the Christian paradigm. Additionally, while the alterity-based approach I have adopted in this book is generative for paying attention to the gaps, silences and exclusions in normative theological constructions, there remains a need for scholarship that addresses the dynamics of intersectionality at play in fantasy's theological storytelling. As theorized by Kimberlé Crenshaw, intersectionality involves attentiveness to the ways that overlapping sites of marginality compound one another in the experiences of individuals (for instance, Black women) so that they become 'greater than the sum' of separate axes of oppression (Crenshaw 1989: 140). While both Schalk (2018) and Thomas (2019) have engaged in impressively nuanced analyses of fantastic texts' relationship to intersectionality, theological studies of fantasy literature have yet to fully consider the implications of this work. While these discussions are beyond the scope of this book, my sincere hope is that the theological reading strategies I have developed create a space for them within the fields of fantasy literature as well as literature and theology.

The open-ended nature of fantasy means that every eucatastrophic conclusion exists in the advent of a transformation that cannot be prefigured in advance. Accordingly, the queer activity of theological re-visioning should be understood as an ongoing activity for which fantasy writing can be a generative starting point and indispensable imaginative resource, but never the final word. It would be tempting to argue for representations of femininity and queerness that humanize gender and sexually marginalized subjects, and for theologies that declare clear and absolute affirmation for such subjects from on high. However, fantasy itself, as well as the deconstructive projects that have informed my discussion of it in this book, casts into doubt whether such representations are desirable. Rather than seek an abstract moral justification for the affirmation of queer people or attempt to construct an ideal or universal queer or feminine subject, fantasy literature can write theology from the body and its desires in a way that can be liberating precisely because it confounds the strictures of conventional theology. In fantasy, not only are the mysterious nature of God and the incarnation reinvigorated with new-found strangeness, but so are our own bodily and sexual lives. Taking cues from Derrida's critique of the phallogocentric subject of theology and philosophy, I have thus favoured theological readings of fantasy that privilege disharmonious conjunctions of sacred and profane, orthodox and heretical, and divine and monstrous. Fantasy's potential to deconstruct and radically re-vision God, sex and gender does not promise easy gratification, but for authors and readers willing to risk opening themselves to transformation in the face of the other, it can work provisionally towards a justice that is still yet to come. In this way, fantasy can recast the story of theology as one of 'joy beyond the walls of the world' (Tolkien [1947] 2008: 75) for those of us living outside the gates of normative Christianity.

Notes

Introduction

1. From one perspective, Tolkien's designation of our own day-to-day reality as the 'Primary World' and fantasy worlds as 'secondary worlds' seems to imply a metaphysical hierarchy. While it is tempting to counterpose a 'primary world' that is 'real' against an unreal 'secondary world', this is fundamentally at odds with the deconstructive approach to fantastic worldbuilding taken up in this book. Indeed, as I argue explicitly in the first chapter and continue to reiterate in further chapters, fantastical 'secondary worlds' can, by their self-conscious fictitiousness, reveal that what is understood as the 'primary world' is itself a contingent textual construction. (This is also why I have chosen not to capitalize 'primary world', as Tolkien does, in my own invocation of the term.) Nonetheless, 'secondary world' is the most commonly used term for fictional worlds in current fantasy scholarship and therefore, while it is to be understood as provisional, it is used throughout this book.
2. Clemente Lisi documents how the threat Bolsonaro and his policies pose to indigenous, feminist and LGBTQ+ rights are intertwined with conservative Catholic and evangelical Protestant ideologies; see Lisi (2019).
3. The most extreme example is the state of Alabama, which in May of 2019 passed a bill calling for a near-blanket ban on abortions in which doctors face a life sentence in prison for performing the procedure. Other states to have passed similarly restrictive laws include Ohio, Kentucky, Georgia and Mississippi. See Presaud (2019).
4. See Ash (2020) for commentary on how these initiatives have been supported by prominent leaders in the Catholic Church in Poland.
5. Arguably among the best of these is Sami Schalk's *Bodyminds Reimagined: (Dis)ability, Race, and Gender in Black Women's Speculative Fiction*, which examines works from a range of speculative genres at the intersections of Black feminism, queer theory, crip theory and disability studies. Equally worthy of mention is Ebony Elizabeth Thomas (2019). Thomas's monograph is a study of race and gender in fantasy, but it also provides a theoretically grounded structural critique of the Western fantastic imagination and the colonial, white supremacist cultural and material conditions that produce the representations she discusses in her study. Notable surveys of current discourse on gender and sexuality in fantasy include Barbini (2018) and Roberts and MacCallum-Stewart (2016).

6 Kenneally's study is a particularly strange case in that it begins by acknowledging that '[q]ueer fantasy's invisibility [. . .] is rooted in [. . .] the tendency of queerness to inhabit the margins, and the power and potential that lies within the hidden' (Kenneally 2016: 8), only to go on to diagnose this 'power and potential' as a problem and curate a 'canon' of queer fantasy using ruthlessly narrow criteria based on visibility and optics.

7 On this point, Eve Kosofsky Sedgwick's ambivalent theorization of the closet can be instructive. As she notes, 'the deadly elasticity of heterosexist presumption means that, like Wendy in *Peter Pan*, people find new walls springing up around them even as they drowse' so that 'there can be few gay people, however courageous and forthright by habit, however fortunate in the support of their immediate communities, in whose lives the closet is not still a shaping presence' (Sedgwick 1990: 68). This will be discussed in further detail in Chapter 4.

8 See Althaus-Reid and Isherwood (2007), Althaus-Reid (2004), Coakley (2002), Fisk (2014), Jantzen (1998), Walton (2007).

9 Indeed, Derrida has noted that Christianity's dominance in Western discourse extends to the discursive categories of 'religion' and 'theology' per se; that is, to speak at all of 'religion' or 'theology' is already to fall back within Christian notions of religious belief and practice as distinct and distinguishable from 'culture'. Derrida calls this phenomenon 'globalatinization' (Derrida [1996] 2002: 44).

10 For theoretical insight on this phenomenon, see Davidsen (2016) and Petersen (2016). Kirby (2013) is particularly lucid, focusing on the Otherkin community as a case study, even though its conclusions tend towards a liberal focus on the 'humanization of the other' (Kirby 2013: 100) that this book does not share.

11 There are a handful of articles, book chapters and blog posts that have begun to make connections between fantasy literature and queer/feminist Christian theologies and therefore serve as important precursors to this book. These include Anderson (2016), which examines how Le Guin's later young adult fiction uses fantasy to unsettle difference-suppressing religious dogmas, as well as Linn Marie Tonstad's guest blog for *Fantasy Matters* on sexual theology in the fiction of N. K. Jemisin (see Tonstad 2011). Additionally, scholarship on the works of Lois McMaster Bujold has often intersected with queer and feminist theologies, as evidenced by several essays in McCormack and Lee (2020), including Lee (2020), Reid (2020) and MacDonald (2020).

12 A typical example is Łaskiewicz (2018), which nominally recognizes fantasy's ability to challenge religious doctrines but is ultimately much more concerned with insisting that fantasy does not pose a threat to Christian orthodoxy as usual. Gray (2013) is theologically and methodologically more rigorous than most studies of theology and fantasy, and even goes some way towards suggesting an inherently deconstructive potential in fantasy (see Gray 2013: 94). However, Gray's adherence

to the methods and vocabulary of systematic theology prevents him from pursuing this point further, and the result is a hint of a more radical project that never fully materializes. Single-author studies written in this vein that are of particular relevance to this study include Chou (2016) and Hilder (2013), which attempt to graft feminist vocabulary onto patriarchal complementarian theology. A notable exception to this rule is Vincent (2012), which theorizes popular fantasy as an imaginative site for exchange, re-visioning and critique across religious difference.

13 See Driggers (2013).

14 This understanding of the relationship between Christian theology and literature is echoed in Philip and Carol Zaleski's recent literary biography of the Inklings, which assesses the Inklings' project as 'a revitalization of Christian imaginative and poetic life' (Zaleski and Zaleski 2015: 510) for which fantasy becomes 'an intimation of a different, higher, purer world or state of being' (Zaleski and Zaleski 2015: 11). While the thoroughness of the Zaleskis' research is impressive and the book is a vital resource for any scholarship on the relevant authors, there is a lingering impression, not uncommon in scholarly projects on the Inklings, that faithfully reproducing the lives, practices and avowed theologies of these early- to mid-twentieth-century fantasists will grant the dedicated scholar or fan privileged insight into ultimate theological truth.

15 A paywalled *Christianity Today* article from 2002 boasts the punchy headline 'Don't Let Your Kids Watch *Buffy the Vampire Slayer*' and portentously states that 'for Christians, there are added obstacles' to enjoying the show due to the presence of witchcraft and queer sexualities, among other 'family-unfriendly' elements. See Hertz (2002).

16 The popular fact-checking website *Snopes* documents one notable instance in which multiple evangelical groups seized on a 2001 article from *The Onion* satirizing the 'Satanic panic' surrounding *Harry Potter* and took it at face value, giving rise to a slew of think pieces and chain emails that have been the primary means by which the controversy spread. See Mikkelson (2001).

17 A particularly egregious example of such handwringing is found in an interview with Richard Abanes on the website of televangelist Pat Robertson's *Christian Broadcast Network*, in which Abanes attempts to adjudicate between 'good' fantasy such as the works of Lewis and Tolkien, and the 'dark', 'occult' and 'anti-Christian' impulses of *Buffy*, *Harry Potter* and *His Dark Materials*. See Elliott (2021).

18 This elision is most clearly articulated in Łaskiewicz's study, which expressly states its avoidance of 'the meanders of Christian diversity' since these 'would require in-depth theological study' (Łaskiewicz 2018: 7), choosing instead to rehearse oft-repeated talking points about fantasy's relation to myth and early-twentieth-century phenomenology of religion (despite the contemporary nature of the primary texts). However, it is also keenly felt in Filmer's *Scepticism and Hope*. In that study, the

actual theological content of fantasy texts does not seem to matter terribly much so long as it articulates a vaguely defined 'hope', even as Filmer's lamentation of 'the proscription of certain religious practices – such as the recitation of prayers in public (state-run) schools in the United States and also in Australia' (Filmer 1992: 140) betrays a forcefully, even reactionary, Christian bias. (It should not go without mention that Filmer's rhetoric regarding the disappearance of religion from Western public life is strikingly similar to that often adopted by homophobic and transphobic political projects, as noted earlier in this introduction.)

19 Contrast, for instance, Jesus's call to abandon traditional family ties in following him in Lk. 14.26 with many contemporary Christians' anxieties over threats to (implicitly white, heterosexual, middle-class) 'family values'.

20 Most relevant to this book, and discussed in-depth in Chapter 4, are the works of Althaus-Reid (2000, 2003, 2004). Walton (2007) also lays crucial groundwork arguing for the necessity for marginalized subjects to take up a deconstructive relationship to theology via literature. Walton (2011b: 37–54) complicates many of the arguments made in her earlier monograph while still maintaining its fundamental aims. Lastly, Sherwood and Hart (2005) showcases many marginalized theologians' engagement with Derrida. Of the essays presented in the volume, Grace M. Jantzen's 'Touching (in) the Desert: Who Goes There?' is a particular standout.

21 Many of Derrida's writings most overtly concerned with religion and theology have been collected in the English translation by Anidjar (2002). The volume includes Derrida's 1996 essay 'Faith and Knowledge: The Two Sources of "Religion" at the Limits of Reason Alone', which grapples with the persistence of religion in the twentieth century, its embeddedness in politics, the status of 'religion' as a uniquely Christian category and its relationship to the scientific age. To name two more such texts directly relevant to this study: *The Gift of Death* (1992) traces a complex genealogy of Judaism, Christianity and Western metaphysics and also turns its attention to mortality, suffering and the ethics of Emmanuel Levinas, by way of reading Abraham's sacrifice of Isaac from the end of Genesis. *Rogues* (2002), meanwhile, continues this engagement with Levinas as it considers the concept of divine sovereignty in the way it informs the sovereignty of nations on a geopolitical scale.

22 Two of the most notable examples of this type of autobiographical reflection are *Archive Fever* (1995) and *Jacques Derrida (Religion and Postmodernism)* (1999) co-authored with Geoffrey Bennington, which includes Derrida's essay 'Circumfession'.

23 An example of the latter is found in Shepherd (2014), which situates itself as a theological engagement with Derrida and Levinas on alterity, only to privilege orthodox Christian understandings of hospitality over and against the former two's interventions into ethics.

24 In 'Psyche: Inventions of the Other' (1987), Derrida explicitly reflects on the gendering of the relation between the same and the other as feminine through the persona of Psyche in Greek mythology. This is particularly relevant to this study given that *Till We Have Faces* is itself a retelling of the myth of Eros and Psyche. Other notable explicit engagements with feminism by Derrida include an interview with Christie MacDonald entitled 'Choreographies' (translated by Peggy Kamuf), in Derrida and MacDonald (1985: 163–86), Derrida (1984).

25 See Spivak (1988: 271–313).

26 See Butler ([1990] 2007).

27 Horstkotte (2004) largely ignores genre fantasy and instead hews closely to authors generally accepted within the established literary canon. Its selection of texts is also, lamentably, overwhelmingly male and white, and when addressing this exclusivity Horstkotte only says, '[t]he thematisation of gender issues in the context of magic realism is not the focus of this study' (Horstkotte 2004: 11, fn. 12). Much more satisfying is Hume (1997: 173–82) (not to be confused with Thomas's aforementioned monograph, also titled *The Dark Fantastic*). Hume retains a sense of deconstruction's concern for marginality and alterity, but both she and Horstkotte unfortunately gloss deconstructive literature as an evacuated space rather than the affirmative movement described by Derrida.

28 The UK's first centre for the study of science fiction and fantasy opened at Anglia Ruskin University in February 2017. In September of 2020, the University of Glasgow also launched its Centre for Fantasy and the Fantastic, following the success of its MLitt programme in Fantasy Literature.

29 See Duncan (2014). It should be stressed that Duncan's argument stems from an overtly queer critical approach, situating practitioners of strange fiction as denizens of 'the city of New Sodom' (Duncan 2014: 3) and claiming that '[t]here is no GENRE of FANTASY, only the fantasy of GENRE' (Duncan 2014: 68).

30 Roz Kaveney has taken up a particularly nuanced and rigorous discussion of Carter's relationship to pulp science fiction and genre fantasy, including a detailed analysis of *The Passion of New Eve*, in her essay Kaveney (2007 [1994]: 184–200).

31 See Mendlesohn (2008).

32 See Armitt (1996), which elaborates on Rosemary Jackson's poststructuralist and psychoanalytic understanding of fantasy but shows, with some success, that its applications extend into the types of worldbuilding fantasy that Jackson derides.

33 An excellently rigorous and widely influential materialist reading of fantasy can be found in Zipes (2002).

34 See Gifford (2018).

35 A detailed account of the campaign as of 2015 can be found in VanDerWerff (2015).

Chapter 1

1. While the trauma experienced by Tolkien, White and Lewis stems from the two World Wars, Shippey notes that Le Guin's fiction is in constant dialogue with the destruction of indigenous peoples and cultures by American settler colonialism, which her anthropologist parents documented extensively in their work.
2. Tolkien is clearly playing on two definitions of 'catastrophe' here, in the classical sense of a final event or dénouement and in the sense of a disruptive and cataclysmic event. He counterposes eucatastrophe with 'dyscatastrophe' or an end marked by destruction and despair, stating that '[i]t does not deny the existence of *dyscatastrophe*, of sorrow and failure: the possibility of these is necessary to the joy of deliverance; it denies (in the face of much evidence, if you will) universal final defeat' (Tolkien [1947] 2008: 75). The anticipation of eucatastrophe, therefore, necessitates a radically open structure, and its arrival does not cancel out dyscatastrophe but transforms it.
3. It should be noted that Le Guin herself refutes this reading of Tolkien's fiction in a 1977 review of C. S. Lewis's *The Dark Tower*, stating that '[t]hough Tolkien seems to project evil into "the others", they are not truly others but ourselves' (Guin [1977] 1989: 242–4).
4. While Derrida uses this passage to describe Francis Ponge's poem 'Fable' specifically, in the context of the essay the 'Fable' serves as an illustration of deconstruction's performative movement. Just as 'Fable' enacts the breaking of the mirror it describes by laying bare the limits and contradictions of that mirror (i.e. its own structure and language), deconstructive writing uses its own reliance on language to expose the limits of language and open towards the other outside of language and possibility.
5. Or, as Orual puts it, 'like all these sacred matters, it is and it is not' (Lewis 1956: 268).
6. The most comprehensive discussion of Taoism in Le Guin's fiction can be found in Erlich (2010), but it is also explored in Bittner (1984), Bucknall (1981), Clarke (2010), Oziewicz (2008) and Rochelle (2001).
7. Derrida engages in extensive wordplay with these words in 'Psyche: Invention of the Other'.
8. Genly's words here quote the German Jewish existentialist Martin Buber almost verbatim. Buber theorizes that all life and identity are constituted by two terms: '*I–It*', which deals with the realm of experience, and '*I–Thou*', which 'establishes the world of relation' (Buber [1923] 1937: 6). As with the eventual nature of Genly's relation with Estraven, Buber argues that '[t]he relation to the *Thou* is direct. No system of ideas, no foreknowledge, and no fancy intervene between *I* and *Thou*' (Buber [1923] 1937: 11). Similarly to Levinas, Buber figures the *I–Thou* relationship as religious in structure, for 'just as prayer is not in time but time in prayer, sacrifice not in space but space in sacrifice, and to reverse the relation is to abolish the reality, so with the man [*sic*] to whom I say *Thou*' (Buber [1923] 1937: 8–9).

Chapter 2

1 Moreover, as I argue in Chapter 4, the novel's worldbuilding also anticipates many of the queer and trans theories of gender that have arisen out of Cixous's project in the intervening years.
2 The sexual aspect of the Foretelling will be discussed in more depth in Chapter 4, as it relates to deviance from gender and sexual norms.

Chapter 3

1 My position regarding the possibility of a resistant reading of Irigaray is similar to that of Grace M. Jantzen, who argues that 'if we affirm that lesbians and gay men also are "real" women and men, then such a heterosexist reading [of Irigaray and Feuerbach] can be rejected while retaining the crucial point: that human selves are sexuate selves, and that if there is to be a divine horizon for human becoming, sexuality cannot be left out of it' (Jantzen 1998: 94). Moreover, as will become clear in Chapter 4, the ways in which some queer and particularly trans theologies have adapted Irigaray's notions of becoming deconstruct the possibility of the sexuate self as a 'real' and unified whole.
2 For readings of Irigaray's overarching project that focus on her engagement with the divine, see Joy (2006) and Martin (2000). For a reading of Irigaray's work as a re-visioning of Levinasian ethics of alterity, see Leonard (2000). For an examination of Irigaray's treatment of mysticism, see Kitty Scoular Datta, 'Female Heterologies: Women's Mysticism, Gender-Mixing and the Apophatic' in *Self/Same/Other*. For a comprehensive overview of the debate as to the usefulness of Irigaray's invocation of the divine for feminist theology, see the conclusion to Joy's *Divine Love*, 142–60. For a discussion of the necessity of a deconstructive, against-the-grain reading of Irigaray for feminist theology, see Armour (1997: 193–214). For elaborations of feminist theologies based in part on Irigaray's philosophical project, see Althaus-Reid (2004), Althaus-Reid and Isherwood (2007), Coakley (2002), Jantzen (1998) and Walton (2007).
3 For further elaboration on the relationship between Irigaray's ethics of sexual difference and restorative justice, see Irigaray ([1989] 1994).
4 This tendency within feminist writing was also prominently explored in speculative fiction texts from the 1970s through the 1990s. Marge Piercy's *Woman on the Edge of Time* (1976) draws a stark contrast between the oppressively hierarchical conditions of the contemporary New York inhabited by its protagonist, Connie Ramos, and the androgynous, anarchist and cooperative future utopia of Mattapoisett, from which Connie receives visions throughout the novel. A text examining similar themes

of anarchist and ecofeminist utopia, albeit from a more essentialist and lesbian separatist standpoint, is Sally Miller Gearhart's *The Wanderground* (1979). Marion Zimmer Bradley's highly influential *The Mists of Avalon* (1983) also adopts an essentialist stance, staging a retelling of the Arthurian legend in which women are caught between the nurturing but dying pagan religion of the Mother-Goddess and the violent, patriarchal Christianity adopted by Arthur and his knights. For related discussions, see Filmer (1992), especially Chapter 11 (127–37), as well as James (2012: 62–78).

5 It is worth noting that devouring, absorption and assimilation into the self occur throughout Lewis's fiction as motifs associated with hell. In *The Screwtape Letters*, for instance, the demon Screwtape transforms into a centipede out of rage at his nephew and declares, 'In my present form I feel even more anxious to see you, to unite you to myself in an indissoluble embrace' (Lewis 2001 [1942]: 121). In *That Hideous Strength*, the deputy director of the demonic N.I.C.E. plots to make anti-hero Mark complicit in the organization's agenda by declaring that he 'would open [his] arms to receive – to absorb – to assimilate this young man' (Lewis [1945] 2005: 332).

6 'Body' is placed in quotation marks in this passage to highlight the 'body' as a philosophical construct in contrast to essentialized notions of embodiment.

7 Lacan elaborates his theory of the mirror stage in the opening chapter of *Écrits*, stating that the moment that 'the human child [. . .] can finally recognize his own image as such in a mirror' (Lacan [1966] 2002: 3) establishes 'the symbolic matrix in which the *I* is precipitated in a primordial form' (Lacan [1966] 2002: 4). Although Eve is an adult woman, the imagery of birth pervading Beulah invites a comparison with Lacan's theory; note, for instance, that Lacan's archetypal child is implicitly male.

Chapter 4

1 Two notable examples in particular have surfaced in recent years, one from the Protestant world and one from the Catholic. In August of 2017, the evangelical Council on Biblical Manhood and Womanhood posted the Nashville Statement, an open letter on Christian sexuality and gender roles that states, 'WE DENY that God has designed marriage to be a homosexual, polygamous, or polyamorous relationship' (see *Nashville Statement* (2017) https://cbmw.org/nashville-statement/ (accessed 29 June 2021)). Meanwhile, in June 2019, as the LGBTQ+ community was commemorating the fiftieth anniversary of the Stonewall Riots, the Vatican's Congregation for Catholic Education published a document entitled 'Male and Female He Created Them' opposing transgender identities. The full text of this can be found at Staff (2019).

2   For a more thorough historicization (and problematization) of the development of post-Stonewall queer politics in the United States through the latter days of the AIDS crisis, see Berlant and Freeman (1993: 193–229).
3   Alyson Escalante's viral essay 'Gender Nihilism' is one of the more notable recent examples of such a critique, cautioning that 'the ever expanding list of personal preferred pronouns, the growing and ever more nuanced labels for various expressions of sexuality and gender, and the attempt to construct new identity categories more broadly' can be the means by which 'we ensnare ourselves in countless and even more nuanced and powerful norms' (Escalante 2016).
4   A comprehensive overview of these varying perspectives can be found in Stryker and Whittle (2006) and Stryker and Aizura (2013).
5   A good introduction to the legal, political and economic concerns of transgender politics is Giles (2019), which posits the myriad practical considerations involved in gender transition as forms of labour 'to produce genders survivable under capitalism, at least for another year' (Giles 2019: 4) and advocates a project of 'gender communism' (Giles 2019: 6) to undo these conditions. Giles's manifesto was first distributed as a zine at the Dundee Centre for Contemporary Arts exhibition 'Seized by the Left Hand', which displayed artworks and performances inspired by or thematically linked to *The Left Hand of Darkness* from December 2019 through March 2020.
6   One trans scholar who has begun to make crucial interventions on this front is M. W. Bychowski. Her essay 'On Genesis' connects Tolkienian subcreation to 'the process of assigning meaning to bodies' (Bychowski 2019: 443) that occurs when Adam names the animals in the Garden of Eden in order to posit a theology of trans liberation. Within this trans-liberative framework, fantasy as not only a theological but a divinely ordained act affirms gender and transition as important for forming self-identity and meaningful social relations, while continuing to resist Christian arguments for gender essentialism. See Bychowski (2019).
7   Thomas outlines the difficulty, necessity and radical potential of deconstructively unpicking the colonial and white supremacist underpinnings of the Western fantastic imagination (especially as they intersect with gender) at length in *The Dark Fantastic*, arguing that '[l]iberating the fantastic from its fear and loathing of darkness and Dark Others not only requires new narratives for the sake of endarkened readers. It requires emancipating the imagination itself' (Thomas 2019: 29).
8   It remains to be seen what the lasting consequences of the Covid-19 pandemic will be for queer theology. Certainly, at the time of writing, it seems to present an impasse, having simultaneously made thinking communion in terms of gathered bodies difficult while also presenting an opportunity to revisit queer theory's own origins as arising out of a global pandemic. Going forward, queer theology will

need to resist the discourses of purity and cleanliness, especially those surrounding the bodies of sexual and racialized 'others', that have emerged amid the twenty-first-century public health crisis, as well as give renewed attention to the multiple traumas of disease, isolation and loss of community, and the unequal distribution of wealth, access to medical care and the ability to safely shelter in place that have shaped many queer people's experiences of the pandemic.

9 For a video recording, see London Drag Shows, 'Sasha Velour – As I Love You (Gollum Mix) @ The Powder Room, Brighton – 19/01/2018', *YouTube* (22 January 2018). https://www.youtube.com/watch?v=JEwH0JjCNh4 (accessed 8 March 2021). Special thanks goes to Naomi Berry for pointing me towards this performance.

10 For a more in-depth, and even more ambivalent, queer reading of Sauron's gaze in *The Lord of the Rings*, see Battis (2004).

11 For one example, see Tonstad's critique in *God and Difference* of 'womb-wound' imagery associated with Christ and the crucifixion, which 'derives from the ancient image of the birth of the church out of the spear-wound in Jesus' side' (Tonstad 2016: 13). In Tonstad's view, this symbolically naturalizes and sacralizes women's suffering by attributing it to the fundamental nature of Christ – especially when it is deployed to position Christ as 'feminine' – rather than positioning it as an effect of worldly injustice and sin.

Monstrous messianisms

1 Though not explicitly commenting on fantasy fiction, Huw Lemmey has recently referred to this phenomenon in broader popular media as 'gay stories for straight allies' (Lemmey 2021: 16 of 22 paras) because of the way queer life is instrumentalized in these narratives 'to confer some moral benefit, to offer a fable, for a straight life' (Lemmey 2021: 18 of 22 paras).

Bibliography

Althaus-Reid, Marcella, *From Feminist Theology to Indecent Theology: Readings on Poverty, Sexual Identity and God*. London: SCM Press, 2004.

Althaus-Reid, Marcella, *Indecent Theology: Theological Perversions in Sex, Gender and Politics*. London and New York, NY: Routledge, 2000.

Althaus-Reid, Marcella, *The Queer God*. London and New York, NY: Routledge, 2003.

Althaus-Reid, Marcella and Lisa Isherwood, *Controversies in Feminist Theology*. London: SCM Press, 2007.

Altizer, Thomas J. J., 'History as Apocalypse', in *Deconstruction and Theology*, 147–77. New York, NY: Crossroad Publishing, 1982.

Anderson, Elizabeth, 'Ursula Le Guin and Theological Alterity', *Literature and Theology* 30, no. 2 (June 2016): 182–97.

Armitt, Lucie, *Theorising the Fantastic*. London: Arnold, 1996.

Armour, Ellen T., 'Crossing the Boundaries Between Deconstruction, Feminism, and Religion', in *Feminist Interpretations of Jacques Derrida*, edited by Nancy J. Holland, 193–214. University Park, PA: Pennsylvania State University Press.

Ash, Lucy, 'Inside Poland's "LGBT-free" zones', *BBC* (20 September 2020).

Attebery, Brian, *Stories About Stories: Fantasy and the Remaking of Myth*. New York, NY and Oxford: Oxford University Press, 2014.

Attebery, Brian, *Strategies of Fantasy*. Bloomington, IN: Indiana University Press, 1992.

Barbini, Francesca T. (ed.), *Gender Identity and Sexuality in Current Fantasy and Science Fiction*. Edinburgh: Luna Press Publishing, 2018.

Battis, Jes, 'Delany's Queer Markets: *Nevèrÿon* and the Texture of Capital', *Science Fiction Studies* 36, no. 3 (November 2009): 478–89.

Battis, Jes, 'Gazing upon Sauron: Hobbits, Elves, and the Queering of the Postcolonial Optic', *Modern Fiction Studies* 50, no. 4 (Winter 2004): 908–26.

Berlant, Lauren and Elizabeth Freeman, 'Queer Nationality', in *Fear of a Queer Planet: Queer Politics and Social Theory*, edited by Michael Warner, 193–229. Minneapolis, MN and London: University of Minnesota Press, 1993.

Bittner, James, *Approaches to the Fiction of Ursula K. Le Guin*. Ann Arbor, MI: UMI Research Press, 1984.

Blyth, Ian, and Susan Sellers, *Hélène Cixous: Live Theory*. New York, NY and London: Continuum, 2004.

Bourke, Liz, 'Striking and Ambitious Fantasy: *The Raven Tower* by Ann Leckie', *Tor.com* (26 February 2019). https://www.tor.com/2019/02/26/book-reviews-the-raven-tower-by-ann-leckie (accessed 3 March 2021).

Bradley, Marion Zimmer, *The Mists of Avalon*. New York, NY: Ballantine Books, 1983.

Braidotti, Rosi, *Nomadic Subjects: Embodiment and Sexual Difference in Contemporary Feminist Theory*. New York, NY: Columbia University Press, 1994.

Buber, Martin, *I and Thou*, translated by Ronald Gregor Smith. Edinburgh: T. & T. Clark, [1923] 1937.

Bucknall, Barbara J., *Ursula K. Le Guin*. New York, NY: Frederick Ungar Publishing Co., 1981.

Butler, Judith, *Gender Trouble: Feminism and the Subversion of Identity*. New York, NY and London: Routledge, [1990] 2007.

Butler, Judith, *Undoing Gender*. New York, NY and London: Routledge, 2004.

Butler, Judith, *Gender Trouble: Feminism and the Subversion of Identity*. New York, NY and London: Routledge, [1990] 2007.

Bychowski, M. W., 'On Genesis: Transgender and Subcreation', *Transgender Studies Quarterly* 6, no. 3 (August 2019): 442–7.

Caputo, John D., *The Prayers and Tears of Jacques Derrida: Religion without Religion*. Bloomington, IN: Indiana University Press, 1997.

Carnell, Corbin Scott, *Bright Shadow of Reality: C. S. Lewis and the Feeling Intellect*. Grand Rapids, MI: Eerdmans, 1974.

Carter, Angela, *The Passion of New Eve*. London: Virago Press, [1977] 2012.

Cheng, Kai Thom, 'i Shall Remain', in *Maiden, Mother, Crone: Fantastical Trans Femmes*, edited by Gwen Benaway, 97–107. Winnipeg: Bedside Press, 2019.

Chou, Christine Hsin-Chin, 'The Sacred Space Within: Toward a Psychology of Religion in C. S. Lewis' *Till We Have Faces*', in *Literature and Theology* 30, no. 2 (June 2016): 1–17.

Cixous, Hélène, 'Coming to Writing', in *'Coming to Writing' and Other Essays*, translated by Sarah Cornell, Deborah Jenson, Ann Liddle, and Susan Sellers, edited by Deborah Jenson, 1–58. Cambridge, MA and London: Harvard University Press, [1986] 1991.

Cixous, Hélène, 'The Laugh of the Medusa', *New French Feminisms*, translated by Keith Cohen and Paula Cohen, edited by Elaine Marks and Isabelle de Courtivron, 245–64. Brighton: Harvester Press, [1975] 1980.

Cixous, Hélène, *A Portrait of Jacques Derrida as a Young Jewish Saint*, translated by Beverley Bie Brahic, New York, NY: Columbia University Press, [2001] 2004.

Cixous, Hélène, 'Sorties', in *The Newly Born Woman*, translated by Betsy Wing, edited by Hélène Cixous and Catherine Clément, 63–132. London: I. B. Tauris Publishers, [1975] 1986.

Clarke, Amy M., *Ursula K. Le Guin's Journey to Post-Feminism*. Jefferson, NC: McFarland & Co., Publishers, 2010.

Coakley, Sarah, *Powers and Submissions: Spirituality, Philosophy and Gender*. Oxford and Malden, MA: Blackwell, 2002.

Cohen, Jeffrey Jerome, 'Monster Culture (Seven Theses)', in *Monster Theory: Reading Culture*, edited by Jeffrey Jerome Cohen, 3–25. Minneapolis, MN and London: University of Minnesota Press, 1996.

Crenshaw, Kimberlé, 'Demarginalizing the Intersection of Race and Sex: A Black Feminist Critique of Anti-Discrimination Doctrine, Feminist Theory and Antiracist Politics', *University of Chicago Legal Forum* 1 (1989): 139-68.

Datta, Kitty Scoular, 'Female Heterologies: Women's Mysticism, Gender-Mixing and the Apophatic', in *Self/Same/Other: Revisioning the Subject in Literature and Theology*, edited by Heather Walton and Andrew W. Haas, 125-36. Sheffield: Sheffield Academic Press, 2000.

Davidsen, Markus Altena, 'The Religious Affordance of Fiction: Towards a Catalogue of Veracity Mechanisms in Supernatural Narratives', *Religion* 46, no. 4 (October 2016): 521-49.

De Lauretis, Teresa, 'Queer Theory: Lesbian and Gay Sexualities, an Introduction', *Differences* 3, no. 2 (Summer 1991): iii-xviii.

Delany, Samuel R., *Tales of Nevèrÿon*. London: Grafton Books, [1979] 1988.

Derrida, Jacques, 'Faith and Knowledge: The Two Sources of "Religion" at the Limits of Reason Alone', *Acts of Religion*, translated by Samuel Weber, edited by Gil Anidjar, 40-101. New York, NY and London: Routledge, [1996] 2002.

Derrida, Jacques, *The Gift of Death*, translated by David Wills. Chicago, IL and London: University of Chicago Press, [1992] 1995.

Derrida, Jacques, 'Letter to a Japanese Friend', in *Derrida and Différance*, translated by David Wood and Andrew Benjamin, edited by David Wood and Robert Bernasconi, 1-6. Evanston, IL: Northwestern University Press, [1983] 1988.

Derrida, Jacques, *Margins of Philosophy*, translated by Alan Bass. Brighton: Harvester Press, [1972] 1982.

Derrida, Jacques, *Of Grammatology*, translated by Gayatri Chakravorty Spivak, 2nd edn. Baltimore, MD and London: Johns Hopkins University Press, [1967] 1997.

Derrida, Jacques, 'Psyche: Invention of the Other', in *Acts of Literature*, translated by Catherine Porter, edited by Derek Attridge, 310-43. New York, NY and London: Routledge, [1987] 1992.

Derrida, Jacques, *Rogues*, translated by Pascale-Anne Brault and Michael Naas. Stanford, CA: Stanford University Press, [2002] 2005.

Derrida, Jacques, 'Women in the Beehive: A Seminar with Jacques Derrida', *Differences* 16, no. 3 (Fall 2005): 138-57. Reprinted from *subjects/objects* Spring 1984.

Derrida, Jacques, *Writing and Difference*, translated by Alan Bass. London: Routledge and Kegan Paul, [1967] 1979.

Derrida, Jacques and Christie MacDonald, 'Choreographies', in *The Ear of the Other: Texts and Discussions with Jacques Derrida*, translated by Peggy Kamuf, edited by Claude Levesque and Christie MacDonald, 163-86. Lincoln, NE: University of Nebraska Press, 1985.

Derrida, Jacques, John D. Caputo, Kevin Hart, and Yvonne Sherwood, 'Epoché and Faith', in *Derrida and Religion: Other Testaments*, edited by Yvonne Sherwood and Kevin Hart, 27-50. New York, NY and London: Routledge, 2005.

Dick, Maria-Daniella, and Julian Wolfreys, *The Derrida Wordbook*. Edinburgh: Edinburgh University Press, 2013.

Donaldson, Mara E., 'Orual's Story and the Art of Retelling: A Study of *Till We Have Faces*', in *Word and Story in C. S. Lewis: Language and Narrative in Theory and Practice*, edited by Peter J. Schakel and Charles A. Huttar, 157–70. Eugene, OR: Wipf and Stock Publishers, 2007.

Downing, David C., *Into the Wardrobe: C. S. Lewis and the Narnia Chronicles*. San Francisco, CA: Jossey-Bass, 2005.

Driggers, Taylor, 'Modern Medievalism and Myth: Tolkien, Tennyson, and the Quest for a Hero', *Journal of Inklings Studies* 3, no. 2 (October 2013): 133–52.

Duncan, Hal, *Rhapsody: Notes on Strange Fictions*. Maple Shade, NJ: Lethe Press, 2014.

Elliott, Belinda, 'Harry Potter: Harmless Christian Novel or Doorway to the Occult?', *CBN*. https://www1.cbn.com/books/harry-potter-harmless-christian-novel-or-doorway-to-the-occult (accessed 29 June 2021).

Erlich, Richard D., *Coyote's Song: The Teaching Stories of Ursula K. Le Guin*. Rockville, MD: Borgo Press, 2010.

Escalante, Alyson, 'Gender Nihilism: An Anti-Manifesto', *Libcom.org*, 2016. https://libcom.org/library/gender-nihilism-anti-manifesto (accessed 29 June 2021).

Filmer, Kath, *The Fiction of C. S. Lewis: Mask and Mirror*. Houndmills, Basingstoke: Macmillan; New York, NY: St Martin's Press, 1993.

Filmer, Kath, 'Of Lunacy and Laundry Trucks', *Literature and Belief* 9 (1989): 55–64.

Filmer, Kath, *Scepticism and Hope in Twentieth Century Fantasy Literature*. Bowling Green, OH: Bowling Green State University Popular Press, 1992.

Fisk, Anna, *Sex, Sin, and Our Selves: Encounters in Feminist Theology and Contemporary Women's Literature*. Eugene, OR: Pickwick Publications, 2014.

Gearhart, Sally Miller, *The Wanderground: Stories of the Hill Women*. London: Women's Press, [1979] 1985.

Gifford, James, *A Modernist Fantasy: Modernism, Anarchism, and the Radical Fantastic*. Victoria, BC: ELS Editions, 2018.

Giles, Harry Josephine, *Wages for Transition*. Edinburgh: Easter Road Press, 2019.

Gilman, Greer, *Moonwise*. London: Penguin, 1991.

Gray, Mike, *Transfiguring Transcendence in Harry Potter, His Dark Materials and Left Behind*. Göttingen and Bristol, CT: Vandenhoeck & Ruprecht, 2013.

Halberstam, Jack, *The Queer Art of Failure*. Durham, NC and London: Duke University Press, 2011.

Halberstam, Jack, *Skin Shows: Gothic Horror and the Technology of Monsters*. Durham, NC and London: Duke University Press, 1995.

Hall, Donald E., *Queer Theories*. London: Palgrave Macmillan, 2003.

Hertz, Todd, 'Don't Let Your Kids Watch *Buffy the Vampire Slayer*', *Christianity Today* (1 September 2002). https://www.christianitytoday.com/ct/2002/septemberweb-only/9-16-31.0.html (accessed 29 June 2021).

Hilder, Monika B., *Surprised by the Feminine: A Rereading of C. S. Lewis and Gender*. New York, NY: Peter Lang, 2013.

Holland, Nancy J., 'Introduction', in *Feminist Interpretations of Jacques Derrida*, edited by Nancy J. Holland, 1–22. University Park, PA: The Pennsylvania State University Press, 1997.

Horstkotte, Martin, *The Postmodern Fantastic in Contemporary British Fiction*. Trier: Wissenschaftlicher Verlag Trier, 2004.

Hume, Kathryn, *Fantasy and Mimesis: Responses to Reality in Western Literature*. New York, NY and London: Methuen, 1984.

Hume, Kathryn, 'Postmodernism in Popular Literary Fantasy', in *The Dark Fantastic: Selected Essays from the Ninth International Conference on the Fantastic in the Arts*, edited by C. W. Sullivan III, 173–82. Westport, CT and London: Greenwood Press, 1997.

Irigaray, Luce, 'The Age of the Breath', in *Luce Irigaray: Key Writings*, translated by Katja van de Rakt, Staci Boeckman, and Luce Irigaray, 165–70. New York, NY and London: Continuum, 2004a.

Irigaray, Luce, 'Divine Women', in *Sexes and Genealogies*, translated by Gillian C. Gill, 55–72. New York, NY and Chichester: Columbia University Press, [1987] 1993.

Irigaray, Luce, 'The Fecundity of the Caress', in *Feminist Interpretations of Emmanuel Levinas*, edited by Tina Chanter, 119–44. University Park, PA: Pennsylvania State University Press, [1993] 2001.

Irigaray, Luce, 'The Redemption of Women', in *Luce Irigaray: Key Writings*, translated by Jennifer Wong and Jennifer Zillich with Luce Irigaray, 150–64. New York, NY and London: Continuum, 2004b.

Irigaray, Luce, *Speculum of the Other Woman*, translated by Gillian C. Gill. Ithaca, NY: Cornell University Press, [1974] 1985.

Irigaray, Luce, *Thinking the Difference: For a Peaceful Revolution*, translated by Karin Montin. London: Athlone Press, [1989] 1994.

Irigaray, Luce, 'Toward a Divine in the Feminine', in *Women and the Divine: Touching Transcendence*, translated by Mary Green, edited by Gillian Howe and J'annine Jobling, 13–26. New York, NY and Basingstoke: Palgrave Macmillan, 2009.

Jackson, Rosemary, *Fantasy: The Literature of Subversion*. London: Routledge, [1981] 1988.

James, Edward, 'Tolkien, Lewis, and the Explosion of Genre Fantasy', in *The Cambridge Companion to Fantasy Literature*, edited by Edward James and Farah Mendlesohn, 62–78. Cambridge: Cambridge University Press, 2012.

Jantzen, Grace M., *Becoming Divine: Towards a Feminist Philosophy of Religion*. Manchester: Manchester University Press, 1998.

Jantzen, Grace M., 'Touching (in) the Desert: Who Goes There?', in *Derrida and Religion: Other Testaments*, edited by Yvonne Sherwood and Kevin Hart, 375–92. New York, NY and London: Routledge, 2004.

Jemisin, N. K., *The Broken Kingdoms*. London: Orbit, 2010b.

Jemisin, N. K., *The Hundred Thousand Kingdoms*. London: Orbit, 2010a.
Jemisin, N. K., *The Kingdom of Gods*. London: Orbit, 2011.
Jones, Serene, 'Divining Women: Irigaray and Feminist Theologies', in *French Feminists: Critical Evaluations in Cultural Theory*, Vol. 3 of 4, edited by Ann J. Cahill and Jennifer L. Hansen, 395–417. London and New York, NY: Routledge, 2008.
Jordan, Elaine, 'The Dangerous Edge', in *Flesh and the Mirror: Essays on the Art of Angela Carter*, Revised and Updated Edition, edited by Lorna Sage, 201–26. London: Virago Press, [1994] 2007.
Joy, Morny, *Divine Love: Luce Irigaray, Women, Gender and Religion*. Manchester and New York, NY: Manchester University Press, 2006.
Kaveney, Roz, 'New New World Dreams: Angela Carter and Science Fiction', in *Flesh and the Mirror: Essays on the Art of Angela Carter*, Revised and Updated Edition, edited by Lorna Sage, 184–200. London: Virago, [1994] 2007.
Kenneally, Stephen, 'Hiding in Plain Sight: The Invisibility of Queer Fantasy', in *Gender and Sexuality in Contemporary Popular Fantasy: Beyond Boy Wizards and Kick-Ass Chicks*, edited by Jude Roberts and Esther MacCallum-Stewart, 8–20. London and New York, NY: Routledge, 2016.
Keegan, Cáel M. 'Getting Disciplined: What's Trans* About Queer Studies Now?', *Journal of Homosexuality* 67, no. 3 (2018): 384–97.
Kirby, Danielle, *Fantasy and Belief: Alternative Religions, Popular Narratives and Digital Cultures*. Sheffield: Equinox, 2013.
Lacan, Jacques, *Écrits: A Selection*, translated by Bruce Fink in collaboration with Héloïse Fink and Russell Grigg. New York, NY and London: W. W. Norton & Company, [1966] 2002.
Łaskiewicz, Weronika, *Fantasy Literature and Christianity: A Study of the Mistborn, Coldfire, Fionavar Tapestry and Chronicles of Thomas Covenant Series*. Jefferson, NC: McFarland & Company, Inc., Publishers, 2018.
Lavery, Grace E. 'Transition Is Not a Theory: From Performativity to Technique', *The Stage Mirror* (18 October 2019). https://grace.substack.com/p/transition-is-not-a-theory-from-performativity (accessed 29 January 2021).
Le Guin, Ursula K., 'The Critics, the Monsters, and the Fantasists', in *Dreams Must Explain Themselves: The Selected Non-Fiction of Ursula K. Le Guin*, edited by Ursula K. Le Guin, 309–19. London: Gollancz, 2018 [2003].
Le Guin, Ursula K., 'The Dark Tower by C. S. Lewis', in *Dancing at the Edge of the World*, edited by Ursula K. Le Guin, 242–4. New York, NY: Grove Press, [1977] 1989.
Le Guin, Ursula K., *The Earthsea Quartet*. London: Penguin Books, 1993.
Le Guin, Ursula K., 'The Fisherwoman's Daughter', in *Dancing at the Edge of the World*, edited by Ursula K. Le Guin, 212–37. New York, NY: Grove Press, [1988] 1989.
Le Guin, Ursula K., 'Is Gender Necessary? Redux', in *Dancing at the Edge of the World*, edited by Ursula K. Le Guin, 7–16. New York, NY: Grove Press, [1987] 1989.
Le Guin, Ursula K., *The Left Hand of Darkness*. New York, NY: Ace Books, [1969] 2010.
Le Guin, Ursula K., *The Other Wind*. London: Orion, [2001] 2002.

Leckie, Ann, *The Raven Tower*. London: Orbit, 2019.

Lee, Regina Yung, 'Untimely Graces: Gender, Failure, and Sainthood in Lois McMaster Bujold's *Paladin of Souls*', in *Biology and Manners: Essays on the World and Works of Lois McMaster Bujold*, edited by Una McCormack and Regina Yung Lee, 13–33. Liverpool: Liverpool University Press, 2020.

Lemmey, Huw, 'Gay Stories for Straight Allies', *utopian drivel* (6 January 2021). https://huw.substack.com/p/gay-stories-for-straight-allies (accessed 5 March 2021).

Leonard, Philip, 'Ethical Alterities?', in *Self/Same/Other: Revisioning the Subject in Literature and Theology*, edited by Heather Walton and Andrew W. Haas, 137–58. Sheffield: Sheffield Academic Press, 2000.

Levinas, Emmanuel, *Alterity and Transcendence*, translated by Michael B. Smith. London: Athlone Press, 1999.

Lewis, C. S., *The Lion, the Witch, and the Wardrobe*. London: HarperCollins, [1950] 2001.

Lewis, C. S, *The Screwtape Letters*. San Francisco: HarperCollins, [1942] 2001.

Lewis, C. S., 'Sometimes Fairy Stories May Say Best What's to be Said', in *Of This and Other Worlds*, edited by Walter Hooper, 71–5. Glasgow: Fount Paperbacks, 1982.

Lewis, C. S., *That Hideous Strength*. London: HarperCollins, [1945] 2005.

Lewis, C. S., *Till We Have Faces: A Myth Retold*. Orlando, FL: Harcourt, 1956.

Lisi, Clemente, '"Tropical Trump" Bolsonaro Beholden to Catholic-Evangelical Alliance', *Religion Unplugged* (5 February 2019). https://religionunplugged.com/news/2019/2/1/brazils-jair-bolsonaro-needs-catholic-and-evangelical-support-to-stay-in-power (accessed 29 June 2021).

Loughlin, Gerald, 'Introduction: The End of Sex', in *Queer Theology: Rethinking the Western Body*, edited by Gerald Loughlin, 1–33. Oxford: Blackwell, 2007.

MacDonald, Meg, 'The Bastard Balances All: The Essential Other in Bujold's Queer Theology', in *Biology and Manners: Essays on the World and Works of Lois McMaster Bujold*, edited by Una McCormack and Regina Yung Lee, 229–47. Liverpool: Liverpool University Press, 2020.

Manlove, Colin N., 'On the Nature of Fantasy', in *The Aesthetics of Fantasy Literature and Art*, edited by Roger C. Schlobin, 16–35. Notre Dame, IN: University of Notre Dame Press; Brighton: Harvester, 1982.

Martin, Alison, *Luce Irigaray and the Question of the Divine*. Leeds: Maney Publishing for the Modern Humanities Research Association, 2000.

Mendlesohn, Farah, *Rhetorics of Fantasy*. Middletown, CT: Wesleyan University Press, 2008.

Mikkelson, David, 'Are Harry Potter Books Sparking a Rise in Satanism Among Children?', *Snopes* (2 December 2001). https://www.snopes.com/fact-check/harry-potter-satanism (accessed 29 June 2021).

Milbank, Alison, 'Apologetics and the Imagination: Making Strange', in *Imaginative Apologetics: Theology, Philosophy and the Catholic Tradition*, edited by Andrew Davison, 31–45. London: SCM Press, 2011.

Moon, Elizabeth, *The Deed of Paksenarrion*. Riverdale, NY: Baen, [1988–9] 1992.

Myers, Doris T., *Bareface: A Guide to C. S. Lewis's Last Novel*. Columbia, MO: University of Missouri Press, 2004.

Oziewicz, Marek, *One Earth, One People: The Mythopoeic Fantasy Series of Ursula K. Le Guin, Lloyd Alexander, Madeleine L'Engle and Orson Scott Card*. Jefferson, NC and London: McFarland & Co., 2008.

Petersen, Anders Klostergaard, 'The Difference Between Religious Narratives and Fictional Literature: A Matter of Degree Only', *Religion* 46, no. 4 (October 2016): 500–20.

Piercy, Marge, *Woman on the Edge of Time*. London: Women's Press Ltd., 1979.

Presaud, Ritu, 'Alabama Passes Bill Banning Abortion', *BBC* (15 May 2019). https://www.bbc.co.uk/news/world-us-canada-48275795 (accessed 29 June 2021).

Rayment-Pickard, Hugh, *Impossible God: Derrida's Theology*. Aldershot: Ashgate, 2003.

Reid, Robin Anne, 'The Holy Family: Divine Queerness in *The Curse of Chalion* and *The Hallowed Hunt*', in *Biology and Manners: Essays on the World and Works of Lois McMaster Bujold*, edited by Una McCormack and Regina Yung Lee, 209–28. Liverpool: Liverpool University Press, 2020.

Roberts, Jude and Esther MacCallum-Stewart, 'Introduction', in *Gender and Sexuality in Contemporary Popular Fantasy: Beyond Boy Wizards and Kick-Ass Chicks*, edited by Jude Roberts and Esther MacCallum-Stewart, 1–7. London and New York, NY: Routledge, 2016.

Rochelle, Warren G., *Communities of the Heart: The Rhetoric of Myth in the Fiction of Ursula K. Le Guin*. Liverpool: Liverpool University Press, 2001.

Russ, Joanna, 'The Image of Women in Science Fiction', in *Images of Women in Fiction: Feminist Perspectives*, edited by Susan Koppelman Cornillon, 79–94. Bowling Green, OH: Bowling Green University Popular Press, 1972.

Schalk, Sami, *Bodyminds Reimagined: (Dis)ability, Race, and Gender in Black Women's Speculative Fiction*. Durham, NC: Duke University Press, 2018.

Sedgwick, Eve Kosofsky, *Epistemology of the Closet*. Berkeley, CA: University of California Press, 1990.

Shepherd, Andrew, *The Gift of the Other: Levinas, Derrida, and a Theology of Hospitality*. Cambridge: James Clark & Co., 2014.

Sherwood, Yvonne and Kevin Hart, 'Other Testaments', in *Derrida and Religion: Other Testaments*, edited by Yvonne Sherwood and Kevin Hart, 3–26. New York, NY and London: Routledge, 2005.

Shippey, Tom, *J. R. R. Tolkien: Author of the Century*. London: HarperCollins, 2000.

Spivak, Gayatri Chakravorty, 'Can the Subaltern Speak?', in *Marxism and the Interpretation of Culture*, edited by Cary Nelson, 271–313. Basingstoke: Macmillan, 1988.

Spivak, Gayatri Chakravorty, 'Displacement and the Discourse of Woman', in *A Critical and Cultural Theory Reader*, edited by Antony Easthope and Kate McGowan, 167–80. Buckingham: Open University Press, 1992.

Spivak, Gayatri Chakravorty, 'Feminism and Deconstruction, Again: Negotiating with Unacknowledged Masculinism', in *Between Feminism and Psychoanalysis*, edited by Teresa Brennan, 206–23. London and New York, NY: Routledge, 1989a.

Spivak, Gayatri Chakravorty, 'A Response to "The Difference Within: Feminism and Critical Theory"', in *The Difference Within: Feminism and Critical Theory*, edited by Elizabeth Meese and Alice Parker, 207–20. Amsterdam and Philadelphia, PA: John Benjamins Publishing Company, 1989b.

Susan Stryker and Stephen Whittle (eds), *The Transgender Studies Reader*. New York, NY and London: Routledge, 2006.

Stryker, Susan and Aren Z. Aizura (eds) *The Transgender Studies Reader 2*. New York, NY and London: Routledge, 2013.

Thomas, Ebony Elizabeth, *The Dark Fantastic: Race and the Imagination from Harry Potter to the Hunger Games*. New York, NY: New York University Press, 2019.

Tolkien, J. R. R., and Humphrey Carpenter (ed.), *The Letters of J. R. R. Tolkien*. Boston: Houghton Mifflin, 1981.

Tolkien, J. R. R., and Humphrey Carpenter (ed.), *The Lord of the Rings*. London: HarperCollins, [1954] 2011.

Tolkien, J. R. R., and Humphrey Carpenter (ed.), *On Fairy-Stories*, Expanded Edition. London: HarperCollins, [1947] 2008.

Tonstad, Linn Marie, *God and Difference: The Trinity, Sexuality, and the Transformation of Finitude*. New York, NY and London: Routledge, 2016.

Tonstad, Linn Marie, *Queer Theology: Beyond Apologetics*. Eugene, OR: Cascade Books, 2018.

Tonstad, Linn Marie, 'The Romance of Incarnation–Religion in *The Hundred Thousand Kingdoms*', *Fantasy Matters* (20 October 2011). http://www.fantasy-matters.com/2011/10/romance-of-incarnation-religion-in.html (accessed 18 May 2021), 7 paragraphs.

VanDerWerff, Emily, 'How Conservatives Took Over Sci-Fi's Most Prestigious Award', *Vox* (22 August 2015). https://www.vox.com/2015/4/26/8495415/hugos-sad-puppies-controversy (accessed 29 June 2021).

Vincent, Alana M., *Culture, Communion, and Recovery: Tolkienian Fairy-Story and Inter-Religious Exchange*. Newcastle upon Tyne: Cambridge Scholars Publishing, 2012.

Walton, Heather, 'Introduction', in *Literature and Theology: New Interdisciplinary Spaces*, edited by Heather Walton, 1–4. Farnham, Surrey: Ashgate, 2011a.

Walton, Heather, *Literature, Theology, and Feminism*, edited by Heather Walton. Manchester and New York, NY: Manchester University Press, 2007.

Walton, Heather, 'When Love Is Not True', in *Literature and Theology: New Interdisciplinary Spaces*, edited by Heather Walton, 37–54. Farnham, Surrey: Ashgate, 2011b.

Ward, Graham, *Barth, Derrida, and the Language of Theology*. Cambridge: Cambridge University Press, 1995.

Warner, Michael, 'Introduction', in *Fear of a Queer Planet: Queer Politics and Social Theory*, edited by Michael Warner, vii–xxxi. Minneapolis, MN and London: University of Minnesota Press, 1993.

Yang, Neon, *The Ascent to Godhood*. New York, NY: Tor, 2019.

Yang, Neon, *The Black Tides of Heaven*. New York, NY: Tor, 2017a.

Yang, Neon, *The Descent of Monsters*. New York, NY: Tor, 2018.

Yang, Neon, *The Red Threads of Fortune*. New York, NY: Tor, 2017b.

Zaleski, Philip and Carol Zaleski, *The Fellowship: The Literary Lives of the Inklings: J. R. R. Tolkien, C. S. Lewis, Owen Barfield, Charles Williams*. New York, NY: Farrar, Straus and Giroux, 2015.

Zenit Staff, 'Full Text of Vatican Document Providing Schools with Guidance on Gender Issues', *Zenit* (2019). https://zenit.org/articles/new-vatican-document-provides-schools-with-guidance-on-gender-issues (accessed 29 June 2021).

Zipes, Jack, *Breaking the Magic Spell: Radical Theories of Folk and Fairy Tales*, Revised and Expanded Edition. Lexington, KY: The University Press of Kentucky, 2002.

Index

ACT UP 139
AIDS 139, 140
alterity 14, 23–4, 137, 138
   ethical encounter with 5, 30–3, 44–6, 55–7, 63–5, 66, 77, 172, 182
   fantasy's capacity to evoke 21, 36–40, 66, 71–2, 75, 78–9, 112, 182, 187
   gendered 16, 19, 56, 69–102, 113, 198, 200
   impossibility of representing 36–40, 46–7, 52–3, 71, 79
   marginality of 30–3, 71, 78, 180, 197–8, 201
   monstrous 51, 75, 81–4
   non-human 188, 201
   of the other (*see under* other)
   as queerness 140, 182
   racial 200
   religious 8
   sexual 19, 172, 198, 200
   theological dimensions 7, 20, 23–67, 69–102, 112, 144, 182, 197
Althaus-Reid, Marcella
   critique of decency 173, 182, 197
   deconstructive approach 23, 26, 198
   queer theology of 1, 7, 138, 144–53, 156, 174, 179, 183, 185, 196
   on sainthood 169
   and scriptural interpretation 12
   and spiritual practice 199
   on women in Christianity 71, 103, 111
androgyny 95–6, 143
Annunciation 110–11
apocalypse 40, 132, 138, 153–8
assimilation
   feminist resistance to 74, 110, 116, 118, 126
   in LGBTQ+ politics 2, 152
   of the other 31, 111, 172, 176

Attebery, Brian
   definition of fantasy 6, 18–21, 24, 34–9, 66, 161
   gendering of fantasy 70, 77–9
   on *Till We Have Faces* 85

belief
   Christian 4, 10–11, 34, 38, 51
   in God 10, 25–6, 59, 88
   loss of 48, 124
   as theological principle 61, 63, 82, 85, 106, 115, 196
Bible 157
   1 Corinthians 49
   Genesis 148–9
   Gospel of John 148, 199
   Isaiah 127
   Romans 79
binarism
   conceptual 27, 45, 49, 51, 58–63, 94–102
   as a facet of patriarchy 72–84, 111, 176–9
   gender 7, 72–84, 94–102, 141–3, 160–4, 169–74, 176, 193
   as hierarchical relation 32, 51, 72–84, 94–102
   as structure of Western logic 70, 72, 111
bisexuality
   in the classical sense 94, 96–7, 174
   as sexual orientation 96, 147, 151, 198
body
   alienation from 72–3, 88–9
   of Christ (*see under* Christ)
   communion with 151–2, 155–8, 168, 174, 182–3
   desires of 1, 145
   as discursive construction 73, 103, 181

feminine   85, 106, 111, 128, 131
figurations of   22, 147, 162, 171, 197
gendered   141, 145, 149, 159–64
of God (*see* incarnation)
instability of   57, 80–1, 95, 170, 177, 196
modification of   190
monstrous   1, 51, 80–1
multiplicity of   151–2, 155, 162, 177–83, 196
as origin   128
politic   62
regulation of   1, 138, 150, 162
theology of   107–8, 112, 145–53, 155–8, 161, 186, 202
writing from   73–6, 78–9, 86, 103, 106–7, 186, 202
Braidotti, Rosi   6, 21, 80–2
Buffy the Vampire Slayer   10
Butler, Judith
  critique of legislated identity   160, 192
  on drag culture   139, 141, 159–64, 167–8, 171, 174, 181
  indebtedness to deconstruction   16, 17
  theory of gender   141–2, 159–64, 175, 177, 179
  as a transgender thinker   143

capitalism   6, 36, 145–52, 160, 173
castration   128–31
Chesterton, G. K.   9
childbirth
  feminist reclamation of   80–1, 105, 197
  reimaginings of   96, 149
  as social expectation   81, 117
  subversion of   89, 91
Christ   14, 71, 110
  body of   103, 152–3, 154–6, 175, 182–3
  crucifixion of   153
  figures in fantasy   113–26, 127–36, 156–8, 166, 196, 199
  incarnation of (*see under* 'incarnation')
  life of   14, 154, 185
  as marginalized subject   34, 154, 156–8, 166, 175, 183, 185, 199
  as queer   147, 156–8

resurrection of   154–6
second coming of   138, 153–6
as woman   113–26, 127–36, 156–8
as word-made-flesh   107
Christianity
  apologetics   9–12, 22, 23, 185
  Catholicism   37, 106, 152
  dismantling of (*see under* deconstruction)
  evangelical   10, 42–3, 168
  feminist interpretations of   103–36, 137
  hegemony of   2, 8–9, 13, 23, 26, 32, 69, 145, 199
  mystical expressions of   105, 108, 115
  patriarchal   11–12, 70–1, 75–6, 79, 103–5, 157
  queer interpretations of   144–58
  sexual oppression within   1–3, 11–12, 138, 145–53, 197
  theology (*see* theology)
  traditions   1, 4, 56, 187, 193, 196–7, 202
  and Western metaphysics   2, 34, 40–4, 70, 157, 195
  women in   1–2, 11–12, 70–1, 103–36
church
  as body of Christ   151, 154–5
  conservatism of   144
  early writings   9
  hierarchies in   152
  LGBTQ+ inclusion in   2–3, 7, 144, 183, 201
  limits of   154–5, 175, 198
  marginalization within   12, 106, 152, 175
  reimagining   16, 76, 106, 151–2, 154–8
cisgender
  assumptions of doctrine   1, 11, 26, 138, 151–3, 162, 183, 185
  bias in feminism   17, 109, 113, 124, 132
  construction of reality   23, 141, 159, 163, 170–1, 185
  as default   140–2, 159, 163–4, 170–1, 173
  subject(s)   69, 138, 149, 171

Cixous, Hélène
    anti-essentialism 74
    critique of binarism 72, 74, 87–9, 95–7, 101
    écriture feminine 6, 70–7, 79, 83–4, 85, 101, 103, 137, 186
    elaboration on deconstruction 70–3, 93, 159, 175
    engagement with religion 6, 70, 75–6, 95
    and the fantastic 75–6, 77–84, 101–2, 103, 109, 110, 161
    Judaism 8, 70, 75
    reclamation of femininity 70–7, 85–6, 97–9, 102, 106, 109, 137, 170
    and suppressed femininity 73–4, 89–90, 93–4, 137
closet 3, 152, 162, 163–4, 198
Cohen, Jeffrey Jerome 21, 36, 51–2, 80–2
colonialism 146, 152, 196, 199, 200
community
    ethical 63–4, 115, 169, 178
    as a feminist principle 103, 105, 110, 115, 118, 122
    queer 181
    religious 19, 78, 82, 84, 151, 155, 174
    transgender 144
consensus reality 18, 40, 43, 66–7, 82, 185

death 13, 79, 119–20, 123, 172, 181–2, 197
    of God (*see under* God)
    woman as 81, 120
deconstruction
    definitions 28–30
    différance 14, 28, 29–30, 33, 51, 63
    and ethical alterity 5, 24, 30–40, 46, 56, 65–7, 71–2, 98, 137, 172, 182, 185
    event 28, 38, 49, 54, 185
    and fantasy 5–6, 17–20, 23–67, 69, 71–2, 112, 114, 126, 133–5, 136, 137, 138, 153, 158–9, 185–7, 188, 193, 197, 202
    fantasy criticism's resistance to 5, 26–8, 34–6
    and feminism 6, 16–17, 69, 72, 74, 79–80, 84, 98, 101–2, 103–4, 106, 107, 112, 114, 123–4, 126, 133–5, 175, 186, 202

    of gender 7, 139, 142, 149, 158–62, 167–8, 183
    implications for Christianity 4–6, 8–9, 12–16, 23–8, 32–4, 65–7, 106, 137, 144, 145, 149, 153–4, 158–9, 183, 185–6, 201, 202
    and Judaism 8
    and metaphysics 8, 14, 25, 28–9, 33–4, 38, 41–2, 62, 69, 70, 72, 136, 196
    nihilistic readings 13, 26, 29, 65
    and queer theory 141–2, 144, 153, 173, 183, 186, 201, 202
    theological resonances 6, 12–16, 23–8, 30–40, 65–7, 71, 137, 153–4, 185–6, 188, 193, 202
    trace 29–30, 63, 132, 179, 197
The Deed of Paksenarrion (Moon) 79
de Lauretis, Teresa 139–41
demonic 10, 79, 81
Derrida, Jacques, *see also* deconstruction
    body of work 5, 12–17, 23–4, 26–40, 58, 63, 65–7, 69–70, 72–3, 159, 185, 202
    on Christianity 34
    engagement with theology 5, 8, 13–14, 24, 28–9, 33, 42, 202
    on feminism 16
    Judaism 8, 13
    Levinas's influence on 30–2, 39, 46, 54, 57, 64
    and monstrosity 51
    and postmodernism 17
    on Psyche 48–9
    on religious faith 25, 33, 56, 59–60
    on state power 62
    theology's engagement with 12–16, 33–4
    treatment of God 25–6, 28–9, 31–3, 59, 65, 106
difference
    as alterity (*see under* alterity)
    association with darkness 46–7, 57, 61–3, 108
    communion with 148, 154
    cultural 56, 64, 141
    as *différance* (*see under* deconstruction)
    erasure in discourse 29

gender 8, 16–17, 18, 21, 56, 73, 80–2, 85, 95–6, 100, 106, 109, 137–8, 153, 170
  marginalization of 8, 18, 26, 31, 42–3, 72–4, 104, 137, 182
  marked 29, 178
  monstrous 21, 36–7, 51, 80–2
  of the other (*see under* other)
  preservation of 182–3
  racial 21, 141
  relation to identity 3, 31–2, 65, 71–2, 77, 106, 110–11, 140, 197
  religious 8, 56
  sexual 8, 18, 21, 56, 64, 77, 82, 95–6, 100, 102, 106, 112–13, 137–8, 140–1, 153, 172
  within communities 139–40
  'woman' as symbol 17, 70, 73, 80–2, 108, 137, 197
divinity
  access to 15, 106
  authority of 26, 62, 152, 196
  command of 24
  desire for 108
  encounter with 44, 53, 109, 118, 121–2
  feminine 7, 81, 103–36, 138, 156–8, 165, 186, 197
  incarnate 20, 103–36, 147, 153
  inspiration by 10
  and knowledge 152, 199
  and the law 8, 11, 117, 150
  as *logos* 13, 23
  love of 108–10, 112, 114–15, 124
  masculine 71, 116, 117
  as monstrous 51, 202
  mystery of 44–5, 52, 125
  name of 78
  nature of 48, 54, 118, 119, 122
  as sovereign 4, 11, 32, 42, 45, 50, 65–6, 79, 157, 196
  truth of 10, 29
doctrine
  exclusivity of 1–2, 8, 11–12, 150, 198
  fictional 54, 123, 179, 196, 198–9
  limits of 54, 185
  orthodox 15, 25, 144, 145, 152, 185
  revision of 152
domesticity 11–12, 97, 117

doubt 25, 59, 61, 66, 121
drag
  families 181
  fantastic 158–64, 176–83, 197
  literary text as 170, 176
  performance 139, 141, 151, 158–64, 169, 173, 174
  and sainthood 164–9
  and theology 5, 7, 146, 151, 158–64, 180, 182–3, 184, 186
dragons 1, 34, 36, 39
  and queer embodiment 7, 155, 162, 176–83, 185
  women as 6, 70, 81–4, 102, 123, 185
dualism 95, 110, 172, *see also* binarism

écriture féminine, see *under* Cixous, Hélène
embodiment
  fantastic 155, 158–9, 161–4, 171, 176–84, 187, 198
  gendered 161
  as human existence 115, 129, 148, 151, 153, 182
  in politics 143
  queer 3, 7, 138, 162, 171, 176–83, 198
  in religious observance 121, 148, 158, 165, 169, 187, 197
  of social roles 42, 133, 178
  and subjectivity 21, 73, 162, 171, 173, 176
  transgender 142–3, 160
  women's 74–5, 87, 109, 133
Enlightenment 30, 41–2, 62, 141
Eros 39, 44, 49, 113–16, 126
eroticism
  as feminine 98–9
  and horror 19
  and pleasure 103, 105, 118
  as political framework 195
  and ritual 155, 174
  as theological basis 108–10, 113–18, 121, 125, 155, 196, 198, 200
eschatology 61, 154
ethics
  of alterity (*see under* Levinas, Emmanuel)
  encounter with the other (*see under* other)
  in fantasy 66, 196

feminist 69, 77, 99, 109, 132
  implications of theology 11, 13, 85, 99, 123–4, 151, 153
  of love 77, 112
  queer 142, 151, 173, 182
  relational 57, 60–1, 85, 123, 153
eucatastrophe
  deconstructive reading 37–8, 48–9, 54, 66–7, 74, 114, 124, 138, 181, 185, 202
  defined 37–8, 185
  feminist interpretations 73–4, 104, 109, 117, 155
  limits of 112
  as open-ended 65, 126, 158
  queer theological reading 138, 153–5, 158, 194, 200, 202
  and religious observance 54, 153–5, 158
  subversion of 135
Eucharist 144, 152, 153–8, 168, 182, 184
Eve 40–4, 71, 126–36, 148–50, 164–9

fairy tale(s)
  and fantasy 19, 40, 42
  female archetypes in 70, 75, 166
  as theological storytelling 48–9, 124
faith
  and certainty 56
  consolation in 47, 91
  as ethical relation 31–3, 56, 64–5, 66–7
  profession of 2, 10, 25, 108, 138
  relationship to fiction 5
  as risk 14, 25–6, 56, 59–61, 64–5
  traditions 26, 106, 183
  as unknowing 47–50, 59–61, 66–7, 90
fall of humanity 71, 91, 148–50
family
  fantastical models 57, 96–7, 181, 191, 195
  normative 12, 144, 152, 173, 181
  queer 178, 181
  reconfiguration of 76–7, 181
fantasy
  applicability of 4, 171, 174, 184
  artifice of 37, 43, 67, 132, 134, 168, 184, 186

  conservative tendencies in 20
  as deconstructive 5–6, 12, 17–19, 23–67, 69, 71–2, 74, 107, 124, 126, 135, 137–8, 185, 188, 202
  definitions 17–22, 34–40
  elusiveness of 18–19
  ethics of 34–40, 55, 63, 65–7, 109, 185
  and Faërie 133
  and gender 3–4, 6–8, 17, 21, 42, 70, 72, 74–6, 77–84, 85, 88–90, 94–5, 99, 101–2, 103–5, 107, 109, 112–13, 114, 124, 126, 132–3, 136, 137, 143–4, 161–4, 165, 168, 169, 171, 174, 177, 183–4, 185–7, 190, 191–2, 200–2
  as parody 4, 40, 127
  as queer 3, 5, 7–8, 21, 137–84, 185–7, 191–2, 195, 200–2
  relation to theology 1–12, 17, 19, 20–1, 23–4, 26–8, 34–40, 41–4, 48, 53–55, 65–7, 72, 76, 77–80, 84, 85, 88, 94, 101–2, 103–5, 109, 112–13, 114, 124, 126, 136, 137–9, 143–4, 145–64, 165, 169, 176, 183–4, 185–7, 188, 193, 195, 200–2
  representation of women in 78
  and science fiction 19, 134
  textual construction of 38–40, 43, 65, 114, 127, 180, 195
femininity
  association with earth 87–8, 115
  as darkness 84, 87–8, 93, 99, 123
  disruptive 5, 70, 79, 83, 85, 94, 98, 102, 123, 129, 166
  divine 7, 103–36, 137, 186
  in drag 164, 165
  of literature 77–80, 84
  in men 74
  monstrous 80–4, 98, 120
  normative 17, 85, 111–12, 113–15, 117–26, 127, 132–6, 161, 165
  as nurturing 86–7, 105, 113, 122
  reclamations of 73–4, 79, 94–101, 102, 104–13, 122–3, 127, 133, 137, 165–6, 197
  of religion 88–90, 97–8, 120
  repressed 73–4, 82, 84–94, 102, 106–7, 119, 124, 129, 137
  in social structures 94–101, 102

stereotypes of 86–7, 93, 97, 124,
  134–5, 170–1
and subjectivity 7, 70, 74, 85–6, 103,
  105, 130, 202
subjugation of 42, 72, 79, 149, 158
submissive 85, 88, 113
transgender 156, 164–9, 171
and writing (*see under* Cixous, Hélène)
feminism
  Anglo-American 16, 105
  deconstructive (*see under*
    deconstruction)
  exclusions within 17, 104–5, 107,
    111–12, 114, 135
  history of 100, 110
  in literary criticism 6, 70–84, 94,
    100–1
  and monstrosity 80–4
  as political commitment 11, 16–17,
    24, 69–70, 93, 95, 100, 103–4, 128,
    134, 137
  queer critique of 141, 149–50
  shadow 173–5
  and subjectivity 71, 101–2
  and theology (*see under* theology)
fertility
  as feminine attribute 58, 94, 97
  personified 40, 45, 120, 126–7
Filmer, Kath
  criticism of deconstruction 26–8,
    35–6, 39
  critique of C. S. Lewis 85–6, 91–2
  on fantasy and religion 1, 10
finitude 14, 120, 128, 132, 182, 183
folklore 35, 41
future
  of feminism 98, 131, 132
  and the other 37–8, 59, 60–1, 63–4,
    66, 98

gay 2, 42, 139, 140, 151, 163–4
gay and lesbian studies 139
gaze
  divine 116, 122, 196
  monstrous 80, 83
  of the other 166
  patriarchal 73, 80, 107–8, 112, 116,
    121, 125, 196–7
  scientific 97, 116

  of the self 51, 64, 80, 116, 125, 196
  and surveillance 163
  textual 134, 166
  theological 84, 134
gender
  alterity (*see under* alterity)
  binary (*see under* binarism)
  categories 3, 17, 27, 74, 88, 138, 142,
    160, 164–9, 190–1, 201
  in Christianity 1–5, 7–8, 11, 17,
    21–2, 77–80, 94, 103–4, 108, 112,
    117, 136, 138, 144–58, 185
  dissidence 88, 138–44, 145–53,
    158–64, 165–9, 181, 184, 186, 187,
    191–5
  essentialism 74, 79, 107, 123–4, 132,
    137–8, 149, 160
  femininity (*see under* femininity)
  fluidity of 56, 94–101, 156, 162,
    169–76, 177–83, 197–8
  hierarchies 11, 20, 31, 34, 85, 94, 117,
    152
  and labour 12, 96
  in language and discourse 70–7, 95,
    99–102, 170–5
  and marginality 1–5, 8, 10, 16, 18,
    21, 23, 31, 34, 69–102, 106–8, 136,
    137–8, 140, 164–9, 177–9, 185, 200,
    202
  masculinity (*see under* masculinity)
  performativity 7, 141–2, 159–62,
    164–9
  pronouns related to 56, 100–1, 170,
    192
  rethinking 3–5, 7, 17, 19–22, 40,
    77–80, 94–102, 104, 105, 110, 136,
    138–9, 141–4, 145–53, 158–62,
    169–76, 177–83, 184, 191–5, 201–2
  transition (*see under* transgender)
genderqueer 143, 160–1, 164, 171, 174,
  194
God
  authority of 25
  belief in 10, 14–16, 25–6, 28, 41,
    58–9, 61
  death of 13, 29, 65
  as dominant 32, 85, 196–7
  feminine figurations of 5, 79, 84,
    85–6, 103–36, 147–50, 156–8

image of   11, 22, 144, 166
incarnation of (*see under* incarnation)
and *logos*   25, 28
as other   2, 25–6, 31–4, 38, 50–1, 59, 65–7, 71, 79, 86, 106, 138, 152–6, 184, 202
patriarchal concepts of   69, 78, 85, 106, 110–11, 113, 116, 152, 166, 196–7
queer figurations of   137–8, 144–58, 180, 183–4, 186, 197
sovereignty of   31–4, 42–3, 67, 109, 196–7
submission to   85
will of   57, 103, 193
word of   106
goddess(es)
feminist interest in   104
in miscellaneous fantasy texts   104, 156–8, 195–8
in *The Passion of New Eve*   40, 126–36
as stereotype   82, 84, 102, 107, 111
in *Till We Have Faces*   45, 47, 52–4, 84–94, 102, 113–26, 136
gods
in Carter   40–1, 127, 129
in general fantasy   36, 39, 56, 84, 137
in Jemisin   195–200
in Leckie   187–91
in Le Guin   82
in Lewis   44–55, 84–94, 113–26

Halberstam, Jack   7, 21, 143, 172–6, 184, 194
Harry Potter (Rowling)   10
healing   102, 115, 118, 150, 154, 156–8
heaven
exile from   156–8
fantasies of   53, 117, 128
longing for   11
purity of   81
in theology   147, 193
hegemony
Christian (*see under* Christianity)
discursive   69, 133, 146, 180
of gender   140, 146, 163
political   32, 39, 152, 163, 173, 196
and realism   43, 133
theological   23, 26, 69, 145, 199

heresy   10, 195, 199, 202
heterodoxy   9, 78, 162, 199
heteronormativity
and the closet   164
construction of reality   140–1, 153, 183
in cultural representation   159, 164, 170–1, 173–4
in literary criticism   3, 79
in social structures   138, 178
in theology   113, 138, 145–6, 183
heterosexuality
bias in feminism   17, 79, 124, 141
construction of reality   23, 141, 159
as default subject   21, 69, 140–2, 159–60, 163–4, 169, 171–2, 183, 198
as divine ideal   12, 94, 109, 124, 138, 151–3, 185
and the gaze   165
heterosexism   11, 152
of theological structures   1, 11–12, 26, 113, 138, 145–53, 157, 159, 162, 166, 169, 181–2, 185, 196
Hilder, Monika B.   11, 85, 89–90, 92, 113
His Dark Materials (Pullman)   10
holiness
of the body   1, 116–17, 153, 174, 180, 183–4, 198
as darkness   44, 46–7, 66, 84, 94, 116
as fiction   165
horror of   46–7, 50, 88, 98
mystery of   53, 88
and sovereignty   42, 50
vocation toward   79, 179
Holocaust   30
homophobia   8, 162–3, 181
homosexuality   147, 152, 172, 174, 198
humanism   30
Hume, Kathryn   18

identity
constructed   89, 159–64, 168, 193, 198
gender   3, 17, 23, 56, 74, 138–9, 141–2, 144, 156, 159–64, 165–7, 170–6, 183–4, 186, 190, 192–3, 198, 200–1

instability of 51, 56–8, 129, 140–2, 144, 156, 158–64, 167–8, 173–5, 177–9, 182–3, 184, 192, 198
intermingling of 110, 114, 116
national 57–8, 61–2, 96
normative 71, 140–1, 154, 162, 165, 200–1
politics of 3, 74, 141
religious 13, 144
of the self 2–4, 20, 31, 64, 71, 106, 129, 175
sexual 3, 17, 23, 56, 138–9, 142, 144, 151, 156, 170–6, 183–4, 186, 190, 200–1
idolatry 25, 32, 106, 148
impossibility
of determinate meaning 13–14, 25, 29, 63, 66, 132, 159, 171, 179
and fantasy 2, 18–19, 24, 35, 37, 39, 71, 90, 155, 162
of God 14, 25–6, 32, 65
of the other 24, 32, 34, 38–9, 49, 65–6, 74, 98
incarnation
of Christ 12, 34, 51, 151, 183, 185, 195, 199, 202
feminist relationship to 5, 7, 20, 79, 103–36, 137–8, 185–6, 202
masculine 106, 151, 166
in queer theologies 137–8, 147, 156, 158, 164, 166, 183, 185, 198–9, 202
Inheritance trilogy (Jemisin) 158, 186–7, 191, 195–200, 201
intersectionality 201–2
Irigaray, Luce
and deconstruction 17, 106, 136
and feminist theology 6–7, 103–36, 137–8, 185–6, 197
revision in queer theology 138, 147, 155
'i shall remain' (Cheng) 3, 143, 145, 156–8, 196

Kaveney, Roz 135, 166–8

Lacan, Jacques 130
Le Guin, Ursula K.
and Christianity 4, 146
Earthsea series 2–4, 7, 19, 82–3, 139, 155, 162, 169, 176–84, 194, 200

on fantasy 6, 24, 35–6, 66, 76
The Left Hand of Darkness 2–4, 6–7, 19, 24, 39, 44, 55–66, 70, 78, 84, 94–102, 139, 162, 169–76, 184–5, 191, 196, 200
relationship to feminism 6, 73, 76, 89, 100, 110
and Taosim 58, 99, 172
L'Engle, Madeleine 9
lesbian 2, 42, 139–40, 147, 149
Levinas, Emmanuel
ethics of alterity 5, 24, 30–2, 35, 39, 46, 56–7, 63–5, 172, 182, 185
influence on Jacques Derrida 15, 24, 30–2, 39, 54
Judaism 8, 30
on subjectivity 31, 45
Lewis, C. S.
as a Christian fantasist 1, 4, 9–10, 26
The Chronicles of Narnia 1, 10, 44, 51, 53, 87
The Screwtape Letters 210 n.5
That Hideous Strength/Cosmic Trilogy 41–2, 44, 53, 87, 117–18
as a theorist of fantasy 35
Till We Have Faces 2–4, 6–7, 19, 24, 39, 44–55, 57–8, 65–6, 70, 78, 84–94, 97, 102, 105, 109, 113–26, 129, 136, 137, 185, 188, 196
liberalism 30, 36, 64, 186, 200
logocentrism
deconstructive critique of 28–9, 76
necessity for deconstruction 30, 66–7
and patriarchy (*see under* phallogocentrism)
and reason 86–9
relationship to theology 42–3, 77, 85, 87, 148
violence of 31, 71, 80, 103
love
between persons 55–6, 90–3, 118, 175, 191
erotic 50, 52, 92–3, 108, 110, 114, 116–18, 121, 125, 147, 152–3, 168, 172, 193, 196–7, 200
of God 15, 114, 147, 152, 154, 157, 197
of nation 57–8, 97
normative concepts of 112, 124

of the other 66, 77, 106, 108, 110,
    114–15, 123–4, 200
of self 106–7, 110–11

MacDonald, George 9
magic
    and fantastic imagination 11–12, 36,
        166, 193–4, 198–9
    and femininity 78, 166
    and gender 191, 198
    and science 134, 191
    as theological knowledge 176–80,
        193–4, 199
    thinking 78, 158
marriage
    in *Earthsea* 178
    gay 2, 200
    heteronormative 12, 99
    in *Till We Have Faces* 50, 86
Marxism 20, 189
Mary, Mother of Jesus
    feminist rehabilitation 110–11, 117
    as impossible ideal 71, 106, 110–11
    in *The Passion of New Eve* 128, 131
    in queer theology 147
masculinity
    and authority 69, 85, 96, 117, 166
    and the body 149, 158, 166, 171
    as default 56, 80, 95–6, 99–101, 106,
        111
    and God 85, 88, 106, 113, 117, 185
    and logic 5, 71–7, 78–9, 84, 98, 108,
        117, 132
    normative 161, 164, 168
    and subjectivity 111–12, 122, 128–30
    in women 79, 89–90, 92, 124
Medusa 75, 80, 83
Mendlesohn, Farah 19
messianism
    deconstructive 14, 38, 66–7, 74, 185
    and eucatastrophe 37–8, 66–7, 73–4,
        109, 153–8, 185
    in feminism 73–4, 113, 128–9, 136
    queer 7, 153–8, 175, 183
    triumphalist 4, 61, 66–7
The Mists of Avalon (Bradley) 104
modernity 35, 41–2, 45, 62
    crises of 35
    rational 45, 62, 81
    secular 28, 41–2, 88

monasticism 58, 98, 180, 193–4
monstrosity
    as alterity 21, 36, 39, 50–2, 75, 82,
        185, 197
    bodily 1, 80–4, 85, 159, 164, 177–9,
        183–4, 197
    divine 21, 40, 50–2, 66, 93, 102, 120,
        156, 184, 197, 202
    feminine 70, 75, 80–4, 85, 89–90, 93,
        98, 102, 120, 127, 137
    queer 159, 162–4, 177–9, 183–4, 197
Moonwise (Gilman) 104
motherhood
    as divine archetype 40, 43, 82, 84, 87,
        107, 111, 126–35, 165–6, 198
    as patriarchal ideal 71, 72, 117–18, 135
    perversion of 91
    reclamations of 85–7, 89, 105,
        109–11, 118, 123, 126–35
    subversive 80, 87, 128–31
mysticism
    Christian 108, 115
    in *The Left Hand of Darkness* 56, 59,
        61, 64, 97, 175
    in textual interpretation 26
    in *Till We Have Faces* 44, 52, 114
myth
    as cultural imaginary 4, 40–4, 56,
        75–6, 96, 126–36, 146
    fantasy's reliance on 19, 35, 39, 40,
        104, 113–14, 133, 146, 162
    nationalist 188
    revisions of 44, 49, 83, 114, 124–6,
        127, 131–2, 136, 137, 149
    of self 43, 90, 128, 133–6, 166
    as theological storytelling 48, 53–4,
        65–6, 146, 150, 162, 176–7, 181, 188
mythopoetics 26, 35, 72, 104, 162

nationalism 31, 43, 57–9, 61–2, 96,
    188–9
non-binary
    identities 83, 143, 160–1, 171, 180, 192
    social structures 84, 94–101, 102,
        169–76, 180

oppression
    in Christianity 8, 12, 33–4, 71, 173,
        185
    class 191, 193

heteronormative 140–2, 146, 152–3, 165
intersectional 140, 202
patriarchal 16, 73–4, 135, 166
in Western discourses 3, 20, 25, 38, 66
within feminism 17, 111, 135
orthodoxy
challenges to 78, 145–53, 193, 202
deconstruction of 8, 23, 26, 32, 69, 193
exclusivity of 9–12, 145–53, 158, 185
as normative 8, 14–15, 37, 202
other
advent/approach of 24, 37–8, 48–50, 54, 60, 66, 73, 98, 124, 154, 158, 182
communion with 5, 32–3, 35, 54–5, 59, 67, 109–10, 132, 153–5, 168, 176, 183
encounter with 35, 38, 46, 63–5, 98, 108–9, 168, 172, 185
face of 15, 22, 24, 31–2, 36, 50, 63–5, 87, 153, 172, 181, 202
fear of 3, 57
as feminine/woman 5–6, 69–84, 86, 98, 102, 106, 109, 166
as God (*see under* God)
hospitality toward 29, 58, 96
impossibility of representing 18, 21, 33, 37–40, 44–55, 57, 66, 71, 155
love for 66, 77, 93, 106, 110, 123, 183–4, 194, 200
marginalized 1–2, 9, 15, 33–4, 41–3, 47, 65, 69–84, 88, 133, 138, 142, 153, 158, 175, 179, 186
openness to 5, 14–15, 20, 37, 45, 56, 58–61, 65–7, 77, 96–8, 111, 113, 130, 185
as the other gender 106–10, 123, 130–2
in psychoanalysis 24, 106
queer 138, 142, 153–5, 162, 166, 169
self and 31, 63, 110, 128, 172, 175
suffering of 32, 64
violence toward 15, 31–2, 36–8, 65, 79

The Passion of New Eve (Carter)
and Christianity 6, 40–4, 65–6, 146, 153, 200
and deconstruction 24, 39, 40–4, 62, 65–6, 107

drag in 7, 139, 164–9, 176, 184
as fantasy 2–4, 6, 19, 185–6
and feminist theology 7, 105, 107, 109, 113, 126–136, 137, 149
patriarchy
absence of 95
cis-hetero- 26, 142, 146, 160, 163, 171
construction of reality 23, 70, 75–6, 82, 105, 127, 150, 173
in fantasy 20, 76, 82–3, 86–94, 97–8, 102, 135
as hierarchy 7, 130, 149, 157
and religious authority 29, 75, 88, 116, 125, 152, 196
and religious doctrine 1, 6, 11–12, 23, 26, 75, 79, 103, 106, 110, 113, 124, 150
sexuality under 109, 129
in theology 70, 75–6, 79, 84, 102, 103–4, 110–11, 113, 117–18, 120–2, 124–6, 128, 135, 146, 157, 166, 181, 196
and Western discourse 16–17, 73–5, 77, 81–2, 84, 85, 87, 90, 93–4, 99–102, 107, 110–11, 118, 120–1, 126, 128–31, 133–4, 135, 158, 170, 196
phallocentrism 73, 112, 130
phallogocentrism
feminist critique of 73, 76, 82, 84, 85, 94, 96, 107, 111
and sovereignty 70
and the subject 67, 84, 129–30, 202
and theology 43, 70, 101, 104, 107, 114, 122–3
of Western discourse 16, 29, 42, 66, 69–70, 85, 88–9, 97, 101–2, 126, 134
phallus
imagery in fantasy 83, 89, 126–8, 130, 134, 156
as structuring motif 29, 102, 111, 130
polyamory 151, 196
postcolonialism 146, 200–1
poststructuralism 4, 77, 93, 105, 111
pregnancy 80–1, 98, 171, 199
prophecy
in fantasy 61, 98, 114, 120, 132–3, 136, 180, 194
in theological traditions 4, 38, 75

Index

purity
  deconstructive resistance to 8, 13, 28
  feminist critique 110, 114–15
  queer critique 144, 146, 148, 173, 197
  of reason 28, 42
  in theology 14, 61, 69, 144, 197

queer
  affordances of fantasy 1, 3, 5, 21, 137–84, 185–6, 191–202
  approaches to criticism 18, 144, 169–76
  coming out 130, 163–4
  elaboration on feminism 16, 105, 112, 141–2, 175
  embodiment 138, 145, 158–64, 176–83
  individuals 2–3, 7, 24, 138, 165, 171, 174
  marginality of 42, 162, 166, 178–9
  as a marketing category 200–1
  origins and definitions 139–44
  representation in fantasy 3–4, 190–3, 198, 201
  sainthood 165–9
  theology (*see under* theology)
  theory 7, 16, 24, 139–44
  transgender critiques 142–44
Queer Nation 139

race 21, 31, 41, 141, 195, 199–201
The Raven Tower (Leckie) 186, 187–91, 201
reason
  light of 46–52, 57–8, 73, 78, 83, 196
  logocentric 41–2, 57, 119, 134
  patriarchal 73, 77–9, 83, 88–90, 97, 108, 134, 196
  versus faith 45–52, 88–90
recovery 35, 54, 74, 104
redemption
  of love 197
  by messianic grace 91, 113, 126, 154, 199
  of self 53, 104, 109, 120–3
  of the world 12, 40, 112, 126, 129, 131–2, 136
relativism 21, 27, 65

religion(s)
  authority of 2, 70, 75, 146, 152
  as cultural imaginary 4–6, 9, 21, 39, 40–4, 104–13, 124, 131–3, 146, 159, 162
  and deconstruction 8, 13–17, 23–8, 33, 39, 53, 56, 58–61, 65–7, 69, 71
  devotion to 5, 37–8, 66
  doctrine 1–2, 25, 123, 144, 198
  dogma 138
  exchange between 8, 31, 56, 193, 201
  and fantasy 1, 6, 9–12, 17, 20–1, 23–4, 27–8, 36–9, 40–67, 76, 84–101, 104, 109, 113–36, 146, 162, 164–84, 185–202
  feminine 88–90, 97–102, 103–36
  fictional 19, 36, 39, 44–64, 78, 84–94, 97–101, 104, 113–26, 169–70, 174–5, 179, 187–200
  institutional 1–3, 33, 104, 108, 115, 144, 152, 162, 169, 196
  language of 1, 8, 44–55, 56, 117, 131, 188
  orthodoxy (*see under* orthodoxy)
  participation in 2–3, 19–20, 37–8, 44–55, 69, 78, 84, 138–9, 145, 153, 156, 185, 189, 199
  patriarchal 6, 23, 26, 75–6, 79, 84, 94–5, 106, 118, 124
  queer 144, 152, 159, 169–70, 174–5
  ritual 49, 53, 55, 98, 179
  and the state 2, 43, 61, 138, 146, 153, 196, 200
  vocation 79
  without religion 31, 33, 56, 58–61
reproduction
  and heterosexuality 12, 152, 159, 166
  and patriarchy 2, 118
  queer refusal of 153–4, 173
  as theological ideal 144, 151, 185
RuPaul's Drag Race 160

sacrament 12, 145, 151, 153–8, 168, 184
sacrifice
  ritual 45–9, 54–5, 87–8, 114, 124–5, 187
  as sin 107, 154
  of sovereignty 31, 194
  as virtue 13, 165

sainthood 85, 165–9
salvation 8, 41, 138, 157–8, 185
Sasha Velour 143, 162–4
secondary world(s)
　affordances of 1, 10
　conservatism in 20, 191
　as deconstructive 19–20, 23–4, 37–9, 57–8
　and feminism 77, 99, 102, 104
　instances of 56, 60, 64, 95, 150, 179, 188, 191, 192, 195–6, 198, 200
　provisionality of 19, 36–8, 40, 58, 99, 101, 112
　queer potential 3, 138–9, 158, 162, 169–71, 183, 192–3, 201
　and religious longing 35
secularism 27, 31, 88, 134, 199
secularization 13, 41, 199
Sense8 155
sexuality
　and desire 1, 107–8, 144–5, 171, 185, 195, 200
　deviant 138, 139–40, 145–7, 151–3, 174, 178
　fluidity of 56, 95, 141, 197–8
　and identity 3–4, 17, 142, 151, 153, 190, 201
　imagery of 90, 98
　marginal 2–3, 8, 10, 18–19, 21, 23, 31, 136, 137–8, 140, 145, 153, 185, 202
　orientation 2–4, 96, 138–9, 142
　and pleasure 50, 76, 117–18, 147, 156, 198
　reclamation of 76, 82, 109, 145–7, 165
　reconfiguring 3, 19–20, 22, 40, 100, 149–50, 156–8, 169–76, 185, 190, 191–2, 198, 201–2
　regulation of 11–12, 55, 71, 92, 117, 129, 144–7, 152, 153, 159
sexual violence 83, 96, 152, 166, 177
sex work 2, 156
Shippey, Tom 35
signification
　deferred 13, 29–30, 38–9, 46, 51, 58, 63, 66
　in drag 141, 160
　feminist 104, 108
　of identity 3

logocentric 28–9, 31, 72, 117
　in theology 12–13, 201
sin 91, 107, 148–9, 154, 199
soul
　classical concept of 41, 91, 93, 113–14
　in fantasy 82, 196
　in feminism 86, 109, 118, 121
spirituality
　formation of 93, 113
　generalized 9, 27, 41
　in practice 15, 40, 108, 146, 154, 199
Spivak, Gayatri Chakravorty 17, 29, 69, 112
Stoicism 45–7, 88
subjectivity
　alternative 21, 84, 96
　embodied 73, 162, 173, 176–84
　feminine 7, 17, 69–71, 74–5, 79, 82–6, 89, 102, 103, 105–7, 110–11, 120, 128–32, 202
　heterogeneous 82, 114, 119, 130, 132, 163, 172, 176–84
　marginal 3, 10, 20, 38, 55, 141, 161, 177, 180, 186, 202
　patriarchal 16, 29, 67, 69, 71, 75, 80, 96, 111, 128–30
　queer 3, 151, 162–4, 171, 176–84, 202
　sovereign 2, 21, 24–5, 28, 31–2, 34, 41, 67, 105, 120, 130, 182, 186, 194, 197, 200, 202
　unified 29, 32, 34, 49, 140–1, 154, 186

Tales of Nevèrÿon (Delany) 147–50, 195
Tensorate series (Yang) 143, 186–7, 191–5, 200–1
theology
　beyond Christianity 193, 201
　and deconstruction (*see under* deconstruction)
　as depicted in literary texts 40–55, 58–65, 84–94, 97–101, 105, 113–36, 147–50, 156–8, 164–83, 187–200
　ecological implications of 189–90, 201
　and economics 145, 147, 152, 156–8, 189–90, 195, 201
　feminist 1–3, 5–7, 12, 17, 21–2, 23–4, 69–102, 103–36, 137–8, 158, 185–7, 195, 201–2
　heterosexual 8, 11–12, 113, 138, 146, 159, 164–6, 169, 181–2, 185

indecent 7, 138, 144–53, 189, 201 (*see also* Althaus-Reid, Marcella)
limitations of 52, 126, 175
negative 33
patriarchal (*see under* patriarchy)
queer 1–3, 5, 7, 9, 12, 21–2, 23–4, 136, 137–84, 185–7, 195–6, 201–2
relationship to literature 1–12, 75–80 (*see also* fantasy)
systematic 52
Tolkien, J. R. R.
  Catholicism 4, 9–10, 37
  The Hobbit 10, 35
  The Lord of the Rings 4, 11–12, 35, 162–4
  misogyny 91
  'On Fairy-stories' 1, 5–6, 24, 35–9, 54, 66, 70, 81–2, 109, 153, 185, 202
Tonstad, Linn Marie
  critique of inclusion 2–3, 144, 201
  critique of suffering 166
  reading of Irigaray 138
  on theology and literature 158, 204 n.11
  theology of failure 7, 9, 138, 144–5, 153–8, 168, 175–6, 182, 183–4
transcendence
  in fantasy 11, 40, 44
  metaphysical 14, 28, 31, 34, 75–6, 78, 98, 117, 120, 127, 133, 135, 141, 146–7, 165, 182, 199
  via the other 7, 31, 109, 168
transgender
  individuals 81, 138, 142–3, 145, 147, 160–1, 171
  representation in fantasy 156, 167–8, 190–3
  theory 105, 142–4
  transition 130, 168, 192–3
  transsexuality 143, 147
  transvestism 167
transphobia 8, 163, 181
Trinity 144, 153, 196

unreality
  of fantasy 20–1, 78–9, 104, 133, 162
  and femininity 78–9, 104, 133
  queer 162, 165–6, 179, 184
utopia 41, 55, 64, 162, 174, 191–2

vagina 98, 111, 130
virginity 71, 109–11, 131, 135

Walton, Heather
  on feminism 16, 104
  indebtedness to deconstruction 26
  on literature and theology 4–6, 70, 77–80, 87
The Wanderground (Gearhart) 210 n.4
White, T. H. 35
Williams, Charles 9
Woman on the Edge of Time (Piercy) 209 n.4
womb 87, 91, 128–30, 136, 148–9, 155
women
  in Christianity (*see under* Christianity)
  divine (*see under* femininity)
  as individuals 2, 11, 24, 47, 84, 99, 145, 153, 171, 174, 202
  internalized misogyny in 73, 82, 84–94, 113
  language of 85, 94, 108, 110–11
  as metaphors 16–17, 70, 75, 77–81, 83, 102, 107, 197
  monstrous (*see under* femininity)
  non-unity of 16–17, 111–12, 138, 141, 165–7, 175
  as other (*see under* other)
  representation in fantasy 78–9, 85–6, 91
  subjectivity of 16, 69, 79, 85, 106, 131
  subordination of 16–17, 70–4, 79, 80–1, 85, 103, 106–7, 109, 117, 124–5, 166–7, 176–80
  as unified category 96–7, 105, 111, 165
  and writing 73, 77–80 (*see also* Cixous, Hélène)
worldbuilding
  as deconstructive 34–5, 44, 137, 186
  in *Earthsea* 177, 180–1
  and feminism 76, 109, 161
  in the *Inheritance* trilogy 195, 200
  in *The Left Hand of Darkness* 58, 94–6, 100–1, 102, 169, 171–2, 176
  in *The Passion of New Eve* 127
  in the *Tensorate* series 191, 194–5
  in *Till We Have Faces* 46

www.ingramcontent.com/pod-product-compliance
Lightning Source LLC
Chambersburg PA
CBHW062142300426
44115CB00012BA/2011